S0-BAM-026

Birth Place	Occupation	Religion	Burial Place	Location of Papers [b]	(Birth - Death)
Virginia	Lawyer	Episcopal	Detroit	BN, BU	(1811-1843)
Connecticut	Lawyer	Congregational	Detroit	BN, BU	(1780-1861)
Connecticut	Lawyer	Episcopal	Brazil [3]		(1809-1853)
New Hampshire	Lawyer/business		Constantine	BN, BU	(1802-1870)
Maine	Lawyer	Methodist	Ann Arbor	BN, BU	(1804-1896)
New York	Lawyer		Adrian		(1813-1883)
Massachusetts	Lawyer		Kalamazoo		(1796-1859)
Pennsylvania	Lawyer		Detroit	BU	(1807-1880)
New York	Teacher	Episcopal	Corunna	BU	(1817-1855)
New York	Lawyer		Brighton	BN, BU	(1808-1861)
New York	Farmer/lawyer		Pontiac	BN, BU	(1815-1864)
New York	Lawyer		Jackson	BN, BU	(1818-1894)
Massachusetts	Lumber	Christian Church/Universalist	Flint	BN, BU	(1804-1869)
Rhode Island	Business	Episcopal	Detroit		(1814-1892)
New York	Business	Unitarian	Detroit	BN, BU	(1832-1881)
New York	Lawyer/banker	Presbyterian/Episcopal	Adrian	BN, BU	(1825-1886)
Detroit	Business/lumber	Episcopal	Saginaw	BU	(1829-1896)
New York	Farmer	Presbyterian	Flint	SA, BU	(1815-1896)
Ohio	Lumber		Detroit	BU	(1836-1907)
Ohio	Farmer	Presbyterian	Coldwater	SA	(1824-1905)
New York	Farmer	Episcopal	Hamburg	SA	(1826-1894)
Pennsylvania	Farmer	Presbyterian	Lapeer	BN, BU	(1841-1926)
Maine	Business/shoes	Baptist	Detroit	BN, BU	(1840-1901)
New York	Business/lumber	Methodist	Saginaw	SA	(1837-1906)
England	Business	Methodist/Episcopal	Farmington	BN, BU	(1865-1923)
Indiana	Publisher	Presbyterian	Duck Island	BN, SA	(1860-1949)
New York	Educator		Big Rapids	BN, BU, SA	(1853-1928)
Vermont	Business/banker	Episcopal	Lexington	SA	(1862-1934)
Macomb County	Lawyer		Detroit	SA	(1873-1953)
Manistee	Lawyer/business		Ionia	SA	(1872-1936)
Saginaw	Lawyer	Presbyterian	Arlington, Va.	BN, SA	(1894-1968)
Alpena	Banker/business	Episcopal	Alpena	BN, SA	(1877-1949)
Grand Ledge	Politics	Congregational	Grand Ledge	BN, BU, SA	(1885-1939)
Harbor Beach	Lawyer		Harbor Beach	BN, BU, SA	(1893-1949)
New York	Farmer/teacher	Methodist/Episcopal	Charlotte	BN, BU, SA	(1859-1943)
Kingston	Engineer	Episcopal	Troy	BN, SA	(1898-1986)
Illinois	Lawyer	Catholic	Southfield	SA	(1895-1971)
Nebraska	Lawyer	Methodist	Hastings	BN, SA	(1894-1953)
Detroit	Lawyer	Episcopal		BN, BU, SA	(1911-)
Canada	Lawyer	United Church of Christ		BN	(1925-)
Mexico	Business	Mormon		BN, SA	(1907-)
Traverse City	Business	Congregational		BN, SA	(1922-)
Pleasant Ridge	Lawyer	Unitarian			(1942-)

Notes:
a Party designations are D for Democrat, R for Republican, W for Whig and F for Fusionist.
b Designations of repositories of gubernatorial papers are:
  BN: The Michigan Historical Collections located at the University of Michigan's Bentley Historical Library, Ann Arbor, 48109-2113.
  SA: State Archives, Department of State's Michigan History Bureau, Lansing, 48919. (In addition to above holdings, the State Archives has 139 feet of 1810-1910 Executive Office records, saved from the 1951 fire that destroyed other holdings of the Archives.)
  BU: Burton Historical Collection, Detroit Public Library, 5201 Woodward, Detroit, 48202.
1 Leading up to Michigan's admission to statehood in 1837, population of the Michigan Territory was 4,762 in 1810; 8,927 in 1820; 31,639 in 1830; and 87,278 in 1834.

2 Resigned Feb. 24, 1841, to become U.S. senator.
3 As of 1987, the precise burial place of Gordon, who died of a fall in Brazil, was unknown.
4 Resigned March 3, 1847, to become U.S. senator.
5 Resigned March 7, 1853, to become U.S. secretary of interior.
6 Died March 16, 1939.
7 Became governor March 17, 1939.
8 Resigned Jan. 22, 1969, to become U.S. secretary of housing and urban development.
9 Became governor Jan. 22, 1969.
10 Scheduled to begin 1988.

DETROIT
PUBLIC
LIBRARY

DETROIT PUBLIC LIBRARY

3 5674 00304484 0

STEWARDS OF THE STATE

The Governors of Michigan

To Mollie, Julie and MJN

STEWARDS OF THE STATE

The Governors of Michigan

By
George Weeks

Edited by
Robert D. Kirk

Contributing Authors:
Paula L. Blanchard
Don Weeks

Published by
The Detroit News, a Gannett Newspaper
and the
Historical Society of Michigan
Ann Arbor, Michigan

1987

R353.9774
W418s
c.1

CHASÉ BRANCH LIBRARY
17731 W. SEVEN MILE
DETROIT. MICH. 48235

Copyright © 1987 by Historical Society of Michigan

All rights reserved. No part of this book may be reproduced or transmitted in any form or by any means, electronic or mechanical, including photocopying, recording, or by any information storage and retrieval systems, without permission in writing from the publisher, except in case of brief quotations embodied in articles and reviews.

REFERENCE

First American Edition
Published by Historical Society of Michigan
2117 Washtenaw Avenue
Ann Arbor, Mich. 48104

CHASÉ BRANCH LIBRARY
17731 W. SEVEN MILE
DETROIT. MICH. 48235

ISBN 0-9614344-2-2

Library of Congress Catalog Number: 87-081388

DESIGN: Bauer-Dunham-Barr
ART DIRECTION: Robert Bauer
TECHNICAL DIRECTION: Bill Baker Barr
PRODUCTION: Laura Schultz

Printed in USA by Mitchell-Shear, Ann Arbor, Mich. 48104

Following are the abbreviations, full names and affiliations of organizations that provided pictures for this book:

STATE ARCHIVES	Michigan State Archives of the Bureau of History, Michigan Department of State
BURTON	Burton Historical Collection, Detroit Public Library
BENTLEY	Michigan Historical Collections at The University of Michigan Bentley Historical Library
CLEMENTS	William Clements Library, The University of Michigan
HATCHER	Harlan Hatcher Library, The University of Michigan
CATLIN	George B. Catlin Library, The Detroit News
AP	The Associated Press
UPI	United Press International
COTTAGE BOOK SHOP	Historical Collections of the Cottage Book Shop of Glen Arbor, Mich.
N.C.A.M.	Newspaper Cartoonists' Association of Michigan, from a gallery of pen sketches in 1905, edited by C.O. Youngstrand

MAR '89 CH

Table of Contents

Foreword

About the time Michigan Gov. James J. Blanchard gave his State of the State address in January 1987, Detroit News politics columnist George Weeks was hunched over the hand-scrawled state messages of Michigan's first elected governor, Stevens T. Mason, amid the Burton Historical Collection at the Detroit Public Library. Otherwise, Weeks would have been at the Capitol.

Weeks has been fascinated with Michigan's chiefs of state since, as a youth, he first saw the dashing Kim Sigler sweep into Traverse City in 1948 aboard his own plane, complete with a cigarette holder and spats. Subsequently, Weeks collected quotes, anecdotes and facts about politicians. He was there as a reporter when G. Mennen Williams was governor, and when John F. Kennedy tapped "Soapy" Williams as assistant secretary of state for African affairs. He was there when George Romney ended his presidential bid. And he served as trusted adviser and friend to Michigan's longest-serving governor, William G. Milliken. When Milliken retired, Weeks returned to his first love, reporting the facts of politics, without fear or favor.

Weeks is part of a tradition of Detroit News politics writers, who have traversed the state from New Buffalo to Grindstone City, from Monroe to Escanaba, chronicling the great, the near-great and the would-be great. The News librarians carefully clipped, culled and filed the best of that material, including stories, columns and photos. They also filed the best of The Detroit Free Press over the years. From this core, Weeks produced *Stewards of the State,* with help from his son, Don, and inspiration from his father, the late Don Weeks, an ex-newspaperman and state economic development director who conceived Michigan Week in 1954. From territorial great Lewis Cass, called "Big Belly" by the Indians with whom he negotiated treaties, to James J. Blanchard, Weeks has brought the men who served as governor to life in these pages. He shows them as human beings, sometimes grand, sometimes humbled, sometimes a little daft.

You will meet Mason, called "Young Hotspur" by Andrew Jackson; Albert "Uncle Bert" Sleeper, who provided rubber overshoes to World War I servicemen; Henry H. Crapo, the Flint lumber baron; Chase Osborn, the "Iron Governor" from the U.P. who married his once-adopted daughter; Josiah Begole, who arrived in Michigan with $100 in his pocket; Hazen S. "Potato Patch" Pingree, who wanted to keep his job as mayor of Detroit even after he became governor, and Luren Dickinson, who was Michigan's oldest governor and who appointed the first woman lieutenant governor.

The Detroit News assisted in the production of this book in cooperation with the Historical Society of Michigan as a contribution to celebration of Michigan Week and Michigan's Sesquicentennial, but this is not a Detroit News book. It belongs, in part, to the people who made it possible: the Weeks family, the librarians, the curators of letters and other gubernatorial collections and the photographers who chronicled our governors. But mostly it belongs to the people of Michigan.

Enjoy it.

Benjamin J. Burns
Detroit News Chief Administrative Editor

Acknowledgments

Arrangements for this cooperative project between the Historical Society of Michigan and The Detroit News were made by News Chief Administrative Editor Benjamin J. Burns and Tom Jones, executive director of the society. The News, a Gannett newspaper, is not in the business of publishing books, but many of its employees interrupted their daily work schedules to help this effort.

For that, special acknowledgement is due Executive Editor Robert H. Giles, Managing Editor/News Christina Bradford and Executive City Editor Mark Hass for sanctioning occasional diversions to this effort, and Production Editor Michael J. McCormick for getting the book set into type.

Special thanks to State Editor Henry A. Stokes for permitting the author periodic reprieves from writing The News' politics column during this undertaking, and for doing double duty while Assistant State Editor Robert D. Kirk edited this book. Kirk prodded and polished the author, and coordinated with other News employees who contributed to this undertaking.

Especially helpful were copy editor John Stanley, a history buff and editor of the 1980 edition of The Detroit News Stylebook; Donald Pilette, editorial systems editor; George Rorick, assistant managing editor/graphics, whose staff provided invaluable assistance, and graphics coordinator Laura Varon.

A major source of material for this book was The News' Reference Department and George B. Catlin Library, with special help from former Reference Department Supervisor Diane Rockall, Reference Department Cataloguer Anita Mack, Chief Librarian Betty L. Havlena and Lansing Bureau Librarian William Meister.

Valuable historical and creative assistance was provided by Sam and Robert Breck, consulting editors on this project for the Historical Society of Michigan. Nancy Marshall and Mary Chalmers of the Society staff toiled long hours on the book as well.

Jerry Roe, a member of the Michigan Historical Commission and creator of the Jerry Roe Collections, provided source material at various stages of this project.

Of special help were the staffs of the Michigan State Archives, the Michigan Historical Collections at the University of Michigan's Bentley Historical Library, the Burton Historical Collection of the Detroit Public Library, The Library of Michigan, Public Sector Consultants, Inc., and the Cottage Book Shop of Glen Arbor. Special thanks to Lee Barnett and John Curry at the State Archives, Saralee R. Howard-Filler at Michigan History magazine, and Richard Hathaway at The Library of Michigan. Much of the initial research for this project was done over a period of several years by Don Weeks, who coordinated research and photo selection on the Stewards of the State film produced by the Milliken Foundation in 1982. Some of the visual material on early Michigan governors used in the film was used in this book.

Especially appreciated is the contribution of Paula Blanchard on the changing role of first ladies. She provides a historical and personal perspective on what it is like to live in a glass house where the curtains are so often open — and what it is like to be among a growing number of first spouses who have professional pursuits in addition to their public roles.

As with so many publications, the unsung contributors to this book are the photographers whose names somehow get dropped over the years from credit lines on pictures. There are long lists at the end of this book of the names of writers whose words are used. Unfortunately, many of the early pictures are credited only to such sources as "State Archives" or "Detroit News."

Before many pages, it will be apparent that pictures — and cartoons — reflect much of the story of the stewardship of Michigan.

— *George Weeks*

Publisher's Note

It is entirely appropriate that George Weeks' *Stewards of the State* appears during the height of Michigan's celebration of its sesquicentennial of statehood. The essence of the American republic is the cooperative union of its sovereign states, and so while Michiganians are honoring the anniversary of their state's entrance into the Union, they are at the same time paying homage to the national system created more than 200 years ago.

Michigan and the country have benefited by the leadership of our state's governors. They led Michigan during its perilous colonial era, steered its course through the heady days of territorial growth and statehood, and headed it through the various periods of successes and reverses that have marked its 150 years of statehood. Their attention to state affairs and their leadership abilities have not gone unnoticed nationally. Often those administrative skills have been tapped for the good of the nation and the world.

By and large, they successfully fulfilled the responsibilities of their positions and that is a positive reflection on not only their own abilities and sense of stewardship but also the voters who put them into office. You will find some interesting characters in this book, but you will not find any charlatans or crooks. Most importantly, when you finish the book, we think you will be proud of the governors who have served us so well over the centuries. And that alone is one very important thing to be celebrated during this sesquicentennial period.

There is much about this volume that marks it off from the other political biographies. It is, most notably, a *collective* biography. Every elected governor of Michigan is here, from those who served a matter of months to those whose stewardship covered a decade or more. Additionally, reference is made to Michigan's colonial and territorial leaders.

As reference tools, the charts, tables and photographs make the volume particularly interesting.

Also, special sections on the state's first ladies, the capitols and governors' residences and those often obscure personalities from Michigan's political stage — the lieutenant governors — fill out the book and enhance its interest and value to readers.

Lastly, the liberal use of direct quotes and samples from Michigan's political cartooning history add as much to the book's historical substance as to its eye appeal.

The Historical Society of Michigan is honored to be the partner of The Detroit News in presenting *Stewards of the State* to Michigan and the country. George Weeks has accurately recounted the lives and times of our state's leaders in a book that will be a source of enjoyment and reference for generations to come.

Thomas L. Jones
Executive Director
Historical Society of Michigan

The Great Seal of the State of Michigan was adopted at the Constitutional Convention of 1835. It was designed by Territorial Gov. Lewis Cass from the pattern of the Seal of the Hudson Bay Fur Co.

At the top are the words, *E Pluribus Unum*, from the national motto meaning "from many, one" — formation of the nation from many states. *Tuebor* means "I will defend." *Si Quaeris Peninsulam Amoenam Circumspice* is the State Motto: "If You Seek a Pleasant Peninsula, Look About You."

The American Eagle symbolizes the superior authority and jurisdiction of the United States. Its talons hold an olive branch with thirteen olives, representing the first thirteen states, and arrows symbolizing the nation's readiness to defend its principles. The shield is supported by two Michigan animals, the elk on the left and the moose on the right. The man on the shield shows a raised right hand symbolizing peace, and a gunstock in the left hand indicating readiness to defend the State and Nation.

The encircled words, "The Great Seal of the State of Michigan, A.D. MDCCCXXXV," complete the State Seal. Without them and the circle, the design is used as the Coat of Arms of the State of Michigan.

Deviations from Cass' original design were adopted at various periods of the state's history. Sometimes the animals were lean, sometimes stocky. The eagle looked to the left, and to the right. As late as 1987, official state publications used slight variations in the design. But the present seal, adopted by the Legislature in 1911, harkens back to Cass' original. (See page 4 for the modern design.)

Michigan and the American Governorship

Each and every one of us stands on the shoulders of our predecessors.

— Six- term Gov. G. Mennen Williams[1]

In its first 150 years as a state, Michigan was led by 43 governors as diverse as Michigan itself. Farmers, lumbermen, shopkeepers, lawyers, teachers, conservationists, industrialists. At crucial periods of America's history, men who had been military warriors led the state: two were prisoners of war, two lost legs in battle and one was shot out of the sky.*

They came from many states and from three foreign countries. More than two-thirds of Michigan's governors were born outside of the state.

Gov. G. Mennen Williams (1949-60), a U.S. diplomat and Michigan Supreme Court justice whose public career spanned a third of Michigan's first 150 years of statehood, noted that each governor builds a foundation for those who follow. Michigan's longest-serving governor, William G. Milliken (1969-82), observed in his final State of the State address:

Michigan is what it is today because of the vastness and diversity of its natural resources; because of the vigor and diversity of its human resources; because of foresight of those who led Michigan into statehood and through its difficult times. The splendor that is Michigan today was sculptured by glaciers.

But Michigan's future was honed by its people.[2]

And, in large part, by its governors. Through the stories of its governors — the stewards of the state — much of Michigan's history can be told.

American governors have come a long way since being described in 1778 by James Madison as "in general little more than Cyphers."[3] As Gov. Lew Wallace of New Mexico Territory reflected on his 1887 responsibilities: "The office of governor had so little power that my only function was to count sheep and people for the annual report to Washington."[4]

In the Federalist Papers (No. 70),

Alexander Hamilton said that energy in the executive was a leading element in good government: "A feeble executive implies a feeble execution of government." While the Founding Fathers gave the nation a strong executive at its outset, the powers of today's chief state executives evolved from feeble beginnings.

"Attaining their statehood by a war of independence, the American colonists were imbued with mistrust of authority and the governors of their creation were almost as powerless to serve the people as to frustrate their will," New Zealand political scientist Leslie Lipson wrote in *The American Governor from Figurehead to Leader.*[5] Observed Professor Emeritus Samuel R. Solomon of Eastern Michigan University: "The blunt fact of state government history is that it has taken almost a hundred years for the governor in most states to begin to emerge from the shadows of post-Colonial legislative structure; almost a hundred years to begin to make the governor the master in his, and her, own executive house."[6]

Michigan has had a stronger executive office than many other states, and the office's powers have increased. The state's 1905 Constitution specified (Article VI, Sec. 2): "The chief executive power is vested in the governor." Any suggestion by this language that the governor was chief executive only in the sense of being first among many executives was dealt with in the Constitution of 1963, which took effect Jan. 1, 1964. It said flatly (Article V, Sec. 1): "The executive power is vested in the governor." In several respects, however, executive power remains shared. The 1963 Constitution, for example, maintained the autonomy of university boards, and the attorney general and secretary of state continued to be elected officers, independent of the governor. As Michigan observed its

* Hazen Pingree and Aaron Bliss were in Confederate prisons. Harry Kelly lost a leg in World War I. John B. Swainson lost both legs in World War II. And waist-gunner William G. Milliken bailed out of a B-24 bomber over Europe during the same war.

Five governors spanning four decades gathered at Michigan State University's Kellogg Center Nov. 17, 1981, at a meeting sponsored by the Michigan Historical Commission. Left to right, seated: G. Mennen Williams, Murray D. Van Wagoner and John B. Swainson; standing: George Romney and William G. Milliken.

George Weeks

150th year of statehood, its governor still had statutory and constitutional restrictions on some Cabinet level appointments.

But on balance, the power of the Michigan governor has increased, despite the erosions of the role of states in the federal system and the Michigan Legislature's efforts to blunt gubernatorial powers through means such as its administrative rules committee. As of 1987, Michigan was among only 12 states with constitutional authorization for government reorganization through executive order, subject to legislative review when changes require force of law. While most states have treasurers elected by the people, Michigan was one of only four states where the governor appointed the treasurer. In about a third of the states, governors lacked the power of direct appointment of budget officers granted Michigan governors.[7]

Retiring Oregon Gov. Mark Hatfield complained in 1967: "We have in excess of 100 different boards, agencies and commissions that report to the governor. Many of these are virtually independent of any control by the chief executive."[8]

It was a complaint echoed in 1987 by Gov. James J. Blanchard who, as he started his second term, said Michigan would have more accountability in government if the governor had more power of direct appointment.

The greatest enhancement for Michigan's future chief executives in the 1963 Constitution was in extending their terms from two to four years — without any of the restrictions on serving consecutive terms as imposed by 27 other states. Alfred E. Smith, who served four two-year terms as governor of New York before becoming the 1928 Democratic presidential nominee, observed that in two years, one hardly has time to locate the knob on the statehouse door.[9] Oregon Gov. Tom McCall lamented during his first term in 1967 that getting the votes to govern does not always mean getting the tools to govern: "We have run our (state) government like a pickup orchestra, where the members meet at a dance, shake hands with each other, and start to play."[10]

Under Michigan's 1963 Constitution, life and rule were made vastly easier for governors when voters, as of the 1966 election, began picking the governor and lieutenant governor as a team. As of 1987, Michigan was among 22 states in which a vote for one was a vote for both. GOP Gov. George Romney (1963-69) was the last Michigan governor to have a lieutenant governor who was elected independently — Democrat T. John Lesinski. Romney complained Lesinski was "constantly trying to embarrass me....He enjoyed poking fun at me....I couldn't even delegate ceremonial duties under the circumstances."[11]

Gubernatorial life also was made easier by a substantial improvement in salary. As of 1986, remuneration for Michigan's governor was the fourth highest in the nation, a far cry from earlier days when Austin Blair, Michigan's Civil War governor, and one of its most outstanding stewards (1861-64), received $1,000 a year and was moved later to say: "Now I ask them if they can afford — this great and magnanimous people of Michigan — to give the governors about half as good a salary as they pay to a common dry goods clerk."[12]

Michigan's governors have earned their pay dealing with recurrent economic setbacks; floods, tornadoes and other natural disasters; strikes; riots and other civil strife; wartime mobilizations; the health, welfare, education and public safety of millions of citizens, and otherwise tending to the well-being of a state that in population, size, budget, exports, diversity, complexity and other measurements exceeded many nations.

A 1981 "Gathering of Governors" sponsored by the Michigan Historical Commission highlighted the commonality of concerns spanning the history of Michigan governorship. They inherited problems — sometimes coping, sometimes passing them on. One lingering concern has been economic diversification. Largely because of its dependence on the volatile auto industry, Michigan was hurt harder than any other state by the 1974 Arab oil embargo, and by the prolonged recession of the early 1980s.

Reflecting on those times and Michigan's cycles of recession and rebound, Gov. John B. Swainson (1961-62) recalled the pessimism that prevailed with the decline of the fur industry and then the lumbering business in a past time. Swainson said Michigan would "come back" from the 1980s recession. It did. The "Comeback State" theme was stressed in the 1986 campaign by Blanchard, who was re-elected by a margin of 878,091 votes, surpassing the record of 556,633 by Gov. Fred W. Green (1927-30) in 1928, and carrying all counties except Ottawa.*

Democrat Blanchard said he had corrected an inherited fiscal mess despite adverse national economic policies. (Republicans said Michigan rebounded because of the national economic recovery.) Blanchard said:

"The national debt has more than doubled since 1981. This $2 trillion mortgage on America's future will require $139 billion in interest payments next year

* Blanchard's winning percentage of 68.1 was the highest since Green won with 69.9 percent in 1928. Alexander J. Groesbeck won with 68.8 percent in 1924. Stevens T. Mason won 90.3 percent of the 6,744 votes cast in Michigan's first gubernatorial election in 1835.

Mackinac Island's Grand Hotel, which celebrated its 100th anniversary in 1987, is a favorite meeting place of governors. National governors' conferences were held there in 1927, 1934, and 1945. On the hotel's porch, while attending a 1983 Great Lakes Governors' Conference, are, from the left, Govs. Richard Celeste, Ohio; James J. Blanchard, Mich.; Anthony Earl, Wis., and Rudy Perpich, Minn.

AP

3

— or almost 10 times more than the entire state budget of our state."[13]

As Michigan's first governor, Stevens T. Mason was the only one who could not complain that he inherited problems from his predecessor, but he did complain about the impact of federal policies on Michigan. And Mason's immediate successors complained about his handling of finances.

Blanchard was among six men who became governor after serving in the U.S. Congress. Six had been lieutenant governors. But the best political springboard to the governorship has been the state Senate, where 17 Michigan governors served. Four were speakers of the House. Two governors succeeded in coming back after being voted out of office; three failed in such comebacks. But many had lost various elections before being elected governor. One, William A. Comstock (1933-34), failed in three gubernatorial elections before winning. Six governors were elected to the U.S. Senate and six more failed. Six ended up in the U.S. Cabinet.*

Fifteen U.S. governors have become president — Thomas Jefferson, James Monroe, Martin Van Buren, John Tyler, James K. Polk, Andrew Johnson, Rutherford B. Hayes, Grover Cleveland, William McKinley, Theodore Roosevelt, Woodrow Wilson, Calvin Coolidge, Franklin D. Roosevelt, Jimmy Carter and Ronald Reagan. At least one governor was a major party candidate for president or vice-president in all but seven of the national campaigns since 1788.

But most of the 2,000 or so governors during the first 200 years of nationhood were little noted elsewhere and not long remembered in their own states. This book remembers Michigan's governors in the context of highlights of the state's first 150 years of statehood, and Michigan's place in American history.

The University of Michigan's Joseph E. Kallenbach said qualities needed by a political chief executive include "all those virtues celebrated in the New Testament, *The Compleat Gentleman, The Way to Wealth* and the handbook of the Boy Scouts of America."[14] A study on the American governorship conducted at the Institute of Politics at Harvard University's John F. Kennedy School of Government concluded that while the nation's governors were not exactly Boy Scouts, the modern breed was less frivolous and frolicsome than predecessors — and better equipped.[15]

Many of the nation's early governors were not well equipped. Most of Michigan's were.

Larry Sabato of the University of Virginia wrote: "Many of the governors who served throughout this century have been described as 'flowery old courthouse politicians,' 'machine dupes,' 'political pipsqueaks,' and 'good-time Charlies.'" Sabato concluded — as reflected in the title of his book, *Goodbye to Good-Time Charlie* — that the description no longer fits the American governorship. It seldom did in Michigan.[16]

Washington columnist-author Neal R. Peirce wrote of American governors: "The general quality has risen, and there are fewer showmen, charlatans, and crooks in the barrel than there were a quarter century ago."[17]

Michigan's barrel has had its share of showmen. But few charlatans and fewer-still crooks. Michigan's governorship has been one of the nation's cleanest. Many of Michigan's governors provided models for courageous, creative and constructive leadership.

One reason that Michigan had so few good-time Charlies as governors was that its governors faced so many hard times.

Oregon Gov. McCall liked to say, "A good governor's got to throw himself under the train every now and then."[18]

Cass. Mason. Blair. Pingree. Murphy. Many of Michigan's governors did just that, leading it to statehood and through the difficult times, honing its future.

Coat of Arms

* Territorial Gov. Lewis Cass is included in these figures since much of his federal service was after Michigan became a state.

STEWARDS OF THE STATE
The Governors of Michigan

Colonial and Territorial Governors

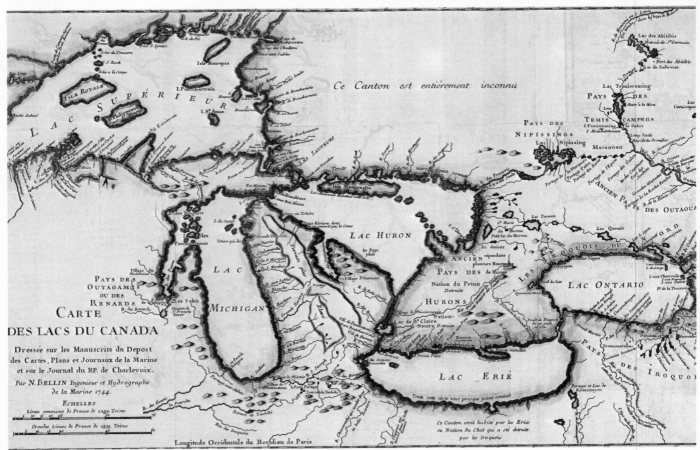

Clements

Colonial Governors

It should be recollected that, under the French and British governments, this (Michigan) was a remote portion of a remote colony, originally settled by adventurers in the fur trade.

— Territorial Gov. Lewis Cass to Michigan's first Legislative Council, June 7, 1824.

Even before Michigan became a state, it had 40 governors under various jurisdictions and three different flags. Michigan was like parts of Africa before that continent's 20th century independence — periodically carved up and passed around.

There were 25 French colonial governors between 1603-1760 — a period of 157 years, longer than Michigan had been a state as of its 1987 sesquicentennial.

Nine British colonial governors ruled Michigan between 1760-92: Two during 1787-1800 when Michigan was part of the Northwest Territory, one when it was part of Indiana Territory in 1800-05, and three governors (and six temporary acting governors) during the 1805-37 period of the Michigan Territory.*

The French period began even before 1620 when French explorers and priests — coming to Lake Superior in New France about the time the Pilgrims landed at Plymouth — were believed to be the first Europeans to see Michigan. It was during this period that Frs. Jacques Marquette and Claude Dablon founded the first mission at Sault de Sainte Marie; Fort Michilimackinac was founded at present-day Mackinaw City; and Antoine de Lamothe Cadillac selected a location on the Detroit River for a trading post that would grow to become the city of Detroit. The period ended with the surrender of Detroit's Fort Pontchartrain to the English in 1760.

One of the most notable governors of the period was Louis de Buade, Count de Frontenac, who served two terms totaling 19 years and encouraged French exploration to the west.

* Some periods overlap and many governors served nonconsecutive terms. In some cases, they had other titles, such as viceroy, governor-general, commander in chief, or acting governor.

During the period of British governors, Guy Carleton (an army brigadier who became a member of the House of Lords) served three nonconsecutive terms. He was succeeded by John Graves Simcoe, a British officer in the Revolutionary War, who in 1791-96 was lieutenant governor of Upper Canada (the future Ontario), with authority extending to Michigan. He was a dedicated imperialist, and argued that a strong military posture would help assure settlement of Upper Canada.[1]

During Simcoe's period, and under provisions of the Constitutional Act by the British Parliament, the first election in Michigan history was held in 1792 to select Detroit area members to the Upper Canada provincial assembly.

Also during the authority of the British governors, the Quebec Act was passed in 1774. It annexed territory extending from the Ohio and Mississippi rivers to what became the province of Quebec, and provided civil government for the first time in the Michigan Territory.

After the American Revolution, the Northwest Territory, of which Michigan was a part, was established by the Ordinance of 1787, which also defined the procedure for obtaining statehood.

Gen. Arthur St. Clair, first governor of the Northwest Territory, had all of present-day Michigan under his control after the departure of British officials in 1796.

When the British evacuated Detroit, St. Clair was out of the territory. Territorial Secretary Winthrop Sargent was acting governor and went to Detroit from the territorial capital in Cincinnati and installed a government.

Sargent established the county of Wayne, which contained all of the present state of Michigan, except the western part of the Upper Peninsula, along with northern Ohio and Indiana, and a strip of eastern Illinois and Wisconsin bordering on Lake Michigan.

In 1800, Gen. William Henry Harrison became governor of the Indiana Territory, which included the western half of Michigan and which was the result of the division of the Northwest Territory. (In 1811, Harrison led 900 troops to victory against the Shawnees at Tippecanoe, Ind. This, and his selection of John Tyler as his running mate, led to a "Tippecanoe and Tyler, Too" slogan that helped Harrison's election to the presidency in 1840.)

Left **John Graves Simcoe**

Middle **Cadillac's Village, Detroit, 1701, first called Fort Pontchartrain**

Bottom **Detroit in 1794, including old shipyard and west gate of stockade. From a painting discovered by Lady Astor in London.**

State Archives

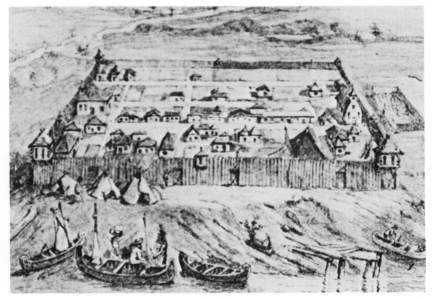

Burton

Burton

Hatcher

The Michigan Territory

Michigan had one of its most distinguished — and one of its most disgraced — governors during territorial days. Today, the size of Michigan is, in large part, the legacy of Lewis Cass, who was Michigan's second territorial governor. He went on to the U.S. Cabinet, the U.S. Senate and made a run for the U.S. presidency.

Gen. William Hull, Michigan's first territorial governor,* got off to a faltering start in 1805 and had a disastrous finish: He was sentenced to be shot for surrendering Detroit to an outnumbered British general in 1812 without a fight, a sentence later set aside by President Madison.

In *Michigan, A History of the Wolverine State,* Hull was described as handicapped at the outset of his term "by his total lack of acquaintance with frontier life and problems. ... In his administration of territorial affairs, Hull seems to have disregarded the fact that a majority of the inhabitants were of French extraction and understood neither the customs nor the language of the Americans."[2]

Petoskey-born historian Bruce Catton described Hull's capitulation to British Maj. Gen. Sir Isaac Brock:

"Hull had more soldiers at his command than Brock had, but Brock knew how to use what strength he had, and Hull — well, Hull was a stout old smooth-bore, with a good record in the Revolutionary War, but he was in decay now and the fire was gone out of him, and when Brock led his men across the river and sent in a demand for surrender, Hull flabbergasted his officers by hanging out the white flag."[3]

One of those officers was Lewis Cass, who had about 300 men some three miles away from Detroit at the time, and who later testified against Hull at the court martial.

* George B. Porter, a member of the Pennsylvania Legislature and brother of the Pennsylvania governor, was named in 1831 by President Jackson as the last territorial governor of Michigan, although there were two subsequent acting governors.

Map of Michigan Territory, 1823

9

State Archives

Lewis Cass

The advantages of the territory are every day more and more known and appreciated. The fertility of our soil, and its adaption to the stable agricultural products of the middle states, promise rich rewards to our citizens. Our climate is highly favorable to hardy and vigorous exertion.

— Lewis Cass, message to Legislative Council, June 7, 1824.

Nearly 200 years after he had come to the state, Lewis Cass still loomed as one of the foremost names in state history and politics, as well as Michigan's most eminent statesman.

A harbinger of the early 1980s' "Say Yes to Michigan" promotion of Gov. William G. Milliken and the mid-1980s' "Yes M!CH!GAN" drumbeating of Gov. James J. Blanchard, Cass was Michigan's first and most important cheerleader. As historian Catton put it, "it developed that the East contained many people who had heard Gov. Cass' siren song and wanted to go to Michigan to live."[4]

Initially, selling Michigan was no easy task. In its early years, Michigan was not considered much of a prize. Settlers heard the soil was bad. Some surveyors said the land was so poor it wasn't worth the cost to survey. On more than one occasion, Cass called for new surveys.

Unfortunately, at the time, much of the land west and south of Detroit was a bog. A warning about unhealthy conditions was put to rhyme in the East:

"Don't go to Michigan, that land of ills; The word means ague, fever and chills."[5]

Cass himself on occasion was Michigan's great surveyor. In 1820, he made an extraordinary voyage by birch bark canoe from Detroit to what is now Minnesota to promote settlement, and to investigate natural resources and meet with Indians. He was accompanied by a party of about 65, including 23 soldiers he recruited at Mackinac Island. Such a trek was not a new experience: long before that trip, and many years before becoming governor, the intrepid Cass had proven his mettle. When only 17, he crossed the Allegheny Mountains on foot, seeking a home in the virtually unexplored "Great West."[6]

The extended travels of Cass would be astonishing to modern governors, who are chairbound in Lansing much of the time except for brief trips away from the capital by limousine, airplane and helicopter.

Cass' 1820 expedition was not brief. It took from May 24 to Sept. 25, and covered more than 4,200 miles. The party traveled up Lake Huron to Mackinac Island (a 14-day trip), and, later, west along the Lake Superior shore. Leaving Lake Superior, Cass traveled via the St. Louis River to seek out the source of the Mississippi River. He returned east by the Wisconsin-Fox rivers portage route, and along the east shore of Lake Michigan to Fort Dearborn at the site that later became Chicago. From there he rode horseback back to Detroit.

Cass promptly reported on the expedition by letter to Secretary of War John C. Calhoun, saying "the journey was performed without the occurrence of a single untoward accident sufficiently important to deserve recollection."[7]

He also shrugged off a tense encounter with Chippewa Indians in Sault Ste. Marie, an incident which deserves recollection. A meeting with a council of Chippewa chiefs broke up when Chief Sa-sa-ba, wearing a British officer's coat, denounced the Americans, threw his war lance into the ground, and kicked aside gifts Cass had laid before him. The Indians then crossed a small ravine and returned to their encampment on a small hill a few hundred yards away where they raised the British flag.

(Although the Indians understandably were suspicious of most white men, they were at the time on relatively friendly terms with the British, who gave them gifts, employed Indian superintendents respected by the Indians and otherwise convinced the Indians they were the lesser of evils.)

Here was how one 19th century account described what happened:

"The governor instantly ordered the expedition under arms, and, calling the interpreter, proceeded with him, naked handed and alone, to Sa-sa-ba's lodge. ... On reaching the lodge of the hostile and violent chief, he, with his own hands, pulled down the British flag, trod upon it, and, entering the lodge, told Sa-sa-ba that the hoisting of that insulting flag was an indignity which would not be tolerated on American soil ...

"The bold and daring course pursued by Gen. Cass had its effect and evidenced a thorough knowledge of the Indian character. They respect bravery ...

"Towards evening, another council of chiefs was convened, and a treaty read and signed by all, except Sa-sa-ba."[8]

The treaty recognized the American right to a four-square-mile tract along the St. Marys River, where Fort Brady was established two years later. Cass, known among Indians as "Great Father of Detroit" and "Big Belly," gradually negotiated far larger treaties with the tribes. Although the territory of Michigan was ceded to the United States by the British in 1783,

Bentley

Indians owned the land of Michigan itself until it was ceded, treaty by treaty.

Michigan gained six million acres in the northeastern Lower Peninsula by the 1819 Treaty of Saginaw. The 1823 Treaty of Chicago gained the state most of the southwestern section of the peninsula. In 1831, President Andrew Jackson appointed Cass secretary of war, and then, in 1836, minister to France. Cass was elected to the U.S. Senate in 1845, resigning when he became the Democratic presidential nominee in 1848. He lost to Whig Zachary Taylor, who won a plurality of the popular votes and 163 out of 290 electoral votes when Cass and ex-President Martin Van Buren, running on the Free Soil ticket, split the Democratic vote. Cass came close to obtaining the Democratic nomination in 1844 and was a leading but losing contender for the nomination again in 1852, when he turned 70.

But Cass, who in 1851 had returned to the Senate, had one more role to fill with distinction — as President James Buchanan's secretary of state. Cass not only made history, he cherished it. He was a founder of the Historical Society of Michigan in 1828.

Geologist and Indian authority Henry Rowe Schoolcraft accompanied Cass on the 1820 expedition, discovering many traces of iron and copper. He was a member of the Michigan Territorial Council.

Painting by Percy Ives

Lewis Cass makes the treaty of Saginaw with Chippewa Indians, Sept. 24, 1819. Percy Ives completed the painting in 1922 to hang in Detroit's new Cass Technical High School, which replaced the original structure on land donated by General Cass in 1860.

School principal Benjamin F. Comfort, author of *Lewis Cass and the Indian Treaties*, said the scene shows Chief Kishkaukou after he told Cass: "We have not asked you to come here. We do not want to sell our lands. We received them from the Great Spirit for our hunting grounds. We want them for our children and our children's children."

Cass replied: ". . .your Great Father, the President. . . is going to give you your share of these lands and pay you for the rest of them and try to make you happy."

STEWARDS OF THE STATE
The Governors of Michigan

The Elected Governors of Michigan

State Archives

Stevens T. Mason (1835-1840)

The time has arrived when Michigan is called upon to act for herself. She has petitioned Congress, again and again, to extend to her the same measure of liberality and justice, which has been extended to all the territories heretofore admitted into the Union as States.

— To the Legislative Council of the territory of Michigan, Sept. 1, 1834.

S tevens T. Mason, who led Michigan to statehood, was one of its most extraordinary political figures. He achieved young and died young.

At 19, he was appointed territorial secretary of Michigan and served periodically as acting governor; at 24 he became the state's first elected governor; at 25 he presided over Michigan's admission to statehood. And then, after leaving office amid controversy and struggling to be a New York lawyer and raise a family, he died at 31.

Of his 10 years in Michigan, eight were spent as a leader. As Michigan celebrated its Sesquicentennial in 1987, Mason still was

recognized the youngest governor in the nation's history.*

While not minimizing Mason's achievements, much of his niche in Michigan history was carved by timely presence in the right place: He had become territorial secretary Aug. 1, 1831, because his father left the job and the state; he often served as acting governor because territorial Gov. George B. Porter frequently was absent over a three-year period, and eventually died of cholera July 6, 1834. He was handy when Henry D. Gilpin's appointment as governor in January 1835 was rejected by the U.S. Senate, which held confirmation power, and Charles Shaler, named acting governor in August 1835, declined the appointment.

Stevens Thomson Mason was born into aristocracy Oct. 22, 1811, in Loudoun County, Va. His great-grandfather, George Mason, was a friend of George Washington and Patrick Henry, and he wrote Virginia's first constitution. His grandfather, after whom he was named, was a U.S. senator from Virginia. His father was John Thomson Mason, a lawyer who in 1830 was appointed by President Andrew Jackson as secretary of the Michigan territory. His mother was the former Elizabeth Moir, descendant of Scottish poet David Macbeth Moir. Mason was a year old when his family moved to Kentucky, where he later attended Transylvania University. He dropped out of school in 1828 and worked as a grocer's clerk to help his family financially.

While widely known as "the boy governor," (he once punched an editor who called him that)[1] a nickname given to the feisty Mason by President Jackson better described his spirit: "Young Hotspur."[2] It was Jackson who appointed Mason as territorial secretary in 1831 when Mason's father moved to Texas. It was Jackson who later removed young Mason, whose aggressiveness in pursuing Michigan's border dispute with Ohio angered official Washington.

On Sept. 15, 1835, Jackson replaced Mason with John S. Horner of Virginia. But

---

* In theory, it is a record that still could be broken. California and Washington have set a minimum age of only 18 for governors. However, in most states, including Michigan, it is 30. Gov. James H. Higgins of Rhode Island was 30 when elected in 1906. Arkansas Gov. Bill Clinton was 32 when elected in 1978. Edward L. Curtis had just turned 25 when he became acting governor of the Idaho territory May 15, 1883. He died at age 31.

Michiganians refused to acknowledge Horner, dubbing him "Little Jack Horner, who fled to a corner." One night in Ypsilanti, citizens pelted his lodging with stones and blobs of horse dung.

Horner, indeed, then fled. The next month, voters approved the Constitution of 1835 and made Mason Michigan's first elected governor.

The mettle of Mason is reflected in the following excerpts from his legislative messages as he led Michigan toward statehood:

Sept. 1, 1834 — Nearly nine months earlier, Congress had rejected as "inexpedient" Michigan's petition for an enabling act to allow it to join the Union. Mason, who on July 6, 1834, had become acting territorial governor upon the death of Porter, called the Legislative Council into special session. He said, "The time has arrived when Michigan is called upon to act for herself," and proposed a special census.

Nov. 17, 1834 — He called another special session to report census results and asked for a constitutional convention to institute a state government. He reported that the Lower Peninsula population "amounts to 85,856 souls" — exceeding the 60,000 required for statehood under the federal Ordinance of 1787, which established the Northwest Territory. It represented a threefold increase over four years. (The official 1834 figure was later set at 87,278.)

Mason said the Ordinance of 1787 "secured to us as a right, that whenever any of the states to be formed in the territory ceded by Virginia to the United States northwest of the river Ohio, shall have sixty thousand free inhabitants, 'such state *shall* (emphasis added by Mason) be admitted by its delegates into the Congress of the United States, on an equal footing with the original states in all respects whatever; and *shall* be at liberty to form a permanent constitution and state government.'"

Although Michigan lacked political clout in Congress, its case was helped because it was becoming the most popular destination for westward-moving settlers. Mason biographer Lawton T. Hemans noted that Michigan's border dispute with Ohio "had at least one beneficial result for the state; it had advertised its prospects and possibilities; it had created an interest throughout the East in the state's resources and people. ... It seemed as though there was hardly a hamlet of New England or New York that

Catlin
First State Capitol, Detroit, about 1840

was not sending its delegation of pioneers."[3] The "Michigan fever" was reflected in the *Michigania* song heard among infusions of pioneers who had become the lifeblood of statehood. It began:

Come all ye Yankee farmers who wish to change your lot.
  Who've spunk enough to travel beyond your native spot.
  And leave behind the village where Pa and Ma must stay.
  Come follow me, and settle in Michigania — Yea, yea, yea, in Michigania.[4]

Jan. 12, 1835 — Mason warned the Legislative Council "the united efforts of the representatives of Ohio, Indiana and Illinois" in Congress were about to succeed in awarding Ohio a disputed 470-square-mile strip of land that included what today is Toledo. He was right — even though Congress had disregarded Ohio's claim to the disputed territory when it admitted Ohio to the Union in 1803, and again in 1805 when the territory of Michigan was established, and Congress provided that Michigan's southern boundary should be

15

that set forth in the Northwest Ordinance.[5]

The ordinance stipulated that "an east and west line drawn through the southerly or extreme of Lake Michigan" would be the north-south dividing line between states in the eastern portion of the Northwest Territory. As a Michigan History Division report noted: "The southerly end of Lake Michigan did lie to the south of Toledo, but in Washington during the 1830s political considerations could bend surveyors' quadrants."[6]

Mason said it was an "unequal contest" that Michigan was waging against Ohio and its congressional allies from Indiana and Illinois. He said the only course was "the speedy assumption by Michigan of a form of state government, when she will not be assumed to protect her soil at the bar of congress, but as a sovereign state will defend it before the supreme judicial tribunal of the country." He said:

"The question before you is not so much how you can make Michigan a rich or wealthy state, as how to make her a free, sovereign and independent state, possessing all the privileges and rights of the other states."

Aug. 17, 1835 — In a special session of the Legislative Council called to report on the dispute with Ohio, Mason said: "If the demand of Ohio is tamely submitted to, what becomes of the rights of the states? Surrender once to the sordid grasp of a state seeking empire or power, and the period may arrive when one portion of the nation appealing to their own strength will prescribe laws for their weaker neighbors."

He had much more to report: During May and June of 1835, a convention wrote the constitution that Mason sought; Ohio Gov. Robert Lucas erected survey marks along the line disputed by Michigan; federal mediators and ex-Gov. Lewis Cass failed to resolve the Michigan-Ohio dispute; Mason ordered the arrest of all Ohioans trying to organize the disputed 520-square-mile territory as an Ohio county; and both states mobilized their militia and exchanged hostilities in essentially bloodless encounters popularly called the "Toledo War" — a misnomer in that it was not a war and the city of Toledo was not yet chartered.

Nov. 3, 1835 — On this day, Democrat Mason was inaugurated as Michigan's first elected governor, having won by a 7,558-814 margin over Whig John Biddle in the October election that also approved Michigan's new constitution. Michigan had

rejected compromise with Ohio, and had begun to function as a state without federal blessing. Its defiant act was etched not only in history, but also in the Great Seal of the State of Michigan, which shows 1835 as the date of Michigan's entry into the Union.

So it was a dramatic moment when Mason, who had turned 24 just 12 days earlier, addressed the first *state* legislative session called in the Capitol in Detroit. He spoke with modesty seldom voiced by a chief executive of any state, saying that he took office with "anxiety induced by a sincere consciousness, that the cares before me are above my ability, and that in venturing upon them I have consulted my capacity less, probably, than the impulses of a premature ambition."

But ambitious "Young Hotspur" already had demonstrated capacity.

Feb. 1, 1836 — A disappointed Mason told the Legislature (The former Legislative Council): "The position which Michigan now occupies with the nation, is a peculiar although not a new one in the history of our government. It is that of a people claiming and exercising all the reserved rights and privileges of an American state, and yet excluded from the bonds of the federal union."

July 11, 1836 — Mason, convinced that Michigan would be admitted to the Union only if it yielded on the disputed boundary question with Ohio, presented Congress' terms to the Legislature: "Were I to consult the first impulse prompted by the feelings which every citizen of Michigan must acknowledge, I might be led into a determination to resist the legislation of Congress," he said. But he called on Michiganians to "discard excited feelings" and avoid action "offering so little hope of gain, but the certainty of permanent loss and lasting injury to ourselves and to the nation."

Reluctantly, Mason accepted the condition that Congress would admit Michigan if it relinquished the disputed territory to Ohio, with Michigan getting the western Upper Peninsula as compensation. Impelling Mason to accept was Michigan's worsening financial condition, and the fact that recognized statehood would mean federal funds to start his internal improvement projects.

A Sept. 26 convention, assembled under a legislative act, rejected the conditions. But another convention, assembled without legislative sanction and known as the

Frostbitten Convention, voted on a cold Dec. 15 in Ann Arbor to accept the congressional terms. President Jackson promptly informed Congress of Michigan's assent based on a convention that "originated from the people themselves." He deemed it "most agreeable" to Congress' intent, and declared: "Your early action upon it is too obvious to need remark."[7]

Jan. 2, 1837 — Mason delivered a long message outlining plans for the new state's education, prison and other programs. Although financial problems were looming, Mason was optimistic as Michigan was about to be admitted as the 26th state:

"The tide of emigration is rapidly extending its course to the remotest borders of the state; unprecedented health has blessed the habitations of the people; abundant harvests have crowned the exertions of the agriculturist; our cities and villages are thronging with an active and enterprising population; and not withstanding the embarrassments which have surrounded us in our relations to the federal Union, social order has been preserved, and the majesty of the law has been supreme."

Michigan's population had increased to 174,619. By the time it reached 212,267 in 1840, Michigan had the largest 1830-40 percentage increase of any state or territory.[8] As an indication of the extent of the 1836 population "tide" touted by Mason, in just one day the ferry boat *Argo* brought 20 covered wagons of immigrants to Detroit; there were 90 steamboat arrivals in Detroit in May, and during June, on an average, a wagon left Detroit for the interior every five minutes during daylight.[9]

Mason's Jan. 2, 1837, State of the State Message included a subject that he focused on throughout his governorship: "Our militia system ... is worse than valueless. ... Too little importance is generally attached to this branch of our state policy." In 1834, he mustered troops at Niles in the southwestern part of the state when it appeared that the Black Hawk War might spill over to Michigan. But Black Hawk, chief of the Sacs and Foxes, was defeated and captured

Election Day in Detroit: Mason is depicted left center in a tall black hat. To the right, a supporter on horseback holds a Mason banner. In the background, opponents carry a banner promising "Provisions for the poor if Whigs carry the day." Some suggested painter T.H.O. Burnham portrayed Mason buying votes.

Detroit Institute of Arts

17

before he reached Chicago. In 1835, Mason sent 1,000 militiamen into the disputed Michigan-Ohio boundary strip. In 1833, the militia patrolled Detroit streets for a week during what Mason biographer Hemans described as "the Negro Riot,"* a disturbance sparked when two blacks who were "fugitives from the services" of a slave owner in Kentucky broke out of jail.[10]

Although he squabbled with, and for a time defied, the federal government on the conditions of statehood, once Michigan became a state, Mason was eloquent in espousing "sacred ties which bind us together as a nation." He challenged citizens of the new state not to let patriotism "be limited by the confines and boundaries of a single state."

"Why," he asked the Legislature on Jan. 2, 1838, "do we permit the value of the Union to be questioned? Why do we listen to contracted and selfish calculations of the balance of power between North and South? Do American citizens already begin to distrust and fear each other? If so, it forebodes little good to our Union."

This was not Michigan Civil War Gov. Austin Blair talking. It was the nation's youngest governor warning its newest state of conflict yet to come. Stevens T. Mason, 26, said "fellow citizens: cling to Michigan, but live and act for your country — *your whole country.*"

W ith statehood secure, Mason was able to devote more effort to the high priority he put on education and development programs. He championed a state-directed free school program, and appointed as superintendent of public instruction John D. Pierce, the pioneer of the Michigan school system. He also championed the University of Michigan, promoting its location in Ann Arbor, and seeking funding in 1837 "which will enable the state to place that institution upon an elevation of character and standing equal to that of any similar institution in the union."

He pushed a state geological survey and appointed Douglass Houghton as the first state geologist; a ship canal around the falls on the St. Marys River at Sault Ste. Marie, and an ambitious internal improvement program which included railroads, roads and a canal network connecting the state's major rivers. The railroads were to reach out westward from Monroe, Detroit and Port

Huron to the east shore of Lake Michigan. One canal was to connect the Clinton River in the east with the Kalamazoo River in the west. The other was to connect the Saginaw and Grand rivers. Later, a separate act provided for a third canal around the falls of the St. Marys River at Sault Ste. Marie.

Mason recommended that the state borrow money to become a subscriber to the stock of private companies that would be organized to build the railroads and canals. But the Legislature preferred to proceed by state action alone.

The act authorized Mason to fund the projects by selling bonds for $5 million to Eastern creditors. But one, Morris Canal and Banking Co., defaulted on its payments to Michigan. Another, the former Bank of the United States, which had purchased three-fourths of the bonds, went bankrupt.

Mason's handling of all this high finance came against a backdrop of national and state money woes. The Panic of 1837 developed after doubts about the soundness of paper money set in when President Jackson issued his Specie Circular. This decreed that only gold and silver would be acceptable payment by new settlers for public land.

Then there was the matter of Michigan's "wildcat banks." As requested by Mason, the Legislature passed a law permitting any 12 freeholders to establish a banking association if they had $500,000 in capital. The original act required specie subscription but the Panic of 1837 prompted Mason to suspend the payment of coin for notes. Currency became scarce, and Michigan's banking system collapsed.

Mason showed amazing foresight when he sought an appropriation for the Soo canal. He was less on the mark with his Jan. 2, 1837, pronouncement to the Legislature that, "The practicability of uniting the waters of Lake Michigan with those of the eastern part of the state has been long conceded." Mason also improved the State Library and promoted the idea of a prison at Jackson. He emphasized the importance of

---

* Michigan's black population was estimated at about 400 in 1833. Well before then, Detroit had become a terminal of the "Underground Railway," assisting blacks in their flight from slavery. At one point in the 1833 disturbance, according to Hemans, "from the bushes that grew near the jail, from barns, and from every means of cover scores of Negroes rushed towards the jail armed with every conceivable kind of weapon. ... A score or more of Negroes were placed under arrest, under an old statute requiring people of their race to give security for their good behavior."

The Detroit News

Mason statue, Detroit, 1925

training prisoners in a self-supporting trade and told the Legislature on Jan. 4, 1838, that failure to stress reformation of offenders would mean "our penitentiary will become the school of vice."

In 1837, Mason was re-elected by a 15,314-to-14,546 vote over Whig candidate Charles C. Trowbridge, a plurality of 768. Mason won Detroit by 38 votes, but lost Wayne County by 68. As would prove true with many subsequent governors, Mason's last term sullied his reputation, and Michigan suffered from the impact of national economic decline. In this case, it was the Panic of 1837. Michigan banks had begun to fail, prompted in part by state banking laws that Mason had promoted.

"Michigan's first governor, who had wielded a special magic, found himself the scapegoat for all of Michigan's problems," Jean Frazier wrote for Michigan History magazine. "He was publicly abused and slandered by the Whigs."[11] Bruce Catton noted that Mason "lost everything — his enthusiasm, his popularity and, finally, his job. He had caused his state to bite off much more than it could chew, and when

the whole business exploded, he got all of the blame."[12].

In opening his Jan. 7, 1839, message to the Legislature, Mason signaled his intention not to run again, saying it was "the last annual communication I shall be called upon to present to the people of the state of Michigan." The words of his father, written in 1835, were prophetic:

"Politics are fascinating, but altogether delusive; and I think a poor broken-down politician the most miserable of society. Even one honorably retiring is soon forgotten, and he sickens from neglect. I have seen so much of this unprofitable life that I look upon your course as full of hazards and disappointments, as that of every politician must be. But take care not to progress too rapidly and be not ambitious of promotion. When it comes regularly and unsought for, it has some stability and secures a foundation to build on.

"You stand infinitely higher as secretary and acting governor, than if you were governor because less is expected from you."[13].

In 1838, Mason married Julia Elizabeth

Phelps, a New York City socialite he met while in New York for negotiations on the $5-million loan. In 1841, they moved to New York. Struggling with a law practice and raising three children, Mason became sick Jan. 1, 1843, and died Jan. 4 of what was widely described as pneumonia. (In a Jan. 5 family letter, his father wrote that a physician "said his case was a suppressed scarlet fever."[14])

Mason was buried in Marble Cemetery in New York City. In 1905, his remains were reinterred in Capitol Park in downtown Detroit, under the foundations of the old Capitol building where he presided as first governor of the new state of Michigan.

Prolific writer

The pen was a mighty instrument for Michigan's first governor. While modern governors have speech writers and computers to help produce their legislative communications, Stevens T. Mason had only his pen and what must have been a barrel of ink.

Vaults at the Burton Historical Collection in the Detroit Public Library contain veto and other messages that Mason penned to the Legislature, some of them with words blotted out and other words inserted. Mason edited as he wrote.

The Burton Collection also contains a treasury of letters that Mason wrote to

Mason letter to his mother

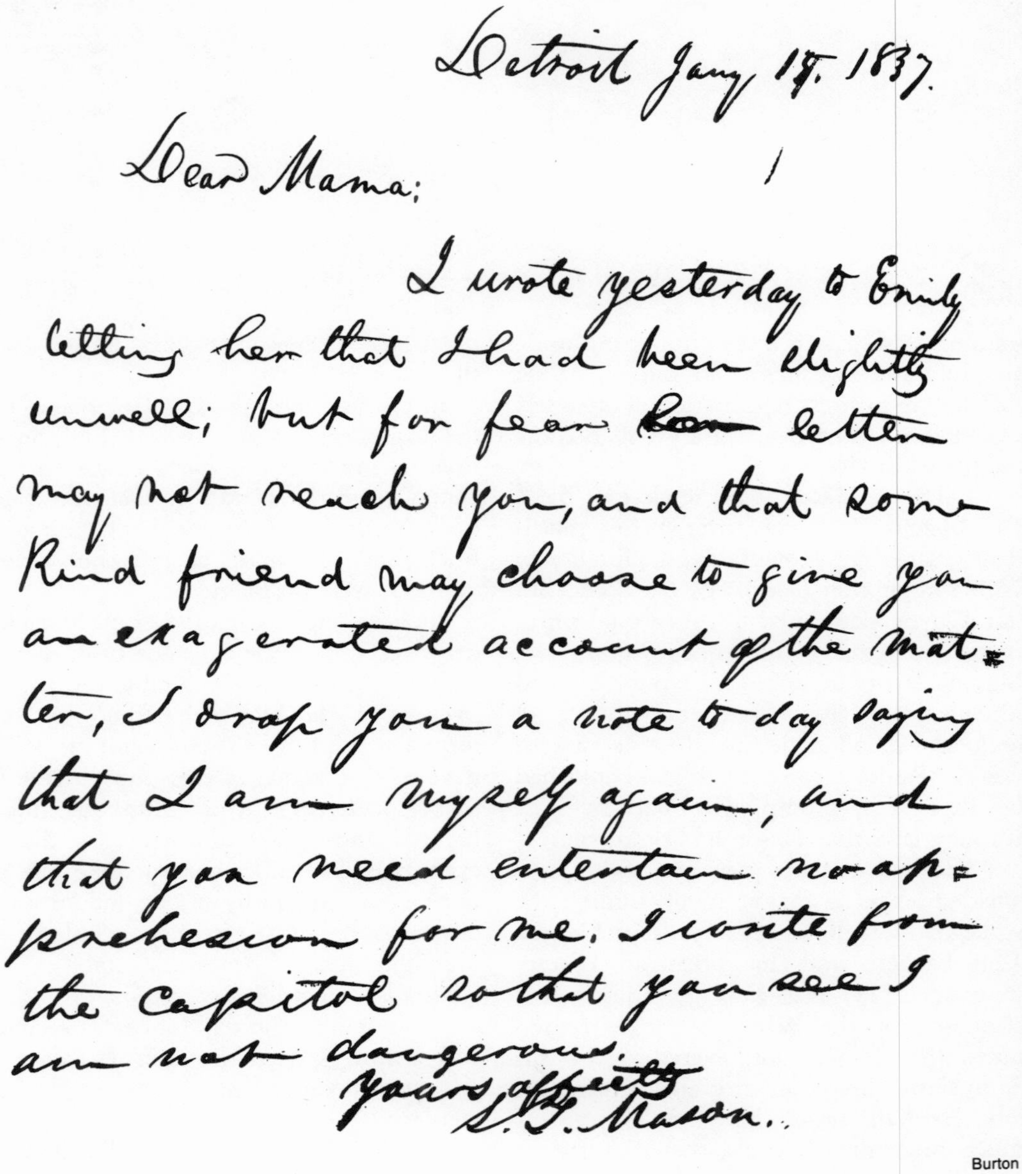

Detroit Jany 14. 1837.

Dear Mama;

I wrote yesterday to Emily letting her that I had been slightly unwell; but for fear that letter may not reach you, and that some kind friend may choose to give you an exagerated account of the matter, I drop you a note to day saying that I am myself again, and that you need entertain no apprehension for me. I write from the capitol so that you see I am not dangerous.

Yours affec'ty

S. T. Mason.

Burton

20

President Andrew Jackson and to his own family.

In a Dec. 15, 1833, "petition" he sent to Jackson, for example, Mason complained that he had been acting territorial governor and Indian commissioner for about eight months, yet had only been paid his regular territorial secretary salary. He noted that George B. Porter, who was Michigan's 1831-34 territorial governor, was still drawing his gubernatorial salary and his pay as Indian commissioner even though he wasn't performing the duties. In his petition asking to be paid for his acting governor responsibilities, Mason said, "he (Mason) does not mention this circumstance in a spirit of envy but merely to show that the governor (Porter) cannot in fairness urge any objection against his claim."*

Another personal financial matter in the Mason papers was a $50 IOU, dated July 9, 1840, from a client Mason represented in U.S. Circuit Court. Presumably, Mason was never paid.

Mason was prolific in writing family letters, and they reflected a gentle sense of humor that did not come out in his official pronouncements.

Letters to his mother began: "My dear Mama." In a Jan. 15, 1837, letter to her, he expressed concern that she might have heard that he had been ill, and "some kind friend may give you an exaggerated account of the matter." But he concluded by saying: "I write from the Capitol so that you see I am not dangerous."

In an Aug. 1, 1839, letter written "Wednesday, 1/2 past 2 p.m.," Mason informed his mother of the birth of a son with "black eyes, black hair." The next day, saying he was doing so "by instruction" of his wife, Julia, he corrected himself, noting the baby's hair was dark brown. He enclosed a lock of hair.

In a March 11, 1842, letter to his father about another birth, Mason said the child had "great proficiency in the arts of sleeping, eating and bawling."

* The document did not indicate what the territorial governor's pay was. But Mason, who became Michigan's first elected governor when the state declared statehood in 1835, had an annual salary of $2,000.

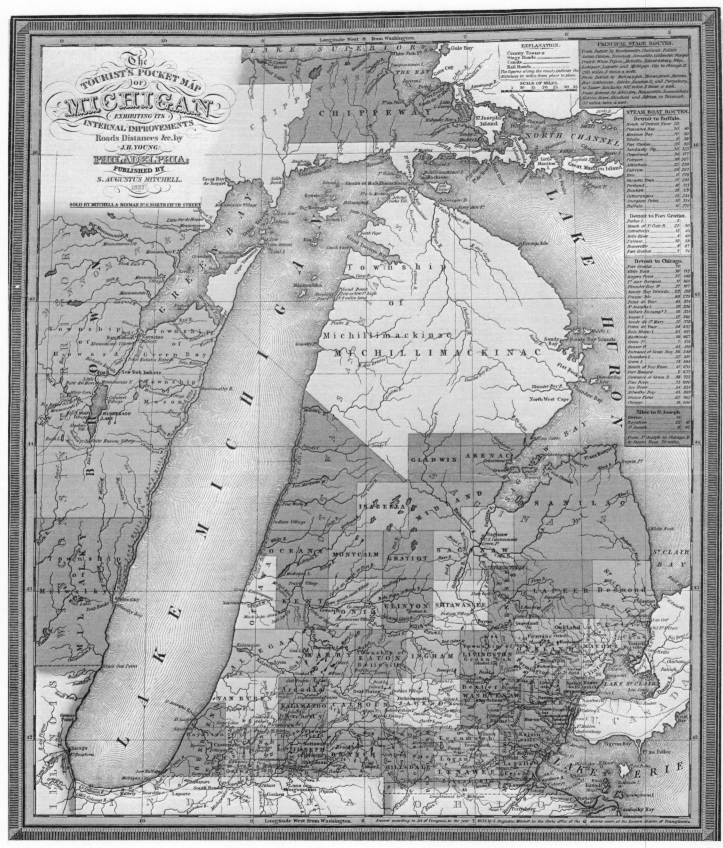

Michigan at statehood

Hatcher

Michigan Bell Telephone Co.

Boom/Bust/Rebound:

From the Start, the Story of Michigan and Its Governors.

Michigan rode into statehood on the crest of an economic boom powered by a land rush and easy credit. But, as was to happen so often throughout its first 150 years of statehood, Michigan and a Michigan governor were riding for a fall. The Michigan cycle began: It went abruptly from boom to bust, largely because of economic forces beyond its border, compounded by excessive spending at home.

The national Panic of 1837 was building when Mason pushed through his ambitious internal improvements program. The mania was not Mason's alone. Legislators and the press were caught up with a mid-1830s development craze that swept from the East.

The Detroit Daily Advertiser on March 9, 1837, called for a system of railroads "as numerous as cotton or woolen factories."

Historians Willis F. Dunbar and George S. May, in *Michigan: A History of the Wolverine State,* said, "Looking back on the boom of the mid-'30s it is difficult to understand why the people of the time failed to recognize the clear signs they were riding for a fall."

But fall they did. Enter William Woodbridge to pick up the pieces.

THE IRON HORSE — An 1837 scene by Artist Robert A. Thom, commissioned by Michigan Bell Telephone Company

State Archives

William Woodbridge (1840-1841)

It can never be either expedient or wise, to undertake more than can be fitly and within a reasonable time, accomplished. But with us in Michigan, we have many things begun, but nothing finished. We have nothing yet productive!

— State of the State Message to the Legislature, Jan. 7, 1841.

H e served Michigan for 36 years, in all three branches of government and eventually joined the U.S. Senate. But William Woodbridge, Michigan's second governor, is remembered, in large part, as a nemesis of its first.

Woodbridge, one of the first leaders of the Whig Party in Michigan and the only Whig to be elected governor, argued that Michigan's 1835 election of Stevens T. Mason as governor was illegal because it had occurred before Congress had approved statehood. In July 1837, at Woodbridge's invitation, Daniel Webster spent four days in Detroit stirring Whig opposition to Mason through bombastic oratory.[1] As a candidate for governor in 1839, Wood-

bridge himself campaigned on a platform of "retrenchment and reform." In his own brief tenure as governor, Woodbridge focused on what he argued was a fiscal mess inherited from both Mason and the national economy.

In his 1841 State of the State message, Woodbridge said, "It appears that during the first four years of our state government, a debt of nearly $400,000 has been created, beyond the means provided for its redemption." Woodbridge hounded Mason on a $5-million internal improvements loan that had gone sour during Mason's administration. A biographical sketch of Mason by Patricia J. Baker, published by the Michigan History Division, said, "Woodbridge drummed up a charge that Mason had accepted money from one of the companies handling the $5-million loan. So thorough was Woodbridge that he even secured a false confession from an associate of Mason, stating that the ex-governor had indeed taken a bribe."[2] But there was no disputing that Woodbridge was the first of a long line of Michigan governors to confront severe budget problems upon taking office.

At the outset of his first year in office, Woodbridge lamented the impact of the nation's money woes on Michigan in a Jan. 4, 1840, legislative message, saying there "still remain evils in the bosom of the state, which no effort, no skill of ours can thoroughly eradicate. ... We have had the misfortune to see our general currency reduced from a condition of the most enviable excellence, to that of almost utter worthlessness."

Woodbridge was not in office long enough to deal with these problems. He resigned Feb. 24, 1841, after being elected to the U.S. Senate,* where he served six years. He earlier had served in the Ohio Senate and Assembly, in the Michigan Senate and in the U.S. Congress as a nonvoting Michigan territorial delegate. He also was a territorial Supreme Court justice, the first of four Michigan governors who served in all three branches of territorial or state government in Michigan.

A subsequent Michigan governor, Robert McClelland, said of Woodbridge: "With

---

* Under the U.S. Constitution, members of the Senate were elected by the legislatures of their respective states, rather than by popular vote, until the 17th Amendment went into effect in 1913.

Wide World

the exception of General Cass, there was no man who did more to mould the character of the state than Governor Woodbridge."[3] Woodbridge, then a member of the Ohio Senate, was appointed by President James Madison as secretary of the Michigan Territory on Sept. 30, 1814, serving until 1828. In 1819, he was elected the first delegate to Congress from territorial Michigan. But Woodbridge, sensitive to criticism that too much power was concentrated in one man, withdrew at the end of his first year as delegate. In 1828, he was named to the Supreme Court, and was a delegate at the convention that framed the Constitution of 1835.

He was elected governor Nov. 4, 1839, by a vote of 18,195-17,037 over Democrat Elon Farnsworth, a Detroit lawyer.

Woodbridge was born in Norwich, Conn., Aug. 20, 1780. His family moved to Marietta, Ohio, in 1791, but he returned to Connecticut to get his degree at Litchfield Law School. He once described himself as "a son of New England. ... I was born in the latter part of the Revolutionary War; I inhaled with my first breath an unconquerable aversion to tyranny."[4]

As a lawyer, he returned to Ohio, where he became prosecuting attorney for Washington County. In 1806, he married Juliana Trumbull. They had four children. When Woodbridge's public career ended in 1847 with his retirement from the U.S. Senate, he settled on his farm near Detroit. Tiger Stadium, at Michigan and Trumbull, is located on a portion of the Woodbridge farm. Although some of his friends raised his name as a possible gubernatorial candidate in 1847, and as a vice-presidential running mate for Zachary Taylor in 1848, he preferred the life of a recluse and gentleman farmer, "mingling in no wise with public men, nor with public things."[5]

Woodbridge, who for months struggled with emphysema, died at age 81 on Oct. 20, 1861, and was buried in Detroit. A 19th century publication said "at the time of his death, he was the oldest and most distinguished member of the Detroit bar."[6]

A story handed down through generations of his family was that one of the responsibilities that weighed most heavily on Woodbridge was the power to grant pardons. "My grandfather, who was one of the governor's sons, told me he (Woodbridge) would walk the floor into the night and pray that he would make the right decision," recalled Mrs. Neil McMillan, great-granddaughter of the governor.[7]

Like Woodbridge, President William Henry Harrison was a Whig. This print shows his 1841 inaugural, to which he rode without a coat. He died of pneumonia a month later. Harrison was governor of the Indiana territory when it included the western half of Michigan.

25

State Archives

James Wright Gordon (1841)

... as ... he celebrated his prospective honors with his loyal friends, the Democrats sealed a compact for his defeat with a half-dozen Whig malcontents.

— From an account of how James Wright Gordon lost a bid for the U.S. Senate.

James Wright Gordon served as governor for less than a year, just 10 months and a week.* He once had a promising future as a politician, but met a mysterious death while in service as a diplomat.

Serving as lieutenant governor, he became governor on Feb. 23, 1841, when Gov. William Woodbridge resigned to go to the U.S. Senate. Like Woodbridge, Gordon was a Connecticut Yankee, born in 1809 in Plainfield. A Harvard graduate, he went to Geneva, N.Y., where he taught and studied law. During Michigan's 1835 land rush, he settled in Marshall. He married Mary Hudun of Geneva, N.Y., and had five children.

Gordon's popularity as a state senator was evident in 1839 when the Whig State Convention gathered in his hometown of Marshall on Aug. 28 to select an election slate. On the first ballot, he was nominated for lieutenant governor. It took three ballots to nominate Woodbridge for governor. Gordon later was elected 18,871-17,782 over Democrat Thomas Fitzgerald, a winning margin only slightly smaller than Woodbridge's.**

In their first year in office, both Gordon and Woodbridge demonstrated ambitions beyond the Capitol. Gordon displayed less than lockstep loyalty to his governor. Both eyed the U.S. Senate. Gordon was viewed at the time as having the best shot because, early on, he appeared to have the support of a majority of Whigs in both houses of the Legislature, which elected U.S. senators in those days and, at the time, was controlled solidly by Whigs. One account said he was the "Whig caucus nominee against Gov. Woodbridge."[1]

What happened was described by Lawton T. Hemans, biographer of Gov. Stevens T. Mason (1835-40):

"There is a tradition, attested by the reminiscence of many an old politician that James Wright Gordon was the clear choice of the senatorial caucus of his party, and that in the late hours of night as in wine and flow of soul he celebrated his prospective honors with his loyal friends, the Democrats sealed a compact for his defeat with a half-dozen Whig malcontents.

"Gordon promptly was nominated in the Senate by the unanimous Whig vote of 11. But in the House, he could never command the vote of more than 20. On Feb. 3, the two Houses met in joint session and the Democrats cast their united support for their old enemy, Gov. William Woodbridge, who was elected with the help of the few Whigs who had deserted their own party choice."[2] (At the time, the House had 52 members; the Senate, 17).

Why would some Democrats throw in with Whig Woodbridge? Because they had no chance of getting the Whig majority to elect a Democrat, and because some of his views coincided with theirs. Why would some Whigs who were known to be anti-Woodbridge, nonetheless vote for him? Because, according to Woodbridge biogra-

---

* William L. Greenly served for 10 months in 1847-48.
** It was not until 1966 that Michigan governors and lieutenant governors ran as a team.

pher Emily George, they hoped "by Woodbridge's election to make Gordon governor, since he would do their bidding."[3]

A 19th century Michigan history book called Gordon "a gentleman of high character and ability."[4] But Gordon lacked high historical visibility and made little impact on the Michigan governorship, beyond routine appointments, requisitions, extraditions, pardons and proclamations. Some state publications merely listed him as "lieutenant governor" for all of 1841, and he was not included in the Michigan Historical Commission's *Governors of the Territory and State of Michigan.*[5]

Yet even a caretaker governor touched many lives and institutions with official actions. In his first month as governor, Gordon made more than 200 appointments.[6] One of his first was an inspector of beef and pork for Allegan County. Two of his last were notaries public for Branch County. One of Gordon's longest public pronouncements as governor was the official 1841 Thanksgiving proclamation. Among his shortest was the call for a special election to fill the vacancy of state Sen. John S. Barry, who resigned in order to run successfully for governor in 1841. He signed his documents "Acting Governor."[7]

One of Gordon's first communications to the Legislature was to inform it that a Pennsylvania bank holding Michigan funds was failing. "The disastrous effects which must inevitably result, not only to the credit of the state, but also to a large and respectable class of our citizens, unless some measure shall be taken to provide for the deficiency thus likely to be produced in the public funds, cannot but be obvious," Gordon said.[8]

After completing Woodbridge's term as governor on Jan. 3, 1842, Gordon's health began to fail. In hopes of restoring it in a warmer climate, Gordon accepted a U.S. consulship in the Brazilian province of Pernambuco, a "rough and tumble place ... whose residents included pirates who terrorized the high seas."[9] Three years after taking up the post, he died in a fall off a second-story balcony in December 1853. His predecessor had met a similar fate. Adding to the mystery was that 20th century historians and diplomats have been unable to locate Gordon's grave — the only Michigan governor whose place of burial has not been determined. U.S. Rep. Carl Pursell, R-Plymouth, became involved in the search at the urging of Jerry Roe, a member of the Michigan Historical Commission, who has crusaded for suitable marking at the burial sites of all Michigan governors. In August 1984, Pursell received a letter from Edward A. Torre, the American consul in Recife, Brazil, saying the consulate was researching the matter because it "has now become a challenge and we are anxious to find out what really happened to our late colleague Mr. Gordon."[10]

State Archives

John S. Barry (1842-1846; 1850-1851)

It cannot be concealed, that embarrassments of no ordinary magnitude oppress the finances of the state. The public debt is heavy, and the immediate demands upon the treasury are beyond its present ability to meet.

— **Inaugural address, Jan. 3, 1842.**

Michigan's only 19th century three-term governor put the state's early financial house in order. The outlook was bleak when John S. Barry took office, but two years later he was able to report:

"Though, for a time, (Michigan's) prospects seemed obscured, the thick cloud is now dispelled and the obstacles removed that impeded her march onward to prosperity. The paper money bubble of former years has burst, and the mania of speculation has subsided."[1]

John Stewart Barry was born Jan. 29, 1802, in Amherst, N.H., and later moved to Rockingham, Vt., where he worked on his father's farm. He married Mary Kidder

in Vermont (they had no children) and moved in 1824 to Georgia, where he was in charge of an academy in Atlanta, practiced law and worked in the Georgia governor's office. He moved to Michigan in 1831, settling in White Pigeon and then Constantine, in southwestern Lower Michigan.

A successful merchant and one of the organizers of the Michigan Southern Railroad, Barry was a member of the convention that wrote the Constitution of 1835. He served in the state Senate in 1835-38, and was elected again in 1841, but resigned the same year to run as the Democratic candidate for governor. On Nov. 1, 1841, he defeated Whig Philo C. Fuller, 20,993-15,449. He was elected again in 1843, by 21,392-14,899 over Whig Zina Pitcher. At the time, there was a constitutional limit to a governor serving more than two consecutive terms. In 1849, he won again, 27,847-23,540 over Flavius Littlejohn, the Whig and Free Soil candidate.

The conservative Barry's early focus was on state finances. The day after his first inaugural, he reported that the state's indebtedness totaled $6,260,286 — an enormous amount for the times, particularly considering that the state's general fund expenditures for fiscal 1842 totaled only $161,514. He instituted a belt-tightening program, and began using proceeds from the sale of university and school lands. He pushed for repeal of all acts authorizing banks to suspend payment of their liabilities in legal currency. There was one story that he helped boost the hard-pressed state treasury by having grass in the Capitol yard cut and sold for hay.[2] By 1843, the debt was down to $3,535,334.

Barry's 1845 reports to the Legislature reflect the costs and size of some government activities as the new state began to function: Jurors were paid $1 a day, plus 6 cents a mile for travel; the state prison had 94 prisoners; there were 50 students at the University of Michigan; the state paid $28,076 for the support of local schools. By 1850, Barry reported "the large amount of $113,187 expended in the state the past year for the promotion of common school education," included operations and construction. There were 102,871 students in the primary schools. At the time, no tuition was charged to attend the University of Michigan, and Barry said, "The whole necessary annual expense of a student at this institution does not exceed $100 and, by practice of strict economy, may be reduced to $70."*

Leaving office in 1852, Barry returned to private life and his mercantile business in Constantine. He ran twice again for governor, losing in 1854 to Republican Kinsley S. Bingham and in 1860 to Republican Austin Blair. He was a delegate to the National Democratic Convention in Chicago in 1864. He died on Jan. 14, 1870, in Constantine, and was buried there.

* By standards of the 1980's, this would hardly buy a single credit hour. The estimated 1986 school year cost to a U. of M. freshman or sophomore was about $7,500. The first credit hour cost was about $145, and about $88 for each hour thereafter.

Bentley

University of Michigan in the 1840's, Mason Hall, named after Gov. Stevens T. Mason

State Archives

Alpheus Felch (1846-1847)

The history of our young republic, numbering now scarcely 10 years of existence as a state, has been crowded with questions of difficulty and embarrassment ... But although in the history of the past we see errors which, in the light of experience, we may now think might have been avoided, yet it is evident that our commonwealth has been blessed with general prosperity, and that her progress has been onward and upwards.

— Inaugural message, January 1846.

Post-statehood financial problems claimed the attention of Alpheus Felch, the third Michigan governor who wrestled with the numbers. He blamed the red ink on the state partaking "in some degree, as did...every other state in the union, of the speculative and extravagant spirit of the times."[1] He also was the second governor in the state's early years to quit the post before completing a term in order to go to the U.S. Senate, and was the second of the first five governors to serve in all three branches of government.

Felch was born Sept. 28, 1804, in Limerick, Maine. He graduated from Bowdoin College in Brunswick and practiced law in Maine for three years before moving to Michigan to practice in Monroe. He married Lucretia W. Lawrence and they had four children. His public service included the Michigan House, 1835-37; state bank commissioner, 1838-39; auditor general, 1842, and Michigan Supreme Court, 1842-45.

In 1845, the quiet, modest Democrat was elected governor with 20,123 votes and a 51 percent margin in a three-candidate race. It was during his term that the Legislature decided to move the capital to Lansing. He promptly took action to withdraw the land from the market, thus thwarting land speculators. While not among its most memorable governors, Felch was among Michigan's most distinguished early public servants. He was a tough bank commissioner when that was just what was needed. "The state banks of the period were, as a rule, corrupt and rotten," wrote Claudius B. Grant.[2]

As Gov. William Woodbridge (1840-41) before him, Felch resigned as governor to become a U.S. senator on March 3, 1847. In the Senate, he successfully fought for legislation for the first canal at Sault Ste. Marie. After six years as a senator, Felch was appointed president of the commission to settle war claims.

Felch ran unsuccessfully for governor in 1856, losing to Republican Kinsley S. Bingham. Also that year, he practiced law in Ann Arbor and later became a law professor at the University of Michigan and president of the State Historical Society.

Felch died in Ann Arbor on June 13, 1896, at age 91 and was buried there. He still holds the record as Michigan's longest-living governor.*

---

* Eight of Michigan's ex-governors, as of 1987, had died in their 80s, 11 in their 70s. Rhode Island Gov. Theodore Francis Green (1933-37) is believed to hold the U.S. gubernatorial record. He died at 99.

Catlin

Felch, who fought for the first canal at Sault Ste. Marie, recognized early on the importance of shipping to Michigan. Shown here are ships at the Detroit riverfront in 1838. The etching is copied from a print by H.L. Meharey, New York.

State Archives

William L. Greenly (1847)

The first political relations of his life were with us, and as soon as he had attained his majority he was by the almost-unanimous suffrages of our people elected to the chief magistracy of our state.[1]

— Announcing the death of Stevens T. Mason, Jan. 15, 1843.

As a state senator from Adrian, it was William L. Greenly who formally announced to the Senate the death of Michigan's first governor. As lieutenant governor, it was Greenly who stepped up March 3, 1847, to act as Michigan's chief executive for 10 months — the shortest tenure for a Michigan governor.* He replaced Alpheus Felch who resigned the governorship for a seat in the U.S. Senate.

William Greenly was born Sept. 18, 1813, in Hamilton, N.Y., and graduated from Union College, Schenectady, N.Y., in 1831. He was admitted to the bar in 1833 and practiced law in Eaton, N.Y., until October 1836, when he moved to Adrian in southeastern Michigan, where he practiced law. After an unsuccessful try for the Legislature in 1837, he was elected to the Senate for a two-year term in 1839 and returned in 1842-43. A Democrat, he was elected lieutenant governor in 1845. Greenly, as did James Wright Gordon, moved from lieutenant governor to the governorship, the second lieutenant governor in six years to become governor.

On March 16, 1847, Greenly signed into law legislation to move the state capital from Detroit, locating it "in the township of Lansing, in the county of Ingham." There was intense competition for the site. But many legislators of the day, who still had memories of battles with the British, argued against keeping Detroit as the capital city. They feared that as a border city, it would be at the mercy of enemy guns in case of war.

"Lansing," said one biographical sketch on Greenly, "was isolated; wilderness accessible only by stage, with the nearest railroad at Jackson."[2]

Greenly also signed legislation to abolish the Court of Chancery and transfer its duties to the Michigan Supreme Court.

During the Greenly administration, Michigan, at a cost of $10,500, furnished a regiment of volunteers for the war with Mexico.

After completing Felch's term Jan. 3, 1848, Greenly returned to Adrian, where he served as mayor in 1858 and was a justice of the peace for 12 years. He died Dec. 2, 1883, and was buried in Adrian. A Michigan Historical Commission publication decribed him as a "scholarly, cultured and genial man."[3]

Greenly was married three times, to Sarah A. Dascomb, Elizabeth W. Hubbard, and Maria Hunt.

* James Wright Gordon, another lieutenant governor who stepped up, served as governor for 10 months and one week. Frank D. Fitzgerald served only two months of his term before dying in 1939, but had served a full term in 1935-36.

Catlin

Logs are sorted and rafted at the mouth of the Muskegon River in the 1840's for delivery to sawmills on the Muskegon Lake. Each log has its owner's mark stamped on both ends.

Burton

Epaphroditus* Ransom (1848-1850)

It seems best ... to dispense with all unnecessary and useless communications. — **First message to the Legislature, Jan. 3, 1848.**

H e was a no-nonsense politician who served only one term as Michigan's governor. But Epaphroditus Ransom was the first one to head both the executive and judicial branches of state government.

Epaphroditus Ransom was born in Shelburne Falls, Mass., in February 1796, the son of a Revolutionary War officer, Ezekiel Ransom. He earned a law degree at Northampton in Massachusetts in 1823; was a member of the Vermont Legislature for several terms. He married Almire Cadwell of Vermont. They had a son who died in infancy. In 1834, Ransom moved to Michigan's Kalamazoo County to practice law. He was appointed a Circuit Court judge, Supreme Court justice, and then chief justice of the Michigan Supreme Court, serving in the latter position in

*Pronounced: ee-paff-row-DIE-tus

1843-47.

Democrat Ransom was elected governor in 1847 by a margin of 24,639-18,990 over Whig James M. Edmunds. He carried all counties.[1] Ransom was the first governor to be inaugurated in the new capital of Lansing. (The Capitol then was a temporary frame building 60-by-90 feet, the second of two buildings used before the present Capitol was dedicated in 1879).

The debt remaining from failure of a $5-million loan for ambitious "internal improvements" during the administration of Stevens T. Mason continued to plague the state. Ransom addressed it periodically as had governors Woodbridge, Barry and Felch before him.

Ransom reported the debt at the end of 1847 was $2,390,599, and said "to make early provisions for the ultimate payment of this debt, both principal and interest, appears to me to be an imperious duty, which we should neither attempt nor desire to avoid."[2] While the debt was heavy, the tax burden was not. After noting higher taxes in New York, Pennsylvania, Ohio, Indiana and Illinois, Ransom said:

"Taxes in Michigan for state and county purposes together have never exceeded in one year, 70 cents for each person in this state, while in some of those enumerated they have been almost double that amount."[3]

Ransom emphasized the importance of road improvements, and succeeded in enacting a toll plank-road law requiring companies to build "good, smooth, permanent roads." (In 1855, the law was changed to allow the use of gravel instead of planks.) The toll? Two cents per mile for two-horse vehicles and a penny per mile for those pulled by a single horse.[4]

Ransom also pushed for development of the Upper Peninsula, saying the potential there was "of such vast magnitude and importance" that it was important to build the long-discussed St. Marys Falls canal to permit shipping in and out of Lake Superior.[5]

In his Jan. 3, 1848, message to the Legislature, Ransom urged road development for the 2,000 or so Hollanders who had settled in Ottawa County the previous year, saying:

"They are a hardy, industrious, frugal, moral and religious people ... in the midst of a wild unbroken wilderness ... without roads, without mills, without mails, without magistrates or police regulations of any kind, and indeed without most of those facilities and conveniences that are deemed indispensably necessary to civilized life, even in its humblest condition."[6]

This appeal was not surprising. Ransom was a leader among a faction of west Michigan Democrats who believed state government placed too much emphasis on the eastern section — a factionalism that long has split Michigan politicians.[7]

The Michigan Agricultural Society was organized while Ransom was governor, and he became its first president.

After his one term as governor, Ransom returned to his home in Kalamazoo County, and later represented it in 1853-54 in the Michigan House of Representatives. He also was an 1850-52 member of the board of regents of the University of Michigan, one of six governors to serve as a U. of M. regent.

In 1857, Ransom was appointed by President James Buchanan as receiver of the Osage land office in Kansas. He died at Fort Scott, Kan., Nov. 9, 1859, at age 62. He was buried in Kalamazoo.

State Archives

The extensive mining of Michigan's Upper Peninsula copper in later years substantiated Ransom's feeling that the area had "vast magnitude and importance." Here is the shaft house at the old Quincy Mine in Hancock.

35

State Archives

Robert McClelland (1852-1853)

During the past year, the people of this state have been most signally blessed with the enjoyment of an unusual degree of prosperity. ... The state is growing rapidly in nearly all the elements of greatness. — **Message to the Legislature, Jan. 5, 1853.**

Of the eight men who had served as governor by the middle of the 19th century, Democrat Robert McClelland was able to give one of the most optimistic reports on the condition of the state.

"The financial condition of the state was never more healthy and encouraging," he said in his 1852 message.[1] There was a surplus in the treasury to help liquidate the troublesome internal improvement bonds, and Michigan's credit rating was on the upswing, as was the value of farmland. Villages were becoming cities.

Robert McClelland was born Aug. 2, 1807, in Greencastle, Pa., son of a prominent physician. After graduating from Dickinson College in Pennsylvania in 1829,

he went to Monroe to practice law in Michigan in 1833. He married Sarah E. Sabine of Massachusetts in 1837. They had six children. He was a delegate to the Constitutional Convention of 1835 — and, then again, to the Constitutional Convention of 1850*.

A member of the University of Michigan Board of Regents, McClelland was elected to the Michigan House of Representatives in 1839. He was House speaker in 1843, one of four Michigan governors to hold that position.** He was mayor of Monroe in 1841 and a member of the U.S. House of Representatives in 1843-45 and 1847-49.

In Congress, McClelland was an advocate of the celebrated "Wilmot Proviso," named after Pennsylvania Rep. David Wilmot, to prohibit slavery in newly acquired territory. As the Civil War approached, McClelland urged moderation and compromise, and as president of the Democratic State Convention in 1850 succeeded in getting passage of a resolution urging compromise.[2] A former law partner, I.P. Christiancy, wrote: "As a politician, (McClelland) was eminently cautious and conservative, and when he thought his party was going to extremes in any direction, he used his best efforts to restrain them."[3]

In 1851, McClelland defeated Whig Townsend E. Gridley by a vote of 23,827-16,901 to win the one-year term specified in the Constitution of 1850. He was re-elected in 1852 to a two-year term 42,798-34,660 over then-Whig Zachariah Chandler, the Detroit mayor who in 1857 became the first Republican U.S. senator from Michigan, serving in the Senate for 18 years.

On March 4, 1853, McClelland was appointed secretary of interior by President Franklin Pierce. He thus was the third

---

* It was this Constitution that set the salaries of state officials, requiring a vote of the people for pay raises. The governor's salary was set at $1,000 — much to the distress of later governors — and stayed there until it went to $4,000 in 1891. The 1850 Constitution also prohibited the Legislature from passing special acts of incorporation, assuring that all corporations would be covered by a general law. It ended a practice of special favors that prompted many vetoes by early governors. The 1835 convention formed the first Constitution of the state. It remained in effect until the Constitution of 1850, which prevailed until the Constitution of 1908 went into effect.

** Others were Kinsley S. Bingham, Charles M. Croswell and John T. Rich.

governor in 12 years who resigned early in order to go to Washington.* He was interior secretary for four years.

In a brief return to public life, McClelland was a delegate to the Constitutional Convention of 1867 (which produced a document that was rejected by Michigan voters, 110,582-71,733.) He died Aug. 30, 1880, in Detroit, where he was buried.

* William Woodbridge and Alpheus Felch resigned to become U.S. senators.

STOCKHOLDERS
OF THE UNDERGROUND
R. R. COMPANY
Hold on to Your Stock!!

The market has an upward tendency. By the express train which arrived this morning at 3 o'clock, fifteen thousand dollars worth of human merchandise, consisting of twenty-nine able-bodied men and women, fresh and sound, from the Carolina and Kentucky plantations, have arrived safe at the depot on the other side, where all our sympathising colonization friends may have an opportunity of expressing their sympathy by bringing forward donations of ploughs, &c., farming utensils, pick axes and hoes, and not old clothes; as these emigrants all can till the soil. N. B.—Stockholders don't forget the meeting to-day at 2 o'clock at the ferry on the Canada side. All persons desiring to take stock in this prosperous company, be sure to be on hand.

Detroit, April 19, 1853.

By Order of the
BOARD OF DIRECTORS.

State Archives

A poster from Detroit calling for a rally of local supporters of the "underground railroad," the system by which slaves fled from bondage for the safe haven of Michigan and often onward to Canada

37

State Archives

Andrew Parsons (1853-1854)

It is a gratification to me that (Michigan's) progress in the way of wealth and prosperity has never been more rapid than during the last two years.

— Final message to Legislature, Jan. 3, 1855.

Andrew Parsons, the third lieutenant governor to step up after the resignation of a governor, served for a year and nearly 10 months. He was to be Michigan's last Democratic governor for almost 30 years.

In his final legislative message, Parsons reported a balance of $553,004 in the treasury, and urged that it be used to accelerate liquidation of the state's indebtedness of $2,339,392 even though it was not yet due:

"A large surplus in the treasury should be avoided. It is not politic to tax the people to obtain money to loan to banks, or lock up in the treasury vaults; it would be safer in the people's hands, and likely to be more prudently and profitably managed by them."[1]

Parsons pronounced the St. Marys Falls canal at Sault Ste. Marie, which opened June 15, 1855, "one of the best of the kind in the world," and said of the minerals that would be shipped through it: "Our mines of copper, and mountains of iron, already being developed in the Upper Peninsula, are scarcely equaled in richness by any on the globe."[2]

Born July 22, 1817, in Hoosick, N.Y., Parsons came to Michigan when he was 17. He married Elvira Rowe of Shiawassee County in 1838. They had two children. She died in 1849, and Parsons six months later married Marella Farrand Stewart of Shiawassee County. They also had two children. Parsons taught school for a few months in Ann Arbor; was a clerk in Prairie Creek in Ionia County; and register of deeds in Shiawassee County, where he was prosecuting attorney in 1848. In 1846, he was elected to the state Senate. He was a University of Michigan regent in 1851, and was elected lieutenant governor in 1852.

Parsons became governor March 7, 1853, when Gov. Robert McClelland resigned to become secretary of the interior.

One matter of controversy during his administration developed when rail interests wanted him to call a special session of the Legislature. "A large sum of money was sent him, and liberal offers tendered if he would gratify the railroad interest of the state and call the extra session," according to the 1873 edition of General History of the State of Michigan. "But he returned the money, and refused to receive any favors whatever from any party who would attempt to corrupt him by laudations, liberal offers, or by threats. ... He refused to call the extra session."[3]

After his stint in the governor's office, Parsons served in the state House of Representatives for the 1855 session. He died June 6, 1855, in Corunna, where he was buried.

Catlin

Mid-1800's scene at Marquette, where ships gathered to take on ore from U.P. mines

The *E. Ward* passes through the Soo Locks shortly after their completion. It was the first vessel to pass through the Locks downbound into Lake Huron.

State Archives

39

Kinsley S. Bingham (1855-1858)

... the laboring and producing classes, those who create the wealth, believe that rather than be swindled periodically by fraudulent banks, they would be far better off with no banks at all.
— **Message to the Legislature, Jan. 7, 1857.**

Ex-Democrat Kinsley S. Bingham was Michigan's first Republican governor. He served for two terms by defeating former Democratic Governors John S. Barry and Alpheus Felch.

By late 20th century standards, he may have sounded un-Republican for criticizing bankers. But he was echoing a theme of early Michigan governors — that greedy banks were gouging the new state and its people.

"The last two years are the only ones in the history of this state in which the people have not been swindled by fraudulent banks,"[1] Bingham told the Legislature in urging strict banking regulations.

Kinsley Scott Bingham was born Dec. 16, 1808, in Camillus, N.Y. He was the son of a farmer, and retained an interest in agriculture throughout his public career. (Legislation establishing Michigan Agricultural College at East Lansing was enacted during his administration.) In 1833, Bingham married Margaret Warden and moved to Michigan, where he purchased a farm with his brother-in-law in Green Oak Township, Livingston County — "on the border of civilization, buried in the primeval forest," as one account had it.[2] His wife died in 1834 after giving birth to a son. Bingham married her sister, Mary Warden, in 1839. They also had a son.

As a Democrat, Bingham was elected to the first session of the Michigan House of Representatives in 1837, was re-elected four times and served as speaker. He was in the U.S. House of Representatives in 1847-1851, where he strongly opposed extension of slavery to new territories. Having earlier been a justice of the peace and probate judge, Bingham ranked among Michigan governors who were in all three branches of government.

At a historic July 6, 1854, convention in Jackson, the Whigs and Free Soilers united on a state ticket that was headed by Bingham as the gubernatorial nominee of the brand new Republican Party. The rally of about 1,500 persons was too big to fit indoors, so it was held "under the oaks" on the outskirts of Jackson. This led to Michigan's claim to be the birthplace of the Republican Party, since it was the first statewide meeting of Republicans in any state, and it produced the first state ticket and platform. Wisconsin claimed an earlier, more localized, meeting at Ripon gave birth to the Republican Party.

In an attempt to block the Republican ascendancy, Democrats nominated former three-term Gov. Barry. Bingham won, 43,652-38,675, giving Republicans a grip on the governorship they would not relinquish until 1883.

"Bingham and the entire Republican ticket emerged victorious, and a Republican majority was elected to the Legislature," wrote Willis F. Dunbar and George S. May. "It marked a complete turnaround in Michigan politics, which up to this time had been almost completely dominated by the Democratic Party. From this date until 1932 Michigan was persistently Republican."[3]

In 1856, Bingham was re-elected by defeating ex-Gov. Felch, 71,402-54,085.

While Bingham was governor, the state Reform School was established, and there were new laws enhancing local government and lumbering. But much of the focus in Michigan, as in the nation, was on the slavery issue. The "Personal Liberty Law" was enacted, directing prosecutors to "diligently and faithfully use all lawful means to protect and defend all persons arrested as a fugitive slave." Michigan prohibited use of county jails to detain persons accused of being fugitive slaves, adopting the controversial "joint resolution respecting slavery in the territories of the United States."

After leaving the governorship Jan. 3, 1859, Bingham went to the U.S. Senate in March. He died Oct. 5, 1861, at his home in Green Oak. He was buried in Brighton.

Under the Oaks, 1854 in Jackson

Bentley

State Archives

Moses Wisner (1859-1860)

This is no time for timid and vacillating counsels, when the cry of treason and rebellion is ringing in our ears.

— **Farewell message to the Legislature, Jan. 1, 1861.**

Michigan, long preoccupied with financial and other problems of early statehood, emerged in the last half of the 19th century as a force in preserving the union that it struggled so hard to join.

No voice was more forceful than that of Moses Wisner, who criticized fellow Republican Abraham Lincoln as being too conciliatory toward the South; opposed efforts to weaken Michigan laws designed to thwart slave traders; and emphasized Michigan's refusal to recognize the right of a state to secede from the Union by declaring "we cannot consent to have one star obliterated from our flag."

In the final words of his last message to the Legislature, Wisner said: "For upwards of 30 years this question of the right of a state to secede has been agitated. It is time

it was settled."[1] To help settle it, upon retiring as governor, Wisner raised the 22nd Michigan Regiment, largely from Oakland County. Commissioned a colonel in 1862, he led the regiment off to Kentucky, where he died of typhoid fever in 1864. In announcing Wisner's death, Gen. G. Granger of the Army of Kentucky wrote: "When his country called for men to fight her battles, he cheerfully gave up the honors and peaceful pursuit of the citizen to undergo the hardships and privations of the soldier's life."[2]

Moses Wisner was born June 3, 1815, in Springport, N.Y., the son of a farmer. After a youth of agricultural labor, he moved to Michigan in 1837 and purchased a farm in Lapeer County. Two years later, he moved to Pontiac, where he studied law and became prosecuting attorney. After Wisner's first wife, Eliza Richardson, died in childbirth in 1844, he married Angeline Hascall in 1848. He failed in bids for Congress in 1854 and the U.S. Senate in 1857, but he was elected governor in 1858, defeating Democrat Charles Stuart, 62,202-56,067.

During his one term as governor, roads were extended into unsettled areas of Michigan; registration of voters was required; and many development projects were advanced, including improvement of the new canal at Sault Ste. Marie.

Reporting on a personal inspection of the canal, Wisner said, "We found the canal in an unsafe condition, so much so that there was imminent danger of the works being washed away ... and the entire commerce of Lake Superior thereby jeopardized."[3]

Wisner campaigned against "the great injustice of excluding our daughters from the state university, at Ann Arbor."[4] He told the Legislature: "We think it necessary to bestow upon our brothers and our sons a high order of instruction, while our sisters and our daughters must be content with such a one as can be obtained from a primary school. This is all wrong. ... It is your duty to give to them the same means of obtaining a high order of education that you have already bestowed upon the sterner sex."[5]

Whether arguing for equal rights for women or against slavery, "his eloquence was that of conviction and action."[6] Wisner was quick to react when Congress passed the Kansas-Nebraska Act of 1854 repealing the

Missouri Compromise and opening the territories to slavery:

"The Missouri Compromise, that our fathers made 33 years before, was abrogated at the direction of the South, that human bondage might be introduced into territories which had been forever dedicated to freedom."[7]

Wisner noted that in 1855, during the administration of Kinsley S. Bingham, Michigan had enacted a law "to protect the free colored citizen from 'forcible removal from the state as a slave' and to punish his kidnapper." He proudly declared: "The foot of the slave has never yet pressed the soil of Michigan since the formation of our government, except in violation of law."[8]

Bingham and Wisner, who gave the Republican Party a proud start in Michigan as its first two governors, were overshadowed in history by Civil War Gov. Austin Blair. But they both contributed to Michigan's role in helping preserve the Union. Wisner died Jan. 5, 1864, in Kentucky, and was buried in Pontiac.

Oakland County Historical and Pioneer Society

Wisner built his home in 1845 and lived there until he died while serving in the Civil War. Today, the Wisner House, pictured here in 1983, is operated by the Oakland County Historical and Pioneer Society and is open to the public.

State Archives

Austin Blair (1861-1864)

Our good Ship of State is driven before a furious gale, and the best navigator can hardly tell what of disaster the next wave may bring. — **Address to the Legislature, Jan. 2, 1862.**

Scarce a battlefield of the war but has drunk of Michigan blood, and the graves of our men mark the camping ground of every army of the Union. — **Address to the Legislature, Jan. 7, 1863.**

Michigan's Civil War governor was an intense champion of human rights and the Union. He mustered Michigan into battle to help preserve both.

From the day of his Jan. 2, 1861, inaugural, Republican Austin Blair began using the office of governor of Michigan to prod Abraham Lincoln into taking a stronger stand against slavery:

"Oh, for the firm, steady hand of a Washington, or a Jackson, to guide the Ship of State in this perilous storm. Let us hope that we shall find him on the 4th of March" — the day Lincoln was to become president.[1]

After devoting the last third of his inaugural address to the secession movement in the South and what was then Lincoln's inclination to compromise on extension of slavery to the territories, Blair said:

"The Union must be preserved and the laws must be enforced in all parts of it at whatever cost. The president is bound to this by his oath, and no power can discharge him from it. Secession is revolution ...

"It is a question of war that the seceding States have to look in the face."[2]

When war erupted just over three months later, Blair, who became one of the nation's foremost Civil War governors, responded.

He responded when Lincoln on April 15 — after the fall of Fort Sumter in South Carolina to Confederate troops — made an urgent call for volunteers to help defend Washington. The First Michigan Infantry Regiment was the first western regiment to arrive in Washington. Lincoln's widely quoted but unverified response was: "Thank God for Michigan." By 1862, Michigan had supplied 21 regiments, six batteries of light artillery, a squadron of cavalry and a number of organized companies of infantry.

Blair also raised $100,000 in subscriptions from bankers and others to equip troops. This was necessary because at least $50,000 in treasury funds turned up missing during the previous administration. As Blair told the Legislature: "There is reason to believe the treasurer is a defaulter to the state in a considerable amount."[3] When hostilities started, Blair later told the Legislature: "Michigan, with more than 100,000 fighting men, had arms for hardly more than 1,000."[4] At the time, Michigan's population was only about 750,000.

Blair and the Legislature responded in 1862 when the federal government set Michigan's share of a special assessment to finance the war effort at $501,063. By then, Michigan already had spent about $600,000 on the war.

And Blair especially was responsive to the plight of wounded Michiganians. He visited them in distant hospitals, and won a special appropriation from the Legislature to help them return home. He also continued to prod: "The loyal states, having furnished adequate means, both of men and money, to crush the rebellion, have a right to expect those men to be used with the utmost vigor to accomplish the object, and that without any mawkish sympathy for the interest of traitors in arms ...

"The object of war is to destroy the power of the enemy, and whatever measures are calculated to accomplish that object, and are in accordance with the usage of civilized nations, ought to be employed."[5]

Blair's attitude was not surprising. Going back to the historic 1854 "under the oaks" Republican convention in Jackson, Blair was an anti-slavery extremist of his day. More than a century later, Detroit News columnist Will Muller wrote: "Austin Blair outshines modern liberals." Muller quoted Blair from a penciled, private autobiography in which Blair reflected on his actions in 1846 as a member of the Judiciary Committee of the state House of Representatives:

"During this session, I made an earnest report from the Judiciary Committee in favor of striking the word 'white' out of the Constitution of the state, as applied to electors, and then took the ground never since abandoned, against all color and race distinctions in the franchise."[6] He also led the successful 1846 effort to have Michigan ban capital punishment.

As chairman of the Michigan delegation at the 1860 Republican National Convention, Blair supported William H. Seward for the presidential nomination. He said the nomination went to Lincoln "greatly to my disappointment."[7]

As all other Michigan governors before him, Blair was not born in Michigan. He was born Feb. 8, 1818, in Caroline, N.Y. He graduated from Union College in Schenectady in 1837 and moved to Jackson, where he started practicing law. He lived briefly in Eaton Rapids, but returned to Jackson, where he was elected to the state House of Representatives as a Whig in 1845. He was elected to the state Senate in 1854, when he was part of the new Republican Party.

In 1860, Blair was elected governor by defeating former Democratic Gov. John S. Barry, 87,806-67,221. He was re-elected in 1862, defeating Byron Gray Stout, a state senator who was a reluctant candidate of the Union Party.[8] Blair won 68,716-62,102.

Blair, who had an annual salary of $1,000 and no expense account for his extensive travels, was somewhat impoverished when he left office Jan. 4, 1865. In

AUSTIN BLAIR
WAR GOVERNOR OF MICHIGAN.
1861. 1862. 1863. 1864.

HE GAVE THE BEST YEARS OF HIS LIFE TO MICHIGAN, AND HIS FAME IS INSEPARABLY LINKED WITH THE GLORIOUS ACHIEVEMENTS OF HER CITIZEN SOLDIERS.

Kendrick Kimbel/The Detroit News

Statue photo as re-touched when published in 1945

Burton

Above **The First Michigan Infantry was the first western regiment to arrive to help defend Washington. Here its colors are presented at City Hall, Campus Martius, Detroit, in 1861.**

Opposite, top **Confederate dead at Rose Woods, Battle of Gettysburg. This photograph has been long identified as the dead of the 24th Michigan, the Iron Brigade. However, Alan Nolan, author of *The Iron Brigade*, accepts the research of William Frassinito, a modern authority on Civil War photography, to the contrary.**

Opposite, bottom **This recruiting poster for the 29th Michigan Infantry seeks volunteers "to finish up the glorious work of putting an end to this unholy and wicked Rebellion."**

1879, in a speech at the dedication of the Capitol in Lansing, Blair said: "Now I ask them if they can afford — this great and magnanimous people of Michigan — to give the governors about half as good a salary as they pay to a common dry-goods clerk."[9]

In 1867, Blair was elected to the first of three terms in the U.S. Congress. In 1871, he failed for the Republican nomination for the U.S. Senate, and in 1872, running as a Liberal Republican endorsed by Democrats, he lost to Republican John J. Bagley in a four-man race for governor.

In 1876, Blair supported Democrat Samuel J. Tilden against Republican Rutherford B. Hayes for president "both because I thought him the stronger man, and because it seemed to me necessary to teach modesty and decency to the Republican Party by defeating it."[10] He later patched up party differences and was an unsuccessful 1887 Republican nominee for the Michigan Supreme Court.

As noted in Michigan History magazine's 1980 special section on 42 governors, "Blair's private life had a full share of tragedy."[11] His first two wives died after giving birth to infants who also died. In 1849, he married Sarah Louisa Horton Ford, who, as first lady during the Civil War, performed hospital relief work. They had five children.

A statue on the Capitol grounds, on the approach to the front entrance, pays tribute to the war governor. The only governor to be honored with such a statue, Blair died Aug. 6, 1894, in Jackson, where he was buried. At the base of the statue is the inscription: "He gave the best years of his life to Michigan, and his fame is inseparably linked with the glorious achievements of her citizen soldiers." He did give his best years. But he earned his wartime fame.

Besides the war, a variety of other issues occupied Blair, including the state prison. He once told the Legislature: "The exercising of pardoning power, I have found the most difficult and trying of all of my duties."[12] In reporting an improvement in prison discipline, Blair attributed it "in great measure to the wise statute giving to every well-behaved convict a liberal deduction from his sentence for his good behavior and orderly conduct. ... His love of liberty is stronger than his fear of the lash."[13]

Timothy H. O'Sullivan/Library of Congress

Rally, Boys, Rally for the Flag
And Avoid the Draft

VOLUNTEERS
FOR THE
29th REGIMENT
OF MICHIGAN INFANTRY
Will be enlisted by the undersigned, who has been duly authorized
by Governor Blair.

SUBSTITUTES
ARE ALSO ENLISTED IN THIS REGIMENT.

$300 GOV. BOUNTY
And LIBERAL LOCAL BOUNTIES, in addition, offered !

TERM OF ENLISTMENT THREE YEARS OR DURING THE WAR.

Come boys, let us strike once more for the old Flag--Let it be ours
to finish up the glorious work of putting an end to this unholy and wicked Rebellion, which has trampled on
the Constitution, violated the laws of the country and nearly destroyed the Union. Let each legacy of our fathers, to us and to posterity. Let us now GIVE
MORE COMPANY to old Column, which will do imperishable honor to ourselves and the name of LIBERTY

N. J. FRINK,
MARSHALL, Aug. 8, 1864   Lieut. 29th Reg. Mich. Vol. Inft., Recruiting Officer.

Burton

State Archives

Henry H. Crapo (1865-1868)

The financial affairs of the state are in a prosperous condition.
— **First message to the Legislature, Jan. 4, 1865.**

The first of several lumber barons to hold the office, Republican Henry H. Crapo was only the second non-lawyer among the first 13 men to be governor of Michigan. He also was the first Michigan governor to proclaim a "paying as we go" policy to finance state operations.

Although he had been mayor of Flint and a state senator before becoming governor, Crapo, according to biographer Martin Lewis, took pride in being different from what he viewed as the ways of politicians. Explaining his appeal as a gubernatorial candidate, he said:

"It is because I am supposed to be a man of business and work, untrammeled and unfettered with old political hacks — a man who says what he thinks — and believes what he says — firm and dedicated, and who will guard well the interests of the state, and make such appointments as her

interests demand, and not such as political partisans clamour for."[1]

In a letter to his son, William, Crapo said "one thing is giving me no little distinction. I rely upon myself, and although I do not reject the advice of others, yet I do not permit the mere politicians to interfere with my policy, or with my appointments." He added: "I talk very little, but work unceasingly."[2]

Henry Howland Crapo was born May 22, 1804, in Dartmouth, Mass., son of a farmer of French descent. While he had little formal education, he read extensively. He lingered for hours around the village bookshop seven miles from his farm, keeping a list of words to look up whenever he could use a dictionary.* He later taught school for 10 years and served as a member of the Massachusetts militia, becoming a colonel. In 1825, he married Mary Ann Slocum. They had a son and nine daughters. He taught himself surveying, becoming a land surveyor and agent. He began making large speculative purchases of western lands, including tracts of pine in Michigan.

His business card said he was a "Dealer in Western lands" who "Offers for sale, on easy terms, 30,000 acres of choice farming lands in the state of Michigan."[3]

In 1856, Crapo moved to Flint, where he began selling lumber and later opened branches at Holly, Fentonville and Detroit. One of Michigan's most successful lumbermen, he also was instrumental in railroad development. He was elected mayor of Flint in 1860, and a state senator in 1863.

While Crapo was a Whig during his earlier years, he became active in the Republican Party after it was formed. In 1864, he was elected governor by a 91,356-to-74,292 margin over Democrat William M. Fenton, a former lieutenant governor who had given $5,000 when former Gov. Austin Blair asked for public subscriptions to help finance Michigan's Civil War troops. In 1866, he was re-elected, 96,746-67,708, defeating Democrat Alpheus S. Williams, a Civil War brigadier general who later became a U.S. congressman.

In his first report to the Legislature,

---

*When he was 18, he assembled the notes in a 125-page cardboard-bound volume he called A Vocabulary in Manuscript by Henry H. Crapo Dartmouth July 29, 1822.

State Archives

Crapo said that total state expenditures for 1864 amounted to $2,004,194, including $478,114 for the general fund and more than $1 million for Civil War funding. The state was left with a cash balance of $440,047. He told the Legislature "rigid adherence" to a "paying as we go" policy on ordinary and incidental state expenses (excluding war expenses), "will preserve the credit and honor of our State, and her finances will never become deranged or embarrassed."[4] He backed up his words with his veto power. He vetoed bills that would have permitted municipal aid to railroads, arguing that they were fiscally unwise, and that acquiring public debt to support privately owned projects was unconstitutional.[5]

Much of Crapo's fight with the Legislature on the projects was conducted from his sickbed. Just before his 1866 annual report to the Legislature, Crapo "was seized with one of his bladder attacks and was unable to deliver the message."[6] The one-hour, 45-minute address was read by Crapo's secretary, Tom Cobb.

Crapo died July 22, 1869, in Flint, where he was buried. He left a legacy beyond his gubernatorial service: The 1,385-acre Crapo farm at Swartz Creek west of Flint was long known nationally as the home of the oldest herd of Hereford cattle on the North American continent maintained by one family on one farm.[7] William C. Durant, a Crapo grandson who spent much time on the farm as a boy, was the president of General Motors Corp., 1916-1920, a company he had established in 1908. Another grandson, Stanford Tappan Crapo, was co-founder of the Huron Portland Cement Co. and general manager of the Flint & Holly railroad that Henry H. Crapo built as an outlet for his lumber. The 402-foot cement carrier *S.T. Crapo,* seen frequently in Great Lakes ports, was named after the governor's grandson.

State Archives

Henry P. Baldwin (1869-1872)

No period in the history of the state has been marked by a more steady and healthful growth in population, and in the wealth of the people, than since the commencement of the last decade. ... The finances of the state are in a prosperous and highly satisfactory condition.

— **First message to the Legislature, Jan. 6, 1869.**

A prosperous businessman and banker, Republican Henry P. Baldwin served two terms as governor and then became the fourth Michigan chief executive to become a U.S. senator.

How prosperous?

When devastating fires swept Michigan in 1871, Baldwin personally contributed $156,876 of the $462,106 raised for a relief fund to aid the 18,000 persons from nearly 3,000 families left homeless.

That was the year of the great Chicago fire. As Baldwin reported to the Legislature:

"While the people of Michigan were engaged in the noble work of furnishing relief to the sufferers in Chicago, the same devouring element was making sad havoc in our own state. Thriving towns, farm and school houses, churches, stock, crops and thousands of acres of valuable timber were consumed."[1]

Extremely hot and dry conditions prevailed throughout the Great Lakes region that October. On Oct. 9, fire swept through the Lake Michigan communities of Holland and Manistee. "Some areas had scarcely any rain since June," observed *Michigan, A History of the Wolverine State.* "In an incredibly short time, the flames had cut clear across the peninsula (from Lake Michigan) to Saginaw Bay and beyond, to engulf large areas of the Thumb region."[2]

Henry Porter Baldwin was born Feb. 22, 1814, in Coventry, R.I. He was orphaned at 12, and clerked in a mercantile establishment until he went into business for himself at age 20. In 1835, he married Harriet M. Day, who later died. He married Sibyle Lambard in 1866. They had seven children.

After moving to Detroit in 1838, Baldwin established a successful shoe business, and became an influential banker, a director of the Michigan State Bank and president of the Second National Bank of Detroit.

One of his major contributions to the state came after he was elected in 1860 to the state Senate. He became chairman of the joint House-Senate committee investigating the condition of the state treasury after it was pilfered by the treasurer during the administration of Moses Wisner. Baldwin's report was the basis of improved management of the treasury.

Republican Baldwin was elected governor in 1868, defeating Democrat John Moore, 128,051-97,290. In 1870, he was re-elected, defeating Charles C. Comstock, former mayor of Grand Rapids, 100,196-83,391.

As governor, Baldwin pressed for funding for the new Capitol and appointed a commission to oversee the work. He also promoted programs of educational, penal and social services institutions. The state Public School for Dependent Children was founded at Coldwater, as was a commission to supervise several state institutions.

"With rare exceptions, the important recommendations of Governor Baldwin received the sanction of the Legislature," according to historian George N. Fuller.[3]

After leaving the governorship Jan. 1, 1873, Baldwin retired to private life. In 1879, upon the death of U.S. Sen. Zachariah Chandler, he was appointed by Gov. Charles Croswell to the vacancy. He failed in an 1881 bid for election to the seat. Baldwin died Dec. 31, 1892, and was buried in Detroit.

Matthew Brady

AP

Left **President Ulysses S. Grant, whose military career included the command of The Detroit barracks in the 1850's**

Right **Michigan was not the only state devastated by the 1871 fire. In Wisconsin, a Peshtigo Fire Cemetery marker notes "the greatest forest fire disaster in American history."**

State Archives

John J. Bagley (1873-1876)

Neither pen nor pencil can fitly describe the transforming that each succeeding year has witnessed; forest to field — marsh to meadow — openings to orchards — hut to home, have followed one another in quick succession.

— **To Legislature on approach of Michigan's 40th birthday. Jan. 4, 1877.**

Midway through his four successful years as governor, John J. Bagley — as had so many other Michigan governors before and since — spoke to the Legislature on Jan. 7, 1875, of the impact that national economic woes were having on Michigan:

"A financial crisis of more than ordinary severity has been encountered by every section of the country, and the best thought of the nation has been taxed for measures of relief — to a large extent unsuccessfully."[1]

But in his final address to the Legislature, Jan. 4, 1877, Bagley said Michigan was "standing today in the midst of ... abundant prosperity." Here was how he described where Michigan stood after its first four decades of statehood:

"An empire in extent with natural resources that seem almost inexhaustible, with means of transportation by land and water unequalled on the globe; a soil that 'tickled with a hoe, laughs with a harvest'; dotted all over with happy homes; schools and institutions of learning with open doors for all; the ills that afflict humanity liberally and kindly cared for; with a history that tells of no gallows ever having been erected in our borders; no slave having ever trod our soil; no treason attained any citizen; all this is our inheritance, ours to preserve and to increase."[2]

Bagley, as all of Michigan's governors before him, was born in the East; as his two immediate predecessors, he succeeded in politics after prospering in business.

John Judson Bagley was born July 24, 1832, in Medina, N.Y. In 1840, he moved with his parents to Michigan, settling first in Constantine and then Owosso. In 1847, he started working in a Detroit tobacco factory, and five years later, at age 21, started his own company. He ultimately made a fortune as owner of the Mayflower Tobacco Co. in Detroit, one of the Midwest's largest producers of chewing tobacco. He was said to have quipped to a Detroit clergyman: "You and I thrive on the sins of the people."[3]

He was one of the founders of the Michigan Mutual Life Insurance Co., serving for several years as its president. He was president of the Detroit Safe Co.; a director of the American National Bank; an incorporator of the Wayne County Savings Bank; vice-president of the American Exchange National Bank; and an organizer of the Merchants' and Manufacturers' Exchange.

Bagley was one of Detroit's police commissioners, a member of the City Council, and a member of the Board of Education.

Originally a Whig, Bagley participated in formation of the Republican Party and became chairman of the Republican State Central Committee. As the Republican candidate for governor in 1872, he easily defeated former Republican Gov. Austin Blair, who was running as a Liberal Republican and with the endorsement of Democrats. The vote was 137,602-to-80,958, with two other candidates receiving a total of about 4,000.

It was different when he sought re-election in 1874. The national depression had turned many voters against men of wealth. There was a Democratic trend in the country, and stirrings of a Democratic comeback in Michigan. But Bagley, Michigan's sixth consecutive Republican governor, had a narrow win, defeating Democrat Henry Chamberlin, a merchant and farmer from Three Oaks, 111,519-105,550. The previous 95-5 Republican majority in the state House was narrowed to 54-46.

As governor, Bagley reorganized the state militia, succeeded in placing railroad regulations under a state commission; enhanced educational and social services institutions, particularly facilities for delinquent and indigent children; reorganized the Boys' Reformatory in Lansing to make it less of a prison and more of a school; and developed the state Public School for Dependent Children in Coldwater for wards of the state. He also succeeded in obtaining legislation that created the state Board of Health and the Fish Commission. He repeatedly warned of declining catches of fish in the Great Lakes, and told the Legislature "every acre of water in the state can be made as valuable as an acre of land."[4]

Strengthening of liquor laws was a special concern of Bagley, who said in his final message to the Legislature: "Intemperance is the danger of the hour. It feeds prison and poorhouse; destroys morals and manhood; and, cancerlike, eats away the life of the individual and the nation. Law will not stop its ravages, but it may be made an instrument that will lessen its evil work."

After his second term, Bagley retired to business and civic life but made an unsuccessful bid for the U.S. Senate in 1881. He died July 27, 1881, in San Francisco, and was buried in Detroit. He was survived by his wife, the former Frances Elizabeth Newberry, daughter of the Rev. Samuel Newberry, a pioneer missionary and educator in Michigan. They had eight children.

N.C.A.M.

Tobacco tycoon Bagley as penned by Fred I. Leipziger of The Detroit News

53

State Archives

Charles M. Croswell (1877-1880)

The excellent financial standing of the state has been maintained, and for the first time the treasury has a revenue equal to all its demands. — **Final message to the Legislature, Jan. 6, 1881.**

He lacked the flair and fame of statehood Gov. Stevens T. Mason or Civil War Gov. Austin Blair. But Gov. Charles M. Croswell, in his businesslike manner, presided at an important milestone for Michigan — getting it out of debt.

In his final assessment of the state of the state that had grown to 1.6 million people, the two-term governor said:

"The state is strong — strong in numbers, strong in resources, strong in its educational and humane institutions, strong in its respect for public virtue, in its devotion to liberty and union, and strong in the hold it has upon the affections of the people."[1]

Charles Miller Croswell was born Oct. 31, 1825, in Newburg, N.Y., son of a papermaker. He was orphaned at age 7 and settled with his uncle in Adrian in southeastern Lower Michigan, in 1837, working as a carpenter's apprentice. In 1852, he married Lucy M. Eddy of Adrian. They had five children. His first wife died in 1868. In 1880, he married Elizabeth Musgrave of Charlotte. They had one child.

Croswell became a lawyer and a partner of Thomas M. Cooley, who later became chief justice of the Michigan Supreme Court. Croswell was elected and re-elected as Lenawee County register of deeds as a Whig. He was a delegate to the Republican founding convention in Jackson in 1854, and became a Republican state senator. He was president of the Constitutional Convention of 1867, and, after being elected to the House of Representatives, became House speaker in 1873.

In 1876, Republican Croswell was elected governor, defeating Democratic state Sen. William L. Webber, 165,926-142,585. Things looked up politically for Republicans as the economy improved. In his re-election bid in 1878, Croswell doubled his winning plurality, getting 126,280 votes to 78,503 for Democrat Orlando M. Barnes and 73,313 for Greenback candidate Henry M. Smith. Republicans won a 30-2 edge in the Senate, and 65-35 in the House.

As governor, Croswell strengthened election laws and programs for the handicapped and disadvantaged. One of his most decisive moves came in July 1877 when workers struck the Michigan Central Railroad Co. in Jackson, stopping all rail traffic in the area. Croswell called out all three regiments of the state militia.

"The trouble was ended fortunately without the destruction of a dollar's worth of property or the loss of life," Croswell reported to the Legislature. "In view of the excited state of feeling that then prevailed among railroad operatives all over the country consequent upon a reduction of wages, and of the fearful outbreaks that had taken place elsewhere, the situation was one of unusual gravity, and the danger imminent."[2]

One Croswell request that was ignored was his urging that the state provide a residence for the governor. "With the small salary affixed to the office, the governor should not be expected to come here and provide himself a home," he told the Legislature in 1879. "... I bespeak this not for myself but for my successors."[3] It was another 90 years before Michigan acquired a residence for its governors.

After leaving office Jan. 7, 1881, Croswell returned to Adrian. He died Dec. 13, 1886, in Adrian, and was buried there.

State Archives

On Jan. 1, 1879, Croswell dedicated Michigan's Capitol in Lansing.

State Archives

David H. Jerome (1881-1882)

It has safely passed the perils that beset young states, and unhampered by debt it is equally free from a tendency to incur it.
— **Final message to the Legislature, Jan. 4, 1883.**

Michigan's first native-born governor, Republican David H. Jerome was another in a line of businessmen who preached prudence in state spending. In his farewell address to the Legislature, Jerome said:

"The state is in admirable financial condition. The policy engrafted upon its legislative practice more than 20 years since, and which has been invariably adhered to in conducting its financial affairs, 'to pay as you go,' or to make provision for needed means before their expenditure is entered upon, has resulted in numerous advantages."[1]

As of Sept. 30, 1882, the Michigan treasury had a balance of $2,057,933.

David Howell Jerome was born Nov. 17, 1829, in Detroit, son of a sawmill owner. He moved to California in 1853 to work in mining and returned to Michigan to settle in Saginaw, where he became a wealthy hardware and lumber businessman and purchased pine tracts in northern Michigan. He married Lucy Peck of Pontiac in 1859. They had three children, two of whom died in infancy.

In 1862, Jerome was appointed by Gov. Austin Blair, with rank of colonel, to raise the 23rd Michigan Infantry, one of six Civil War regiments apportioned to Michigan. He later became military aide to Gov. Henry H. Crapo.

Jerome was elected to the state Senate in 1862 and was a member of the U.S. Board of Indian Commissioners in 1876-81. In 1880, he was elected governor, defeating Democrat Frederick M. Holloway, 178,944-137,671. In his 1882 re-election race, he lost by 4,572 votes to Fusionist Josiah W. Begole, the candidate of Democrats and Greenbacks.

While he was governor, the Michigan School for the Blind was located at Lansing, the Traverse City State Hospital for the Insane* was organized, and railroad construction rapidly increased.

In 1881, a decade after the famous Chicago fire and the blaze that swept across mid-Michigan, a forest fire fanned by a gale ravaged the Thumb counties of Huron, Lapeer, Sanilac, St. Clair and Tuscola. In convening the Legislature for a special joint session Feb. 23, 1882, Jerome said the "calamity" killed 300, left 14,438 homeless, and destroyed 1,480 barns, 50 schools, "and a large number of churches and highway bridges."[2] The 1881 fire resulted in the first disaster relief project of the American Red Cross, which Clara Barton had organized just weeks earlier.[3]

Jerome died April 21, 1886, at Watkins, N.Y., and was buried in Saginaw.

---

* In Michigan's earliest days, before enlightenment regarding mental and physical problems, governors submitted a single legislative program for "the deaf, dumb, blind and insane."

American Red Cross

An 1881 drawing dramatizing nation-wide efforts to aid fire-stricken Michigan

State Archives

Josiah W. Begole (1883-1884)

Draw on me. ... Let no one suffer while I have money.

— An offer to help fire victims, Sept. 17, 1881.

Josiah W. Begole, Michigan's first non-Republican governor in nearly 30 years, had only $100 in his pocket when he first came to the Michigan territory in 1836.

He became a wealthy businessman and his 1881 "draw on me" offer to aid fire victims helped elect him governor in 1882.

Josiah Williams Begole was born Jan. 20, 1815, in Livingston County, N.Y., a descendant of French Huguenots. At age 21, he journeyed to Michigan, traveling by steamer to Toledo and from there to Jackson and Flint by foot.[1] In 1839, he married Harriet A. Miles. They had four children.

In addition to running his 500-acre farm, Begole became involved in banking, carriage-making and lumbering. He was a founder and owner of one of Flint's largest sawmills.

Begole began his political career as a Republican, serving as Genesee County treasurer, state senator and U.S. congressman. But he became an advocate of the platform of the Greenback Party, favoring issuance of large amounts of paper money. In 1882, as the Fusionist candidate backed by both Greenbackers and Democrats, Begole defeated Republican Gov. David H. Jerome, 154,269-149,697, in a five-man race.

Begole's race was boosted in the fire-ravaged Thumb area by the way his campaign publicized his offer to help fire victims. When a shipment of relief supplies he had sent from Flint to the area failed to arrive, Begole wrote a relief agent: "Now, you can draw on me for what you need until these supplies arrive from Port Huron, where they were sent. Let no one suffer while I have money."

Tens of thousands of leaflets containing excerpts from the letter were circulated in the 1882 campaign. But the actual letter could not be found because the man who received it had moved to Chicago. Republicans claimed it was all a myth. (The letter surfaced years later.)[2]

As governor, Begole succeeded in winning legislative approval to create a state Bureau of Labor Statistics. But as an ex-Republican who ousted a Republican governor, Begole faced obstacles in the Republican-dominated Legislature. In his first address to legislators, he said: "I trust the only rivalry between us will be as to who shall labor most earnestly and successfully for the general good."[3]

Just moments earlier, he stepped on some legislative toes by denouncing the acceptance of free passes on the railroads by members of the Legislature. "So long as members can go home weekly, not only without expense, but with a reduction of their board bills, Saturday and Monday will be almost wasted, and the session prolonged by several weeks," he said.[4]

Begole was nominated again in 1884 as the Fusionist candidate but was narrowly defeated by Republican Russell A. Alger, 190,840-186,887.

He returned to his business interests in Flint, where he died June 6, 1896, and was buried.

The Detroit News

Above A wanigan, or cook shanty, floats down the Muskegon River during an 1880's spring log drive.

Left Begole's lost 1881 letter, an issue in his 1882 campaign, was found years later.

in by teams. Now you can draw on me for what you need untill those supplies arrive from Portheuron where they were sent. Let no one suffer while I have money.

J. W. Begole

Michigan Historical Commission

State Archives

Russell A. Alger (1885-1886)

It can be said that our state is practically out of debt; consequently nothing need be said of its credit, because it does not use it, nor is it probable that it will ever have occasion to do so again.
— **Final message to Legislature, Jan. 6, 1887.**

Although he served for only a brief and controversial span, Russell A. Alger ranks among Michigan's most notable governors for the era he represented, and for what he did before and after the governorship.

From orphan to millionaire lumber baron ... from enlistee private to brevet general ... from governor to the U.S. Cabinet, to the U.S. Senate.

Alger was a war hero who later became secretary of war, serving in between in the governor's office. He was foremost among four early lumber men who became rich from Michigan's resources and served in the governor's office during the zesty days of Michigan's timber era.*

Russell Alexander Alger was born Feb.

27, 1836, in Lafayette Township, Medina County, Ohio. His parents died when he was 11. Raised by an uncle, he worked on a farm, attended Richfield Academy, taught country school and studied law. In 1859, he moved to Grand Rapids, where he did well in the lumber business before the nation's pre-Civil War economic problems left him in debt.

In 1861, Alger married Annette H. Henry of Grand Rapids. They had nine children.

Also in 1861, Alger enlisted in the Army as a private in the 2nd Michigan Volunteer Cavalry, and later was commissioned a captain. After several promotions for gallantry, he became a colonel and took command of the 5th Michigan Cavalry Regiment. He fought in 65 battles, and was wounded twice. He resigned in 1864, and was given brevet promotions to brigadier and major general in the U.S. Volunteers in recognition of his war record.

Alger later became a partner in several timber firms, the most successful being Alger, Smith and Co. The firm and his other investments made Alger a multimillionaire by the mid-1880s.[1]

Breaking the pattern of previous Michigan governors who held other public offices before becoming chief executive, Alger was recruited from business to be the Republican nominee for governor in 1884. He defeated Fusionist Gov. Josiah W. Begole, 190,840-186,887, in a four-man race.**

During Alger's term, the Soldiers' Home for veterans was founded in Grand Rapids, and the Michigan College of Mines in Houghton in the Upper Peninsula. The state Board of Pardons was established. The state's strong financial condition was maintained.***

Alger ran the government with economy, the way he ran his business. This pleased

---

* Before Alger, there were Henry H. Crapo, David H. Jerome and Josiah W. Begole. Later, Aaron T. Bliss owned a lumber mill, and Alexander J. Groesbeck worked in his father's sawmill as a teen-ager.

** The Prohibition Party, which had fielded a gubernatorial candidate in five of the previous seven elections with little success, got 22,207 votes, showing a hard core strength that would be maintained for a decade.

*** Even before Alger's administration, Michigan had made provision for liquidating its bonded debt, but since not all of the bonds had matured, they were not all paid until 1890.

some, but others distrusted his motives.

He clearly carried a businessman's attitude into government; in speaking against those who would strike, he told the Legislature that "the honest laboring masses ... will become more and more convinced of the truth that their only true friends are the men who give them such employment as enables them to support their families and themselves, and frequently to engage in business on their own account."[2]

In 1885, violence erupted in a sawmill strike in the Saginaw Valley, where workers wanted their 12-hour work day reduced to 10 hours with no reduction in pay. "Ten Hours or No Sawdust" was their rallying cry.

Alger sent in the militia, and made a personal appearance to urge moderation on both sides. His critics said that he acted to protect his lumbermen friends. In the end, a state law provided for the 10-hour work day.

Alger, who in his first year in office encouraged immigration, came later to favor rigid restrictions. As he left office in 1887, he told the Legislature: "An examination of the records of our asylums, prisons, poorhouses and jails, will startle you when you find the great percent of inmates that are foreign born. Bad people of all classes and conditions, criminals, paupers, partially insane, cripples, aged and infirm, are dumped on our shores, having been sent from foreign countries here because it is much cheaper to pay steerage fare for them across the waters than to keep them ..."[3]

He held a particularly dim view of the "horde of Chinese pagans" who had come to the U.S. West Coast: "They disgrace labor; they will work for wages ... that will not support a white man."[4]

Alger declined to seek re-election in 1886. In 1889, he was elected commander-in-chief of the Grand Army of the Republic, and as such helped improve pensions for Civil War veterans.

Also in 1889, Alger was touted by some for the Republican presidential nomination. But he eventually campaigned for William McKinley, who, as president, named Alger secretary of war.

There was considerable controversy about how the War Department, under Alger, handled logistics during the Spanish-American War. Soldiers complained about the food, calling the canned meat "embalmed beef," and about the wool uniforms they were issued as they embarked

for the tropics. Alger, who ultimately resigned under criticism as secretary, was defended by then-Gov. Hazen S. Pingree, who complained that the criticism of Alger was triggered in large part by New York shipping interests angered by Alger's award of transportation contracts to low bidders from Spain.

In 1902, Alger was appointed by Gov. Aaron T. Bliss to fill the U.S. Senate vacancy created by the death of Sen. James McMillan. Subsequently, he was elected to a full term by the Michigan Legislature. He died in Washington Jan. 24, 1907, and was buried in Detroit.

The Detroit News

B.R. Thomas/The Detroit News/N.C.A.M.

State Archives

Cyrus G. Luce (1887-1890)

For the first time in our history, we can with pride declare that the last dollar of (bonded) indebtedness has been paid.

— **Final message to Legislature, Jan. 8, 1891.**

A farmer was governor when Michigan marked its first 50 years as a state — a farmer who helped lay foundations for the state's emergence as a 20th century industrial power.

Cyrus Gray Luce was born July 2, 1824, in Windsor, Ohio, and spent his early years on the family pioneer homestead. When he was 12, the family moved to Indiana, where he helped clear trees, fence fields and raise crops.

In 1848, Luce bought 80 acres of wilderness near Gilead in southern Michigan's Branch County and started farming. The next year, he married Julia A. Dickinson of Gilead, and began a family. They had five children. (After his first wife died, Luce married Mary Thompson of Bronson in 1883).

Even before moving to Michigan, Luce had an interest in politics. He had been an unsuccessful Whig candidate for the Indiana Legislature. He was more successful in Michigan, being a Branch County township supervisor for 11 years, twice elected county treasurer and serving in both the House and Senate. In six years of legislative service, he was present for every daily roll call, and voted upon the final passage of every bill.[1]

In 1879, Luce was appointed state oil inspector by Gov. Charles M. Croswell, and then reappointed by Gov. David H. Jerome.

As a farmer and public officeholder, Luce was active in the Michigan Grange, and a vocal advocate for legislation that benefited farmers. He repeatedly was elected its grand master.

When incumbent Gov. Russell A. Alger declined to seek re-election, the Michigan Republican Party turned to Luce, the farmer. Farmers were growing in political strength, and there was some voter criticism of the prolonged political rule by lumber barons.

Luce was elected in 1886, defeating Fusionist George L. Yaple, a farmer and ex-congressman. The vote was 181,474-174,042. Luce was re-elected in 1888 over Fusionist Wellington R. Burt, a former lumberman and mayor of East Saginaw, by a margin of 233,580-to-216,450.

Under Luce, Michigan became the first state to create the paid position of state game warden.[2] It was a milestone in a Michigan conservation movement that, among other things, began restoring barren land decimated in the lumber era.

In office, Luce never forgot his roots as a farmer, and supported much legislation to aid farming. But in so doing, he promoted programs that had benefit beyond farming. An example was his plea for property tax relief, an issue still expounded by governors 100 years later. In his first message to the Legislature Jan. 6, 1887*, Luce said:

"Slowly but surely taxation increases, and

---

* It will be noted that incoming governor Luce and outgoing governor Alger submitted 1887 messages to the Legislature on the same day. It was then a constitutional requirement that the outgoing governor, as well as the incoming, report on the condition of the state. The incoming governor would appear in person and the outgoing governor customarily would submit a written message. The requirement for an outgoing governor to submit a concluding report was dropped in the Constitution of 1963.

this is rendered the more burdensome because with the great mass of taxpayers the ability to pay diminishes. In many instances the tax amounts to more than the net income of the property taxes. High taxes necessitate high rents and higher interest, and in this way reacts upon those whose names do not appear on the assessment rolls. Such taxation bears heavily upon agriculture. The farmer's property is all in sight and cannot escape assessment."[3]

In his final message to the Legislature, on Jan. 8, 1891, Luce noted that the income tax had been "advocated by some who seek to relieve property from the burdens of taxation."[4] About 75 years later, Michigan adopted an income tax, but property was not relieved from the burden of taxation.

As Michigan under Luce moved beyond its 50th birthday, its population exceeded two million, immigrants were flocking to its borders for jobs in iron and copper mines, and Luce found himself in a changing world, rural but becoming industrial. He understood the changes and adapted to them.

One hundred years later, the farmer from Branch County was more remembered for heralding the growth of shipping and manufacturing than for his beginnings in the countryside.

Luce fought some losing battles. He failed to get a constitutional ban on the sale of intoxicating beverages. His 1887 legislative lament against carrying of concealed weapons was still being heard in the Capitol 100 years later:

"We are reminded by an almost-everyday occurrence that the habit now so prevalent of carrying concealed weapons brings to our attention the news of murder, manslaughter and accident. Not alone men, but boys of all ages are ready upon the least provocation to use the deadly weapon. Schoolteachers and schoolboys go to their duties and lessons armed. The custom should be prohibited by the most stringent legislation."

After completing his second term, Luce retired to Coldwater, where he was active in the Grange and ran his farming and business interests. He died March 18, 1905, in Coldwater, and was buried there.

Butler Grange Hall, Branch County, 1893; the Grange was a quasi- political farmers' association, many of whose positions were adopted by the Populist Party.

State Archives

63

State Archives

Edwin B. Winans (1891-1892)

The condition of all wagon roads last winter was sufficient proof that our present system of road making is a waste of time and labor. — **First message to the Legislature, Jan. 12, 1891.**

A farmer with populist views, Edwin B. Winans was the first Democrat to be elected governor of Michigan in nearly 40 years.*

With the state on sound financial footing, Winans concentrated in his single term on the "people issues" that helped him end the long Republican grip on the governorship.

"Good wagon roads all the year round would be more to the general advantage, would add more to the value of farm, and yield comfort, convenience, and profit to a larger number of people than any other work for which public money is expended," Winans said in his initial legislative message. "We claim to be a practical people,

but surely our road building has been a failure."[1]

Edwin Baruch Winans was born May 16, 1826, in Avon, N.Y. At age 8, he moved with his family to a Livingston County farm. He attended Albion College for two years and then was lured to California to prospect for gold.

The frontier experience helped shape his populism and later reputation among some 20th century writers as "Michigan's Teddy Roosevelt." When pack horses collapsed under him, he carried supplies on his back. He became a stockholder in the Rough-and-Ready Ditch Co. On one western trip, a stagecoach rolled over, causing a gun he carried to discharge and wound him in the chest and shoulder. As one biographical sketch put it; "Mr. Winans received the contents of his own gun."[2]

In 1855, Winans returned to Michigan to marry a neighbor, Sarah Galloway. As related by former Winans aide Howard Hovey in a 1938 Detroit Free Press account, Sarah did not want to leave Michigan and, pointing to her sister, said: "Take Lib."

"Will you go?" asked Winans.

"Sure," replied Elizabeth Galloway.[3]

They were married in 1855 and had two children. After three years in California, they returned to Michigan to farm in Livingston County.

As a Democrat, Winans was elected to the state House in 1860 and 1862, and to the U.S. House in 1882 and 1884. He also was a probate judge in 1877-81.

In 1890, Winans was elected governor when he defeated Republican James M. Turner, a Lansing railroad baron, 183,725-172,205.

As governor, he succeeded in getting electoral reform but failed in bids for tax reform and reduction in the number of state governing boards. He said citizens believed "public expenditures have increased much more rapidly than the ability of the people to pay, and that our civilization is becoming very expensive."[4]

Winans did not seek re-election, instead retiring to his farm. He died in Hamburg, north of Ann Arbor, July 4, 1894, and was buried there.

* The last Democrat elected was Robert McClelland in 1852.

The Detroit News

Lumber Days: Grayling about 1890

State Archives

John T. Rich (1893-1896)

The financial condition of the State is not all that could be wished. The funds in the State Treasury are practically exhausted ... this will necessitate borrowing of a considerable sum of money ... — **Final message to Legislature, Jan. 7, 1897.**

Like Gov. Edwin B. Winans before him, John T. Rich was toughened by farm life. This stood him well; he had to deal with difficult problems, including election fraud and labor strife. And the state, once again, faced hard times in the wake of a national depression.

In 1893, as Republican Rich later reported to the Legislature, "for the first time in many years, Michigan confronted an empty treasury. This was not caused so much by increased expenditures, as it was by the failure of the legislature of 1891 to levy taxes sufficient to meet what might reasonably have been contemplated would be the needs of the State."[1] Michigan's distress was compounded by the nation's ruinous financial Panic of 1893, which

brought bankruptcies, unemployment and severe depression. Rich met needs, in part, when he induced railroads to advance tax payments. In his four years in office, the state obtained advances and loans totaling $1.9 million.

In the summer of 1894, Rich called out the National Guard when Michigan, like many other states, faced labor strife. Eight companies of troops were mobilized in connection with a railroad strike in Battle Creek and Kalamazoo after what Rich described as "wanton destruction of property."[2] But the troops remained in their armories, and no further disturbance occurred at the time. Later, however, two people were killed in a wreck caused by removal of a rail from the track of the Chicago & Grand Trunk railroad west of Battle Creek on the night of July 16.

That same July, Rich mobilized five companies of Guard troops in Gogebic County in the western end of the Upper Peninsula during a mine strike. They stayed 26 days, but Rich was able to report: "No blood was shed, and good order was maintained," although two or three guardsmen were injured by stones thrown upon their arrival.

In 1893, Rich removed the secretary of state, state treasurer and state land commissioner — all fellow Republicans — "for gross neglect of duty" in which they certified fraudulent returns in a referendum on salary increases for state officers. Rich, who conducted much of the investigation himself, recalled later:

"So many men with political influence were implicated that persons who could give incriminating evidence were intimidated. ... Some men were afraid to be seen talking to me. There were vague rumors that I was in danger of bodily harm. My wife advised me not to walk alone at night between the state house and our hotel."[3]

John Treadway Rich was born April 23, 1841, in Conneautville, Pa., son of a farmer. At age 7, after his mother died, he moved to Elba Township in Lapeer County, where he did chores on a farm worked by his father and uncle. He thought of being a lawyer, but a doctor once said to him: "My boy, if you become a lawyer you will probably die early, but stick to the farm and you may live to a mature age."[4] He stuck to the farm and began a political career as township supervisor, Lapeer County clerk, state representative and House speaker, state senator and U.S. congressman.

In 1892, Rich was elected governor when he defeated Democrat Allen B. Morse, a former Republican, 221,228-205,138. In 1894, Rich was re-elected, 237,215-130,823, over Democrat Spencer O. Fisher, a lumber man and banker. Rich was the first Michigan governor who won with a plurality of more than 100,000 votes.

He did not seek a third term. After leaving office, he was appointed collector of customs in Detroit, and then Port Huron. He was appointed state treasurer in 1908.

Rich died March 28, 1926, in St. Petersburg., Fla., and was buried in Lapeer. He had gone to Florida with his second wife, Georgia Winship. His first wife, Lucretia M. Winship, Georgia's aunt, died in 1912.

Jerry Roe Collections

Drury V. Haight/N.C.A.M.

State Archives

Hazen S. Pingree (1897-1900)

It is your special privilege and duty to bring the so-called "merchant princes" and "captains of industry" in this country to a realization of the fact that our laboring men are something more than tools to be used in the senseless chase after wealth.
— Final message to Legislature, Jan. 9, 1901.

Reformer Hazen S. Pingree, one of the most forceful and extraordinary figures in Michigan politics, was unquestionably its most unorthodox governor.

A Republican, Pingree forged a record of success as mayor of Detroit when he took on the captains of industry, fought for low streetcar and utility rates, built a municipal light plant, bucked political bosses, trimmed fat and graft from city government, and instituted an innovative depression-relief program that included giving people vacant city land and seeds for what became known nationwide as "Pingree's potato patches."

Also, in his mayoral role, Pingree decreed that no one should pay more than 3 cents to ride streetcars. Later, as governor, he continued to battle rail interests, describing them "among the grossest offenders in tax-dodging," intent on "leaching the masses of the people."[1]

The embattled four-term mayor was less of a success as a two-term governor. He never quite fit into Lansing. In fact, he proposed moving the capital back to Detroit, or to Grand Rapids. He called the people of Lansing "parasites ... toadying to the wealthy interests which have conspired to ruin me."

In an angry aside in his last message to the Legislature, Pingree gave a vivid account of the trouble he had getting a decent bath in Lansing and said: "The treatment which the chief executive of this state has received at the hands of the people of Lansing for the last four years, in my opinion, shows that they are not entitled to the gubernatorial residence."[2]

In reference to the common folk he sought to protect, Pingree concluded his message with the prediction that unless there was change in "the present system of inequality, in less than a quarter of a century there will be a bloody revolution in this great country of ours."[3]

The fury of Pingree's rhetoric and passions tended to obscure his record. As governor, he reformed and equalized property taxes, and countered many instances of tax evasion. But Pingree, who preceded the progressive movement, was remembered as governor more for his seeds than his harvest.

Pingree was ahead of his time when he advocated such things as a graduated income tax, the eight-hour workday, and the direct election of U.S. senators — he said there was too much "bribery" in the system of having the Legislature pick them.

The inscription at the base of the bronze statue of Pingree in Detroit's Grand Circus Park reads: "He was the first to warn the people of the great danger threatened by powerful private corporations, and the first to initiate steps for reforms. The idol of the people." But, certainly, not the idol of industry.

Hazen S. Pingree was born Aug. 30, 1840, in Denmark Township, Oxford County, Maine. Earlier generations in England and then America spelled the family name Pengry, Pengrye, and Pingry.

His father was a farmer and cobbler, and Pingree was an itinerant cobbler as a youth. When he was about 20, after less than eight years of formal education, he became a shoemaker in Hopkinton, Mass., learning the trade in which he later would prosper as owner of one of the Midwest's largest shoe factories. It was in Hopkinton that Pingree picked up his lifelong nickname: "Ping."

In 1862, Pingree enlisted as a private in a company of volunteers in Hopkinton that was sent to help defend Washington, D.C., in the Civil War. As part of the First Massachusetts Heavy Artillery, Pvt. Pingree was in the second Battle of Bull Run, where, as he put it, he "first smelt powder" and learned to live on limited rations, eating wagon grease instead of butter.[4] Later, in a skirmish at North Anna, Pingree was captured and spent six months in Confederate prisons.

After his military service, Pingree came to Detroit, where he worked in a boot and shoe company owned by Henry P. Baldwin, who later became governor of Michigan. In 1872, Pingree married Frances Gilbert of Mt. Clemens. They had three children. In 1889, Pingree entered politics as the Republican nominee for mayor, winning that election and three more. In 1892, while still mayor, Pingree tried for the Republican nomination for governor but was blocked by allies of the conservative business community. He tried for the nomination again in 1894, but withdrew.

In 1896, the popularity of "Potato Patch Pingree" was such that Republican leaders wanted him on the gubernatorial ticket to help presidential candidate William McKinley carry Michigan. Furthermore, business leaders in Detroit wanted him out of the city, and they knew the conservative Republican Senate would be able to throttle Pingree's liberal impulses. And that's the way it all worked out — except Pingree tried to remain as mayor of Detroit once elected governor. The Michigan Supreme Court in 1887 ruled against it, and he finally resigned as mayor.*

Pingree was elected governor by a vote of 304,431-to-221,022 over Charles R. Sligh, nominee of the Democratic People's Union Silver Coalition (DPUS). In 1898, he was re-elected by defeating DPUS candidate Justin R. Whiting, 243,239-168,142.

* Newspapers on the same day would sometimes publish proclamations signed by both "H.S. Pingree, mayor," and "H.S. Pingree, governor."

The Detroit News

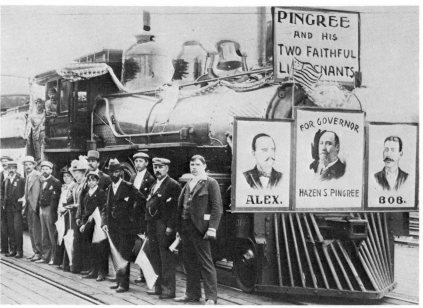

The Detroit News

Top **Pingree in one of his potato patches, 1893**

Bottom **This 1896 campaign train refers to Pingree aides Robert Oakman and Alex McLeod.**

69

The Detroit News

The Spanish-American War broke out during Pingree's first term. To assure that Michigan troops training for the conflict were well cared for, he lived with them in training camp.

In Pingree's last term, members of his administration were tainted by a kickback scandal that involved the sale of unused state military uniforms.* He thought an Ingham County judge was more lenient on the businessmen involved than he was on the state officials, so Pingree pardoned two convicted state officials. All this led to the judge holding Pingree in contempt of court. In a rambling account about the case in his final legislative message, Pingree complained to legislators that another Ingham judge "used to call your governor an old bald headed s.o.b. ... This contempt proceeding is nothing but a conspiracy of these judges against me."[5] The message was the longest and most vehement parting shot a departing Michigan governor left for the Michigan Legislature in the first 150 years of statehood.

Pingree then went off to South Africa to hunt elephants, being quoted as telling the Ingham County bench: "To hell with your court and your contempt."[6] He got his elephant. Proudly writing to The Detroit News, he said, "I trust you will have your artist spread himself on reproducing it, for a man doesn't kill an elephant every day."[7]

Before returning to Michigan, Pingree visited reforestation projects in Germany, where he became ill. Friends took him to London. "I don't want anything to happen to me now," he said. "If they'll only take care of me now, I'm willing to sign a contract with the Almighty to pass away without a murmur at the end of two years. I have so much to do."[8] He was unable to do it.

On June 18, 1901, while in London en route home, Pingree died of what the Associated Press described as "cancerous affection (sic) of the intestines." He was buried in Detroit. The AP's London dispatch was printed in The Detroit News under the headline:

"The Great Commoner Fell Asleep in London."[9]

* It was an example of Pingree having men around him with warped guidelines on ethics. "He was too easily influenced," Charles R. Starring wrote in a paper published by Michigan History magazine in June 1948. "Certain of his lieutenants learned they could appeal to his emotions and prejudices and they did not hesitate to use that approach when they wanted something done for a friend, a client, or themselves."

The Detroit News

Jerry Roe Collections

Opposite At Island Lake training camp near Brighton with Michigan troops preparing for the Spanish-American War. Colonel Cornelius Gardiner, who managed Pingree's potato patches, is seated at right of the pole.

Left Pingree's last photograph, with Eli Sutton in 1901 in South Africa, where Pingree shot an elephant.

State Archives

Aaron T. Bliss (1901-1904)

Michigan enters upon the long highway of the Twentieth century in the van of the procession of the states of this great republic.
— **First message to the Legislature, Jan. 9, 1901.**

Following its first election of the 20th century, Michigan was decidedly Republican as GOP Gov. Aaron T. Bliss addressed a Legislature in which Republicans controlled the Senate by a 31-1 margin and the House by 90-10.

But Bliss, last of a long line of lumber barons to serve as governor, was not so conservative as some business interests hoped he would be when he replaced Republican Hazen S. Pingree, the businessman whose heart was with the common man.

Under Bliss, the Legislature passed and he signed legislation that increased taxes on railroads. It was legislation that Pingree long had sought, but the GOP-dominated Senate refused to pass.

Bliss was born May 22, 1837, in Madison County, N.Y. He was raised on the family farm, attended a nearby school, and clerked in a store in which he ultimately became a partner.

In 1861, he enlisted as a private and went off to the Civil War. He became an officer, took part in the second Battle of Bull Run, and later was captured by Confederate troops. After six months in various stockades, he escaped.

In 1865, Bliss moved to Saginaw, worked in logging camps on the Tobacco River, and became a partner in a sawmill. He then expanded into salt, banking, mercantile and farm enterprises. In 1868, Bliss married Allaseba M. Phelps of Madison County, N.Y. They had no children.

Bliss was elected to the state Senate in 1882, and to Congress in 1888.

In 1900, Bliss was elected governor by a margin of 305,612-to-226,228 over Democrat William C. Maybury, an ex-congressman and mayor of Detroit at the time. Bliss was re-elected in 1902, defeating Lorenzo T. Durand, 211,261-174,077.

When he took office in 1901, Bliss reported there was $1,250,000 in the state treasury. When he left office in 1905, as the first governor to serve a full term in the 20th century, he told the Legislature it would find "a state free from debt, a treasury ample in resource, a commonwealth able to support all legitimate burdens and to discharge every financial obligation." As to future needs, Bliss advised: "If a thing ought to be done, the state cannot shirk its duty, no matter what the expense may be."[1]

Bliss continued the election reform effort stressed by former Gov. Pingree that gave voters, rather than party bosses, control of the nominating process. He called for, but did not win, primary election reform that would have given voters "unrestricted freedom of choice."[2] Said historians Willis F. Dunbar and George S. May: "This was a somewhat belated response to the heavy criticism that had resulted from reports that $750,000 had been spent at the 1900 Republican State Convention, which had nominated Bliss for governor, to buy the votes of delegates for the several wealthy candidates seeking the party's gubernatorial nomination."[3]

On July 6, 1904, at ceremonies in Jackson that marked the 50th anniversary of the founding of the Republican Party,

Bliss commented on the long reign of Republicans in the Capitol: "From the day of Kinsley S. Bingham, with but two exceptions, Michigan has uniformly returned Republican majorities. Under Republican rule the state has written honorable, glorious pages in the national history, and has advanced to a leading position in the union."[4]

In poor health when he left office in 1905, Bliss died Sept. 16, 1906, in Wisconsin. He was buried in Saginaw.

Bill Kuenzel/The Detroit News

Above President Theodore Roosevelt, a periodic and popular Michigan visitor, in Detroit in 1902

Left The first years of the 20th century were crucial ones for Henry Ford, shown here in 1902 with his record-breaking "999" and driver Barney Oldfield, who helped build Ford's reputation as a maker of winning racing cars.

Catlin

73

State Archives

Fred M. Warner (1905-1910)

The people of the State should understand that the deficit was not due to any squandering of their money but solely to the fact that they were not called upon at the proper time to contribute sufficient funds to meet actual needs.

— Final message to the Legislature, Jan. 5, 1911.

Michigan's first foreign-born governor, Fred M. Warner, was also the first to serve three consecutive terms. In his six years as governor, he was around long enough to experience the highs and lows of the financial roller coaster that marked the Michigan governorship throughout its first 150 years.

In his first legislative message on Jan. 5, 1905, Republican Warner said Michigan had paid its share of the expenses of the Spanish-American War, was "practically out of debt," and "the established principle of paying as we go is steadfastly adhered to."[1]

But apparently not steadfastly enough.

In 1908, Michigan had a cash crisis with payless paydays for its employees. The general fund temporarily was depleted because more was drawn for school aid than had been calculated. There was a two-month delay in payment of state obligations. "The greatest inconvenience was suffered by the employees of the state, whose compensation was withheld for a few weeks," Warner told the Legislature in 1909. He explained the deficit developed when the auditor general ruled the Legislature had underappropriated $4 million to the school fund over a period of several years.[2]

Some Michigan governors have blamed financial collapse on legislatures of the opposite party. But in this case, it was an all-Republican show. Republicans controlled the Legislature, having all 32 senators and 95 of 100 House members.

Compounding Michigan's fiscal dilemma was failure of the Chelsea Savings Bank, where State Treasurer Frank P. Glazier had deposited $685,587 in state funds without requiring adequate security. Warner forced Glazier to resign, and replaced him with former Gov. John T. Rich.

But Warner also had some good financial news to report when he began his third term in 1909: "The clouds of depression which for months hung over our country are almost, if not entirely, dispelled, and the business conditions of the state and nation are rapidly assuming their normal state."[3]

Fred Maltby Warner was born July 21, 1865, in Hickling, Nottinghamshire, England, and came to the United States when he was 3-months-old. When his mother died, he was adopted by P.D. Warner of Farmington in Oakland County. After attending Michigan Agricultural College for a year, he worked in his father's store, later taking it over and running it for 20 years.

In 1888, Warner married Martha M. Davis of Farmington. They had four children. In 1889, Warner started a cheese business which was expanded into 12 factories. He also became involved in farming and banking.

Warner spent nine years on the Farmington Municipal Council, served in the Michigan Senate between 1894-98 and was secretary of state for four years beginning in 1900.

He was elected governor in 1904, defeating Democrat Woodbridge N. Ferris of Big Rapids, 283,799-223,571. Ferris,

State Archives

who had run unsuccessfully for Congress in 1882, was himself elected governor in 1912.

Warner was re-elected in 1906, 227,567-130,018, over Democrat Charles H. Kimmerle. After opposition to his management of the state developed, he had a closer race in his final gubernatorial run in 1908. He won 262,141-252,611 over Democrat Lawton T. Hemans, a former state representative (and leading biographer of Gov. Stevens T. Mason).

A number of reforms were enacted during Warner's administration that included a factory inspection law, lower rates for passenger railroads, and a direct primary.

As other governors before him, Warner sent out the National Guard in a strike situation. Two battalions responded to Shiawassee County's request for help during three days of a strike at the Grand Trunk Railroad in July 1910.

After the governorship, Warner returned to farm and business interests, and became president of the Farmington State Savings Bank. In 1918, he entered, but then withdrew, from the GOP U.S. Senate primary.

Warner died April 17, 1923, in Orlando, Fla. He was buried in Farmington.

N.C.A.M.

75

State Archives

Chase S. Osborn (1911-1912)

Although the state had a deficit two years ago to the amount of near a million dollars and was consequently in disgrace, it is now out of debt and has a surplus in the treasury of near a million dollars.
    — **Final message to the Legislature, Jan. 2, 1913.**

H is was only a brief flash in Lansing. But one-term Gov. Chase S. Osborn blazed with an intensity that made the journalist-outdoorsman one of Michigan's most progressive and memorable political figures — and fighters.

"I like the strife and the pawing and the goring and the tragedy and the comedy that form the friction of a public contest," he said. "... I have a good temperament for a row."[1]

The feisty Osborn, Michigan's only governor from the Upper Peninsula, had so many rows that he wrote of himself after leaving office:

"Because of Osborn's independence and temperamental liberalism, he was charged with being erratic, not a few called him

crazy, and everybody agreed to the fact he would not stand hitched."[2]

Much of his trouble was with the conservative wing of his party — a trait he had in common with some earlier and later Republican governors.

Chase Salmon Osborn was born Jan. 22, 1860, in Huntington County, Ind., son of parents who both were physicians. He was a sickly baby, but became robust as he grew up in Indiana's Wabash River country.

While attending public schools he sold newspapers in Lafayette, and learned to set type as an apprentice in a print shop. Osborn, who spent three years at Purdue University, began his newspaper career on the Home Journal in Lafayette. After a brief stint at the Chicago Tribune, he worked on newspapers in Wisconsin, including the Milwaukee Sentinel. As a reporter, he had a reputation for running, not walking, between assignments, and for carrying a hatchet in his belt.

In 1881, Osborn married Lillian Jones of Milwaukee.* They had seven children.

Two years after their marriage, the Osborns moved to Florence, Wis., on the Michigan border, where he bought the Mining News.

It was in this rugged border country that Osborn first prospected for iron, a pursuit that led to the title of his autobiography, *The Iron Hunter,* one of seven books he wrote.

In 1887, Osborn moved to Michigan's Upper Peninsula, where he became publisher of the Evening News in Sault Ste. Marie, where Michigan's first permanent settlement was made in 1668 by Jacques Marquette and Claude Dablon, Catholic priests and missionaries. Osborn said the Soo was expanding "until its country trousers did not reach its ankles."[3]

He owned the News until 1901, when he bought Saginaw's Courier-Herald, which he owned until 1912.

Osborn was postmaster of Sault Ste. Marie in 1889-93 and Michigan's game and fish warden in 1895-1899 by appointment of Gov. John T. Rich — a job that allowed Osborn to remain in the north country and build his reputation as a

---

* In later years, the Osborns were separated. She died in 1948. Shortly before his death in 1949, Osborn married Stella Brunt. She was 34 years younger than Osborn, and had been adopted by him. The adoption was dissolved before their marriage.

Bentley

With Lt. Gov. John Q. Ross before their 1911 inauguration

staunch conservationist.

In 1896, he ran unsuccessfully for Congress, and was a supporter of the winning bid for governor by Republican Detroit Mayor Hazen S. Pingree, whose liberalism Osborn shared. By appointment of Pingree, Osborn from 1899 to 1903 was commissioner of railroads, a job that gave him a political boost. He traveled all 11,000-plus miles of Michigan's track.[4] In this job he also honed some of the progressive regulatory ideas he later pushed as governor.

In 1908, Osborn was chairman of the Michigan delegation to the Republican National Convention which nominated William Howard Taft for president. He also was appointed to the University of Michigan Board of Regents. Political impulses were stirring in Osborn.

In October 1909, Osborn announced that he would seek the 1910 Republican nomination for governor.

Behind most successful politicians there is a political operative. In Osborn's case at the time, it was one of his former editors at the Soo, Frank Knox — a man who went on to become the GOP vice-presidential nominee in 1936 and later secretary of the navy. It was Knox who arranged for Osborn to become chairman of the Michigan delegation in 1908, and began planning the gubernatorial campaign.*

In his primary race, Osborn was critical of incumbent GOP Gov. Fred M. Warner, who backed one of Osborn's two primary opponents. Osborn won the primary and became governor by defeating Democrat Lawton T. Hemans, 209,803-159,770. There also were three minor party candidates.

Osborn went on to become a backer of progressive Republican Theodore Roosevelt for president over Taft. But in his gubernatorial campaign, Osborn sounded more like Franklin D. Roosevelt. Beginning with an October speech in Greenville, Osborn promised to bring Michigan a "New Deal" — which would become the FDR rallying cry two decades later.[5]

Osborn was blocked on much of his "New Deal" by the Republican-controlled Legislature, especially in the Senate. At the outset, the Senate rejected a list of his appointees in favor of a list submitted by

* Other political operatives who played inner circle roles in campaigns of Michigan governors included: Eli Sutton, a son-in-law of Hazen S. Pingree, who, according to Osborn, "seemed to have his ear and his confidence to a greater extent than anyone else"; John S. Haggerty, the Wayne County Republican chairman who was instrumental in Alexander J. Groesbeck's elections until they had a falling out; Larry Farrell, campaign manager and executive secretary to G. Mennen Williams; Joyce Braithwaite, fund-raiser, campaign manager and executive assistant to William G. Milliken; and Ron Thayer, fund-raiser, political strategist and executive secretary to James J. Blanchard.

POLITIKAL BEE

CLARKE

W.W. Clarke/The Detroit News

outgoing Republican Gov. Warner.

However, many of Osborn's programs were passed, including a presidential primary law, Michigan's first Workmen's Compensation Act, and an expansion of state authority over railroads, express companies, banks, insurance companies, telephone companies and the liquor industry.

Much of Osborn's time in office was spent coping with financial problems inherited from the Warner years. In his first message to the Legislature, he vowed to "cut down expenses to bed rock."[6] In his farewell message two years later, he briefly reported on improved state finances and left with the new Legislature a long list of proposed "progressive laws."[7]

Having pledged to be a one-term governor, Osborn did not seek re-election, and went off on one of his many foreign trips. In 1914 he ran unsuccessfully against Democratic Gov. Woodbridge N. Ferris. Helping defeat him were Republican conservatives who felt closer to Ferris' views than Osborn's.

Osborn also was unsuccessful in Republi-

State Archives

can primary bids for the U.S. Senate in 1918 and 1930.*

Another dream Osborn pursued after becoming governor was a bridge across the Straits of Mackinac. He lobbied both state and federal authorities, but he died April 11, 1949, in Georgia; the Mackinac Bridge was completed in 1957. Osborn was buried on Duck Island near Sault Ste. Marie in his beloved U.P.

In a 1939 WWJ radio broadcast on Osborn's 80th birthday, Detroit News writer George Stark said the Iron Hunter name fit the versatile Osborn, "because surely he is an iron man, with all the qualities and ruggedness that attach to the great mines and the great forests of his adopted state."

* The 1918 Senate battle was one of Michigan's most intriguing political episodes. Auto pioneer Henry Ford ran on both party ballots, as was allowed then. In the GOP race, Detroiter Truman Newberry beat Ford, with Osborn a distant third. Ford won the Democratic nomination, then lost narrowly to Newberry. But Ford charged Newberry with spending violations; there was a grand jury investigation; Newberry was convicted but won a U.S. Supreme Court appeal — and then resigned from the Senate.

State Archives

Woodbridge Ferris (1913-1916)

We are entering a new era in statecraft.

— First words to the Legislature, Jan. 2, 1913.

After a run of governors who were lawyers, farmers, bankers, lumbermen, and other barons of business, Michigan elected a governor who was an educator — one who focused on the basics of statecraft.

Democrat Woodbridge N. Ferris lacked the flair of a Blair, Pingree or Osborn. He was, in fact, known as Michigan's "good gray governor." He cultivated an image of always the schoolmaster; rarely the politician.[1]

He was, of course, an effective politician. He was twice elected governor, only the second Democrat to become governor of Michigan since the founding of the GOP in 1854. At age 70, he was elected to the U.S. Senate, the first Democrat from Michigan to serve there after the Civil War.

But Ferris professed to be a reluctant candidate. He was first and foremost for about 40 years an educator. After 15 years as a teacher and principal, he founded in Big Rapids what became Ferris State College.

Ferris was born Jan. 6, 1853, in a log house near the village of Spencer in Tioga County, N.Y. As a youngster in school, he recalled, he got "into mischief and mischief," and had frequent floggings. As a 14-year-old at Spencer Union Academy, he was so dull in English grammar his teacher "called me a blockhead."[2]

He attended the medical department at the University of Michigan for two years but preferred education to medicine and became principal of Spencer Academy in 1874. He held other education positions before moving to Big Rapids with his wife, the former Helen Frances Gillespie of Fulton, N.Y., to establish Ferris Industrial School.* He also became president of the Big Rapids Savings Bank.

In 1892, Ferris was an unsuccessful candidate for Congress and an unsuccessful candidate for governor in 1904, losing to Republican Fred M. Warner.

In 1912, however, conditions were ripe for a Democratic comeback. Incumbent Republican Gov. Chase S. Osborn was not running again and GOP ranks were split between progressives and conservatives. As Ferris told it: "Against my own inclinations and wishes I became a candidate on the Democratic ticket for governor of Michigan chiefly because I believed that as a candidate I could render (Democratic presidential nominee) Woodrow Wilson my largest possible service."[3]

Ferris defeated Republican Amos Musselman 194,017-169,963, with 152,909 votes going to Lucius W. Watkins, the candidate of Theodore Roosevelt's maverick Progressive Party. As it turned out, Ferris did not help Wilson, who was elected president, but ran third in Michigan. Roosevelt, who had Osborn's backing, won all of Michigan's electoral votes. Republican President William Howard Taft came in second in Michigan.

---

* They had three children. Four years after Helen died, Ferris married Mary Ethel McLoud of Indiana in 1921. After Ferris died, his widow became active in politics, periodically running, unsuccessfully, for congressional and other offices. In 1937, she announced her candidacy for the Democratic gubernatorial nomination but later abandoned the idea because, as reported in The Detroit News upon her death in 1954, she said, "being governor of Michigan is a man's job."

Republicans maintained their control of both houses of the Legislature.

In 1914, Republicans again were badly split. Osborn tried a comeback, winning a bitter GOP primary. But then Ferris beat him, 212,063-176,254, in a six-man race. Progressive Henry R. Pattengill finished a distant third with 36,747.

Ironically, Democrat Ferris was able to get enacted some of the election reform and other progressive agenda that Republican Osborn sought, including revision of the primary law. But when the Legislature in 1915 tried to repudiate the reform by requiring enrollment by party, Ferris vetoed it, saying he was opposed to requiring a voter to "advertise his ballots."[4]

His farewell message to the Legislature on Jan. 1, 1917, reflected the Ferris formula for working with a Republican Legislature: "Every state in the Union needs more business efficiency and less partisan politics. The state of Michigan is not owned by any political party."[5]

As other governors before him, Ferris dispatched National Guard troops to help maintain order in a strike situation. The request came from Houghton County, where a copper strike started July 22, 1913, and lasted until April 14, 1914. During a Christmas party for striking miners and their families, 73 persons were trampled and killed when someone yelled "fire" in a crowded hall in Calumet.

"In magnitude and duration, the Michigan copper strike of 1913-1914 was one of the greatest that has occurred in modern times," Ferris told the Legislature in reporting that "not a single life was sacrificed through any action of the Michigan National Guard."[6]

His political advisers had urged him not to send the Guard to the strike scene. But in doing so, he also criticized the mine operators for not properly providing for workers. In the end, it was a political plus for him.

Ferris did not seek re-election in 1916, but did try again in 1920, losing by 392,614 votes to Republican Alexander J. Groesbeck.

In 1922, Ferris was elected to the U.S. Senate. Between Senate sessions, Ferris would return to Big Rapids to lecture. Observed Detroit News columnist Will Muller: "Genius or not in the U.S. Senate, Ferris was genius unadulterated as a teacher. He was raconteur, activist and practical philosopher, and jammed a liberal hod of political science into the minds of his scholars with every course he taught."[7]

After developing pneumonia, Ferris died at age 76 in Washington on March 23, 1928, and was buried in Big Rapids.

A few days before his death, he said, "I know perfectly well that my own successes were due in considerable part to the fact that I chose the good Democratic years. I could not have been elected governor in 1912 except for the split in the Republican party which Col. Roosevelt precipitated."[8]

Bentley

Library of Congress

Top **National Guard encampment at 1913 Calumet copper strike**

Bottom **Ferris State Institute in 1910, which started in 1884 as an industrial school and became Ferris State College in 1963.**

State Archives

Albert E. Sleeper (1917-1920)

Michigan has been called upon to play her part in the great war of the ages. ... We have given unhesitatingly of life's greatest treasure, our Michigan boys.

— Address to Legislature, Jan. 21, 1919.

The second of Michigan's three "war governors," Republican Albert E. Sleeper led the state's mobilization for World War I. He spurred food production and got an emergency $5 million appropriation for war-related expenses. He even provided state soldiers with rubber overshoes at a winter training camp when the U.S. government did not furnish them.*

"Mobilization orders came suddenly and found us unprepared," Sleeper told the Legislature in 1919. "Reports reached us that some of our boys in the various naval training stations were suffering from the cold at night because of insufficient covering. ... We shipped thousands of the best Army blankets obtainable to the points where they were most needed."[1]

Albert Edson Sleeper was born Dec. 31, 1862, on a farm in Bradford, Vt. Educated at Bradford Academy, he moved to Lexington, in Michigan's Thumb, in 1884. He was in the mercantile business and worked as a traveling salesman. He started his own business, buying and selling farm and timber lands. He later established several private banks in small towns in the area.

Sleeper's first public office was as president of the village of Lexington. He then moved to Bad Axe, where his business interests were centered. He became known as "Uncle Bert," a nickname he liked even as governor.

In 1901, he married Mary C. Moore of Lexington, daughter of a lumberman. They had no children.

After being elected to two terms in the state Senate, Sleeper was elected in 1908 as state treasurer, serving two terms.

In 1916, he was elected governor when he defeated Democrat Edwin F. Sweet, a former congressman, 363,724-264,440. He was re-elected in 1918, defeating Democrat John W. Bailey, 266,738-158,142.

It was during Sleeper's administration that an amendment to the state Constitution was passed that provided for limited women's suffrage.**

Sleeper had ambitious plans for economic development and highway improvement, but they were interrupted by the war. Even before war broke out, Sleeper sent a message to President Wilson assuring him of support in the event of war. A War Preparedness Board, with Sleeper as chairman, was established and held its first meeting the day after war was declared. The board helped obtain several hundred tractors for Michigan farmers, bought clothing for enlisted men and provided no-interest loans to needy Michigan officers for clothing and equipment.

In the summer of 1917, Sleeper sent a special force of Michigan State Police, trained to fill in for the departed National

* While several Michigan governors participated in various degrees of preparation and mobilization for military conflicts, the state's most dominant "war governor" was Civil War Gov. Austin Blair. Murray D. Van Wagoner was governor when the nation mobilized after the attack on Pearl Harbor, Dec. 7, 1941.

** In the Constitution of 1850, women's suffrage was rejected, although women were allowed to vote on bond issues.

Guard, to the Upper Peninsula. He told the Legislature: "Agitators on the payroll of enemy powers attempted to foment strife in the iron mining district. ... They hoped to cripple the mines to such an extent that the supply of iron ore flowing down the lakes in a constant stream to the great steel mills, later to be converted into ships and munitions, would be interrupted and the government's war program seriously impaired."[2]

The agitators fled when the police arrived, Sleeper said. Other detachments were sent to guard rail, grain, power and other facilities.

Sleeper had a number of successes, including enhancement of the state park system. But the conservative Republican governor had numerous quarrels with the Republican Legislature. A Detroit News account of the day called them "exceedingly vituperative. A faction of his party persistently denounced him in harsher terms than they used about Democrats."[3]

After leaving office in 1921, Sleeper returned to his business interests in Bad Axe. He died in Bad Axe May 13, 1934, and was buried in Lexington.

Top **As suffragists look on, Sleeper signs a May 8, 1917 state law granting women the right to vote for presidential electors.**

Bottom **Farewells as Michigan goes to World War I**

State Archives

Bill Kuenzel/The Detroit News

83

State Archives

Alexander Groesbeck (1921-1926)

The state treasury has been dug out of the mire of debt and is now on the dry ground of solvency.

— Message to the Legislature, Jan. 4, 1923.

After losing his first bid for governor and then serving four years as attorney general, Alexander J. Groesbeck became one of Michigan's most successful chief executives — politically and administratively.

He reorganized state government, and made it work. He was called aloof as a politician and dictatorial as governor. Yet this Republican won big three times, and built roads and other projects that reflected his vision and skills.

But, as so often happened with the Michigan governorship before and since, the time of Groesbeck's greatest triumphs was followed by a period of discord in his administration and party. He lost his last three bids for governor.

Groesbeck was yet another governor to ride the seesaw of deficit and surplus. In his first message to the Legislature Jan. 6, 1921, he said: "The auditor general informs me that there is a deficit in the state treasury of approximately $6 million, with a strong likelihood that it will be considerably augmented by the close of the current fiscal year."[1]

Two years later, he reported a surplus of $10,165,498 and said: "The depression of two years ago resultant upon the lack of employment has vanished in the smoke of a renewed and stable prosperity and happily with it have also gone most of the isms and nostrums of social and political agitators."[2] Groesbeck's claim of solvency, which he reiterated as he left office, was challenged by his successor.

Alexander Joseph Groesbeck was born Nov. 7, 1873, in Warren Township of Macomb County, son of a sawmill owner who was a Democrat and onetime Macomb County sheriff. He attended public schools in Mt. Clemens, and in Wallaceburg, Ontario, where his father worked for a lumber company. He worked for four years in his father's sawmill, clerked in a Port Huron law firm, and attended the University of Michigan, where he graduated in 1893 with a law degree. He began a highly successful law practice in Detroit.

In 1912, Groesbeck played his first major role in politics. As Republican state chairman, he aligned himself with conservative William Howard Taft in opposition to the Bull Moose wing of Theodore Roosevelt. (In later years, Groesbeck, driven more by individualism rather than ideology, was critical of the conservatism of Calvin Coolidge and Herbert Hoover, and supported Democrats for some key races in Michigan.)

In 1914, Groesbeck tried for the GOP nomination for governor. He lost to former Gov. Chase S. Osborn in a three-man race. In 1916, he lowered his sights, and made a successful election bid to become attorney general. He was re-elected in 1918. Across the country and over the years, being attorney general has proven to be one of the best ways to become governor. That was the case with Groesbeck, as he earned a corruption-busting reputation as Michigan's top lawman.

In 1920, Groesbeck won the GOP nomination for governor in a large field of

W.T. Bailes/The Detroit News

candidates, and went on to defeat former Gov. Woodbridge N. Ferris, 703,180-310,566. The 392,614 plurality was the biggest for a Michigan governor, but it was a record Groesbeck himself would beat.

Two years later, Groesbeck had a closer race, beating Democrat Alva M. Cummins, 356,933-218,252. In 1924, he was elected to a third term over Democrat Edward Frensdorf, 799,225-343,577 — a plurality of 455,648.

As governor, Groesbeck consolidated and centralized government; reorganized the departments of Health, Highways, Public Safety, Conservation, and Agriculture; reformed the Corrections system; established an automobile title system; and created the State Administrative Board — putting the general supervision of the department under a board of elected officials.

Said Groesbeck: "When the Administrative Board Act was passed, a new era in the

Gasoline Tax In Effect

The Michigan State Legislature has passed the gasoline tax law and has made it effective immediately.

As required by law that this Company will, beginning February 1, 1925, collect the Michigan tax of two cents per gallon on all gasoline sales made by it at service stations or through tank wagons.

Standard Oil Company

(Indiana)

910 S. Michigan Ave.   Chicago

Leelanau Enterprise

business administration of Michigan's affairs was ushered in."[3]

While many earlier governors had put an emphasis on good roads, Groesbeck greatly expanded the network, with a tax to pay for them. Said Detroit News writer Carl Muller: "...he uprooted precedent, swept aside archaic inefficiencies and left an ineffaceable record of administrative genius.

"The State Administrative Board stands as one of the monuments to that genius. Greater Woodward Avenue, Grand River, and other highways are monuments to his campaign for the gasoline tax to get Michigan out of the mud."[4]

Noted a Michigan History magazine article: "With a consuming energy and drive, Groesbeck could not establish a structure without directing it."[5] Roads became his goal, and he put in place the structure to improve 6,500 miles of state trunk lines and build 2,000 miles of hard-surfaced roads.

State Archives

Democrats claimed Groesbeck was acting like a czar. A Democratic convention roared approval in 1926 when 1922 gubernatorial contender Alva Cummins called Groesbeck "Mussolini." Other Democrats likened the governor to Caesar and Louis XIV.[6]

Groesbeck had crippling political problems in his third term. Rural leaders objected to the gas tax, and to loss of influence on road construction. A more serious problem came when Groesbeck alienated his longtime close friend and ally, Wayne County Republican Chairman John Haggerty. He had helped deliver votes for Groesbeck, and the governor appointed him to the state Fair Board. When the board refused a Groesbeck request that it fire the fair manager, Groesbeck replaced the entire board, including Haggerty.

Groesbeck biographer Frank Woodford, then chief editorial writer for the Detroit Free Press, said "the repercussions spelled out political disaster for Groesbeck.

"...For years Groesbeck and Haggerty had been on the closest terms. Both bachelors, they were inseparable....More than any other man, Groesbeck listened to Haggerty. As much as anyone could be, Haggerty was closest to being the power behind the throne."[7]

Haggerty supported Fred W. Green for the 1926 gubernatorial nomination. Green won, 397,000-237,339. For the first time in his political career, Groesbeck lost Wayne County. He also lost 56 other counties.

Groesbeck returned to law and business interests, but tried twice more, without success, for the gubernatorial nomination — in 1930 and in 1934.

In 1941, Groesbeck was appointed by Democratic Gov. Murray D. Van Wagoner as chairman of the state Civil Service Commission. In 1948, he quietly supported Democrat G. Mennen Williams in his upset defeat of Republican Gov. Kim Sigler. Asked to list those who helped him pull off the upset, Williams described Groesbeck as "very helpful" in helping him court Republicans disenchanted with Sigler.[8] Groesbeck also supported Democrat George Edwards, who was later appointed to the Michigan Supreme Court by Williams, in his unsuccessful 1949 bid against Republican Albert Cobo for mayor of Detroit.

Groesbeck died March 10, 1953. He was buried in Detroit.

The Detroit News

The Detroit News

Michigan Department of Transportation

Top **Groesbeck pledged to get Michigan out of the mud, which was abundant.**

Middle **A traffic jam on Detroit's Woodward Avenue**

Bottom **1920's highway construction**

LeClear Photo

Fred W. Green (1927-1930)

The state is not paying its bills. ... There are many disturbing rumors in regard to the state's financial condition ...

— **First message to the Legislature, Jan. 6, 1927.**

Michigan's incoming and outgoing governors began 1927 with sharply contrasting views of the state of the state. On Jan. 6, ex-Gov. Alexander J. Groesbeck told the Legislature: "You are not now confronted with deficits and a depleted treasury or with the necessity of devising new methods of taxation to meet and remedy them."[1]

On the same day, Gov. Fred W. Green warned Michigan was in trouble. He announced that he had ordered an audit to find out how deep. Three months later, Republican Green proclaimed a "grave financial situation," and said Republican Groesbeck had left a general fund deficit of $3,302,306.[2]

Groesbeck, who lost to Green in a bitter 1926 GOP primary, fired back that Green's report was based on "a multitude of phony figures." He said the new administration was "giving a circus exhibition of how not to run the government. They have attacked first one thing and another, jumping like jack rabbits from one place to another in a vain and asinine effort to smirch state institutions, state highways and state finances."[3]

So began the administration of one more Republican governor whose biggest feuds were often intra-party.

Fred Warren Green was born Oct. 20, 1872, in Manistee, on the shores of Lake Michigan. The family moved to Cadillac, where he received his early formal education. In 1893, after only 2½ years, he earned a teaching certificate by completing a four-year course at Michigan State Normal School at Ypsilanti. He sold insurance to work his way through the University of Michigan, were he received a law degree in 1898.

Green then enlisted for the Spanish-American War, commanding Company G, 31st Michigan Volunteer Infantry in Cuba. After the war, he practiced law in Ypsilanti, became city attorney, and married Helen A. Kelly of Cadillac. They had a daughter.

Green became a partner in, and later owner of, a furniture company that would make him wealthy. It was moved in 1903 to Ionia, where he was elected mayor in 1912. Green, who had numerous business interests, was an activist in the Michigan Republican Party, serving as treasurer of the Republican State Central Committee for 10 years and as a delegate to several national conventions. In 1912, he broke with party regulars to become a delegate to the Progressive Party convention that gave its presidential nomination to Theodore Roosevelt.

In 1926, Green defeated incumbent Groesbeck to win the GOP gubernatorial nomination. He was elected by defeating Democrat William Comstock, 399,564-227,155. He beat Comstock again in 1928, 961,179-404,546 — a record plurality of 556,633 that was not surpassed until 1986.

Despite his earlier support of Theodore Roosevelt, Green, as governor, was an orthodox Republican with little interest in the reforms of earlier 20th century Republican governors. He complained that the

Administrative Board Act touted by Groesbeck put too much power in the hands of the governor and "made dummies of other members of the board."[4]

An assessment in Michigan History magazine suggested the Green administration "resembled the 'holding operation' that characterized the Calvin Coolidge administration in Washington."[5]

An avid outdoorsman, Green put emphasis on strengthening the Conservation Department, and keeping it out of politics. He also pushed road-building and won legislation to modernize hospitals, and establish a new code of criminal procedure.

One Green action that had a profound impact on Michigan politics was his 1928 appointment of Arthur H. Vandenberg to fill the vacancy created by the death of Sen. Woodbridge N. Ferris. Vandenberg remained in the Senate until his death in 1951.

Green did not seek a third term in 1930. When Atty. Gen. Wilber M. Brucker announced the Monday after Easter that he would seek the GOP nomination, Green was hesitant. Former Gov. Groesbeck already had announced a comeback try. Finally, and somewhat reluctantly, Green announced support for Brucker, who won the primary and the general election.

Green died Nov. 30, 1936, in Munising, in the Upper Peninsula. He was buried in Ionia.

Left **Green, in 1928, promotes commercial air service in Michigan.**

Right **Golfer Green on the Grand Hotel course on Mackinac Island. On the bluff behind Green is the house acquired as the official summer residence of Michigan governors fifteen years after Green left office.**

The Detroit News

Courtesy: Grand Hotel

89

State Archives

Wilber M. Brucker (1931-1932)

While it is beyond our power to change the economic forces which have been responsible for so much distress everywhere, it is our joint duty to apply our best talents to alleviate the present suffering of our people.

— Depression message to emergency session of the Legislature, March 29, 1932.

Once again, a Michigan governor confronted the bust end of the state's nationally propelled cycle of boom and bust. With unemployment hitting 50 percent in many cities, Republican Gov. Wilber M. Brucker called the Senate and House into joint session to deal with the Great Depression.

"Because of its highly specialized industrial structure Michigan suffered sooner and more severely than most of the other states," wrote historian F. Clever Bald, "... more than half a million people were dependent on public funds for their daily bread."[1]

The Legislature adopted much of Brucker's Depression-relief package. The state borrowed $21 million from the federal Reconstruction Finance Corp. for relief purposes. Counties were given a share of the auto weight tax. Cities were allowed higher limits on "calamity bonds" to borrow money to provide relief.

But neither the state nor Brucker were ready for any broad responsibility for welfare. Property taxes, on which the state depended so heavily for revenue, were increasingly delinquent. And Brucker, as Detroit News political writer Will Muller observed, "was deaf to a newer philosophy sweeping the land, a philosophy of government help, social reform, responsibility for the common welfare of man."[2]

As Brucker told the Legislature:

"Direct welfare relief is essentially a local problem. If the state government were to embark upon a program of direct relief out of state funds, the result would be an unwarranted increase in these expenditures, which the localities would themselves have to pay in the end."[3]

Brucker, who won the Silver Star as a World War I infantry officer with the Rainbow Division, fought a losing battle on two fronts as governor — the Depression and his political enemies. The two did him in; he failed to win a second term.

Wilber Marion Brucker was born June 23, 1894, in Saginaw, where his father was a local Democratic leader and two years later was elected to Congress. Brucker graduated from high school in Saginaw, and then went to the University of Michigan, where he worked part-time as a waiter. After getting his law degree in 1916, he served with the Michigan National Guard in the campaign against Pancho Villa on the Mexican border.

Upon his return, war was declared against Germany. He went overseas with the 186th Infantry, 42nd (Rainbow) Division, serving in France at Luneville, Baccarat, the Chateau Thierry offensive in Champagne, at St. Mihiel and in the Meuse-Argonne offensive.

After the war, he practiced law in Saginaw and was twice elected county prosecutor. After backing Green for governor, Brucker was made an assistant attorney general in 1927. Under pressure from Brucker's political allies, Green appointed Brucker attorney general when a vacancy occurred in 1928. That fall he was elected to the position.

In 1930, before Green announced his own intentions, Brucker declared as a candidate for the Republican nomination for governor. In the end, he had Green's support and won the nomination in a tight battle with ex-Gov. Alexander J. Groesbeck, 368,518-364,357. At age 36, he was elected governor when he defeated Democrat William A. Comstock, who had lost to Green in 1926 and 1928. The vote was 483,990-357,664.

Two years later, Comstock reversed the outcome, beating Brucker by 190,737 votes in the Democratic landslide led by President Franklin D. Roosevelt. The magnitude of the 1932 sweep was reflected in the Legislature, where Republicans lost control of both houses.

It obviously was not a vintage year for Republican incumbents.

Brucker returned to law practice. In the 1936 Republican U.S. Senate primary, Brucker defeated Sen. James Couzens, who was supporting Roosevelt's re-election. In the general election, he faced Prentiss M. Brown, a Democratic congressman from St. Ignace. Brucker's billboards proclaimed: "Brucker Knows Michigan." Brown said "Michigan Knows Brucker." Brown won by 196,335 votes.

In 1955, Brucker was appointed by President Dwight D. Eisenhower as general counsel of the Defense Department. Later, Eisenhower made him secretary of the army.

Brucker died at age 74 in Detroit on Oct. 28, 1968. He was survived by his wife, the former Clara Hantel of Saginaw, whom he married in 1923, and a son, Wilber M., Jr., who served as a member of the Wayne State University Board of Governors. Brucker was buried in Arlington, Va., National Cemetery.

Gen. William C. Westmoreland, then U.S. Army chief of staff, said, "The United States Army mourns one of its great leaders."[4] The Detroit News editorialized:

"Among Michigan governors, history will record Wilber M. Brucker as one of the last of the unsophisticates.

"... Those who mourn him now may also mourn the passing of an age when the simple virtues of courage, loyalty, industry and faith were enough to qualify a young man for governor of Michigan."[5]

Left **Detroit firemen help ease Depression hunger in 1931.**

Below **Brucker stands at Herbert Hoover's right during a 1931 presidential visit to Detroit. To Brucker's right is Detroit Mayor Frank Murphy, who later became governor. To Hoover's left is Fred M. Alger, son of former Gov. Russell A. Alger.**

State Archives

Bill Kuenzel/The Detroit News

Michigan Manual

William A. Comstock (1933-1934)

I am happy to report that there has been a material change for the better in the financial situation.

— **Final message to the Legislature, Jan. 3, 1935.**

After three attempts, Democrat William A. Comstock was elected governor in 1933 and then failed to be nominated for re-election. Nevertheless, this Depression-era governor had an action-packed single term.

Within six weeks of taking office, he ordered the state's banks closed for eight days to avoid a collapse. He initiated a 3-percent sales tax, mobilized a responsive Legislature to enact welfare programs and brought about a number of other emergency measures. He signed an old-age assistance program into law.

One thing that made legislators responsive was that Democrats took control of both houses as they, like Comstock, were swept into office in the Democratic landslide. Democrats went from a 1-31

margin in the Senate to control by a 17-15 margin. They were only 2-98 in the House but took control, 55-45. Franklin D. Roosevelt became the first Democratic presidential candidate to win a Michigan majority since Franklin Pierce in 1852.

The long patience of Comstock, who had been Democratic state chairman and otherwise active in the party during the lean years, paid off.

William A. Comstock was born July 2, 1877, in Alpena, son of a lumber dealer and businessman. As a teen-ager, he worked for an electric railroad operated by his father. In 1899, he graduated from the University of Michigan. In 1909, he became president of the State Savings Bank of Alpena, and from 1910 to 1931 had financial interests in several banking and manufacturing enterprises.

In 1919, Comstock married Josephine White Morrison of Detroit. They had one son, and he adopted Josephine's son from a previous marriage. They established their home that year in Detroit, and Comstock in 1924 started a real estate brokerage firm.

Comstock's political career started in Alpena, where he was Democratic county chairman and a city councilman before being elected mayor in 1913. He served a 1914-16 term as an appointee to the University of Michigan Board of Regents.

Comstock was 1920-24 Democratic state chairman, and a Democratic national committeeman in the 1924-30 period. After carrying the party's banner in essentially hopeless gubernatorial races in 1926, 1928 and 1930, Comstock had little trouble getting the nomination when the chances were good in 1932. He defeated incumbent Republican Gov. Wilber M. Brucker, 887,672-696,935. Also fielding candidates were the Socialist, Prohibition, Socialist Labor, Communist, Proletarian and Liberty parties.

As governor, Comstock was an advocate of public works programs for the unemployed.

The Legislature appropriated $24 million over two years for emergency welfare relief. But he told it at a special session in 1934:

"In simple terms the question is, shall we continue the dole for the unemployed, or shall we put them to work on necessary or useful projects at normal wages."[1]

When he left office, Comstock reported a

cash balance in the state treasury of $12,104,882.[2]

While governor, Comstock lived in Ann Arbor because his wife disliked Lansing.[3] Comstock himself began to find Lansing politically uncomfortable because of intra-party feuding. Democrats, who for so long had been shut out of patronage, squabbled among themselves over jobs.

The sales tax was unpopular and Comstock was the first, but certainly not the last, governor to be the target of a refrain voiced by many a merchant: "That will be a dollar, and 3 cents for the governor."

Comstock was confident going into the primary to secure his nomination for re-election in 1934. But he lost a close race to attorney Arthur J. Lacy of Detroit. Comstock said he was relieved that he would no longer have the "grief" of the governorship. "I'm not fooling you when I tell you I feel as if a 10-ton weight had been lifted from my shoulders," said Comstock, who had spent $250,000 of his own money on his many campaigns and those of some other Democrats.[4]

Upon leaving the governorship, Comstock returned to his successful real estate business. He served on the Michigan Civil Service Commission in 1939 and 1940, and was a 1942-49 member of the Detroit City Council.

Comstock died June 16, 1949, in Alpena, where he was buried.

EIGHT-DAY HOLIDAY FOR ALL BANKS IN MICHIGAN

DETROIT ⚡ TIMES

CITY EDITION **EXTRA**

33D YEAR. NO. 137   DETROIT. MICHIGAN, TUESDAY, FEBRUARY 14, 1933   24 PAGES   THREE CENTS

Proclamation Closing Banks to Protect State

Whereas, in view of the acute financial emergency now existing in the city of Detroit and throughout the state of Michigan, I deem it necessary in the public interest and for the preservation of the public peace, health and safety, and for the equal safeguarding without preference of the rights of all depositors in the banks and trust companies of this state and at the request of the Michigan Bankers' Association and the Detroit Clearing House and after consultation with the banking authorities, both national and state, with representatives of the United States Treasury Department, the Banking Department of the State of Michigan, the Federal Reserve Bank, the Reconstruction Finance Corporation, and with the United States Secretary of Commerce, I hereby proclaim the days from Tuesday, February 14th, 1933, to Tuesday, February 21st, 1933, both dates inclusive, to be public holidays during which time all banks, trust companies and other financial institutions conducting a banking or trust business within the state of Michigan shall not be opened for the transaction of banking or trust business, the same to be recognized, classed and treated and have the same effect in respect to such banks, trust companies and other financial institutions as other legal holidays under the laws of this state, provided that it shall not affect the making or execution of agreements or instruments in writing or interfere with judicial proceedings. Dated this 14th day of February, 1933, 1:32 a.m.

WILLIAM A. COMSTOCK, Governor of the State of Michigan.

ERNIE SCHAAF SUCCUMBS TO BRAIN OPERATION AFTER KNOCKOUT

NEW YORK, Feb. 14 — Ernie Schaaf, Boston boxer knocked unconscious in his bout with Primo Carnera Friday night, died at Polyclinic Hospital at 4:20 o'clock this morning.

Mortgage Holiday   *War Supply Bill*
Asked in Nebraska   *Hiked $24,000,000*

STATEMENTS BY OFFICIALS

GOVERNOR COMSTOCK

Under Secretary of Treasury Pledges Fullest Aid of U.S.

ARTHUR A. BALLANTINE

UNION GUARDIAN TRUST CO. DIFFICULTY CAUSES ORDER; BRINGING U. S. AID

Governor William A. Comstock at 3 o'clock this morning issued a proclamation closing all banks, trust companies and all other financial institutions in Michigan for an eight-day period from February 14 to February 21

Detroit Times

93

State Archives

Frank D. Fitzgerald (1935-36, 1939)

We cannot feed the hungry with an empty treasury....It is imperative that we start at once to put our financial house in order ... expenditures have dropped Michigan from a fiscal standing at the top of the list of states to the bottom.

— Message to the Legislature, Jan. 5, 1939.

Republican Frank D. Fitzgerald was a rarity in the politics of Michigan's first 150 years of statehood. He had nearly a quarter century in state government before becoming governor, the only governor to start at the bottom and move up through service in elective office and the bureaucracy.

■ As secretary of state, he was the only state Republican officeholder to survive the Democratic sweep of 1932.

■ He was the only governor to recapture the office when he defeated the governor who had taken it away from him.

■ He was the second and highest achiever in four generations of Fitzgeralds to hold elective office in state government.

■ He was the only governor to die in office.

Although unique among governors, Fitzgerald was like many earlier and later governors when he complained of inheriting a financial mess.

After serving one term, Fitzgerald was defeated in 1936 by Democrat Frank Murphy. Upon taking office after defeating Murphy in a 1938 rematch, Fitzgerald told the Legislature:

"The treasury is deep in the red. Heavy drains upon it in the past two years have thrown it far out of balance. In addition to the actual deficit, we are faced with overdrafts which we must pay from future revenues, such as $10 million appropriated for relief; $6 million appropriated for institutional building, but which is not now available ...

"... We are confronted with debts, including the general fund deficit and other items listed, of $30 million to $50 million."[1]

Frank Dwight Fitzgerald* was born Jan. 27, 1885, in Grand Ledge. His father, John Wesley Fitzgerald, was a hardware merchant and one-term state representative.**

Young Fitzgerald graduated from high school in Grand Ledge, an Eaton County community west of Lansing. He attended Ferris Institute in Big Rapids but did not get a degree, twice going west to work on farms and ranches.

In 1906, his father, who was postmaster in Grand Ledge, hired Fitzgerald as a clerk. Fitzgerald served as a clerk in the state Senate, and then the House, from 1913 to 1919. It was in 1912, however, that he was first elected to public office, as the first Republican to represent Grand Ledge on the Eaton County Board of Supervisors.

While working winters in the legislative branch, Fitzgerald was able to spend the rest of the time as a clerk in the secretary of state's office. In 1919, he was appointed deputy secretary of state. By then, he was living in Lansing near the Capitol with his wife, the former Queena Maud Warner of Mulliken, northwest of Grand Ledge, whom

---

* Fitzgerald's middle name at birth was Thaddeus but he didn't like it and later changed it to Dwight.
** The governor's son, John Warner Fitzgerald, was a state senator, a judge of the Court of Appeals, and a justice of the Michigan Supreme Court, where he became chief justice. John's son, Frank M., extended the Fitzgerald political dynasty when he was elected as a state representative in 1986.

John W. Fitzgerald

95

The Detroit News

Mourners come to the Capitol in 1939 to pay tribute to Fitzgerald.

he married in 1909.

After he worked as an officer in an Oldsmobile dealership in Tennessee, Fitzgerald returned to Lansing in 1923 to become business manager of the state Highway Department, where he served seven years. He was recruited for the highway job by GOP Gov. Alexander J. Groesbeck.

During this period, his only child, John Warner Fitzgerald, was born. Also during the period, Fitzgerald became active in the Michigan GOP in a number of positions, including 1929-30 secretary of the Republican State Central Committee. For this job, Fitzgerald was recruited by GOP Gov. Fred W. Green.

Fitzgerald was elected secretary of state in 1930, and re-elected in 1932.

In 1934, he won the GOP nomination for governor by a lopsided primary victory over onetime mentor Groesbeck. He became governor when he defeated Democrat Arthur J. Lacy of Detroit, 659,743-577,044.

Fitzgerald periodically contended he didn't want the governorship. In 1932, for example, he wisely squelched a move to draft him. He preferred to face the Democratic resurgence as a candidate for re-election as secretary of state, rather than trying for the top job.

After his 1932 victory against the tide, Republicans again began talking about Fitzgerald as a gubernatorial candidate. But he said, "As far as I personally am concerned, I'd rather go back to Grand Ledge and raise potatoes and milk the cows."[2]

Once he became governor, though, he obviously liked the job and sought re-election in 1936. He was defeated, however, in a tight race by Democrat Frank Murphy, who tied himself closely to President Franklin D. Roosevelt. Murphy had a plurality of only 48,919 out of more than 1.7 million votes. Eight minor candidates got about 12,000 votes among them.

Fitzgerald made a comeback bid in 1938, promising "a liberal, progressive administration ... that will be a government that will be a friend to the working man and will do everything in its power to lift him from the bog of unemployment."[3] Fitzgerald regained the governorship by defeating Murphy 847,245-753,752.

As governor, Fitzgerald was a solid administrator, who balanced the budget, yet, for all of his considerable political skills, he was unable to win the sweeping changes he proposed, including increased appointive power.

At the beginning of his second term, Fitzgerald proposed an ambitious agenda that included a ban on sit-down strikes. He was critical of both labor and management, saying, "Certain classes of industry and business have been backward in dealing with labor. ... Certain labor groups, too, have been at fault. Their demands were too abrupt. They cried for the moon."[4]

Before his agenda could be implemented, Fitzgerald died of a heart attack March 16, 1939, in Grand Ledge, where he was buried. He had been ailing at his residence for several days, using an oxygen tent every two hours to ease his labored breathing.

"Hospitalizing the governor was discussed but rejected as too alarming to the public," his grandson, Frank M. Fitzgerald, later wrote in a detailed account of his death.[5]

When a doctor, who had been summoned, rushed to his side, Fitzgerald said, "Let me up. I can't breathe." The doctor administered a heart stimulant.

"Hang on, Frank," the doctor said. "We'll pull you through this one."

"OK, I'll stick," the governor responded. Two minutes later, he was dead.

Michigan was the center of sports attention in the mid-1930's, with Detroit being known as "The City of Champions." In 1935, the Tigers won the World Series, and the Lions were champions of the National Football League. The Red Wings won hockey's Stanley Cup in 1936 and 1939. Joe Louis was 1937-49 World Heavyweight champ. He is pictured here in 1935.

The Detroit News

State Archives

Frank Murphy (1937-1938)

My recent experiences in dealing with industrial unrest confirm the conviction that, basically, the working man of today is only seeking to attain his just and elementary rights.

— **Speech to Knights of Columbus of Boston, April 18, 1937.**

Frank Murphy was a popular Depression-era mayor of Detroit, an activist U.S. attorney general, and defender of civil liberties as a justice of the U.S. Supreme Court.

It was as Michigan's "labor governor," however, that Murphy earned his greatest fame, not all of it favorable, as he himself acknowledged.

Referring to his refusal to use National Guard troops in 1937 to eject auto workers during the landmark General Motors Corp. sitdown strike in Flint, Murphy said in a national radio broadcast:

"Because the government of Michigan refused to employ force in blind and narrow adherence to the letter of the law, it has been said that government was debased in the eyes of the world, that the courts were

flouted and the law ignored.

"But that is far from the truth. The government of Michigan believed then as it does today that obedience to the law and respect for authority are prerequisites to that social orderliness which it was striving peaceably to maintain. But, at the same time, it was confronted by a situation that demanded realistic treatment. To secure the confidence and obedience of many thousands of men under the strain of a conflict of such vast proportions and strong emotions, without causing disaffection and distrust for the institutions of popular government, required methods vastly different from those a sheriff employs in dealing with an ordinary case of trespass."[1]

There was nothing ordinary about the 44-day United Auto Workers strike that started in Flint Dec. 30, 1936, and spread to plants across the country. From it, the UAW won agreement to bargain exclusively with GM over the wages and working conditions of 200,000 workers. Since the UAW at the time represented only about 5 percent of the workers, it was a breakthrough for what was to become the most powerful union in Michigan.

The strike at GM plants in Flint already was in progress when Murphy was inaugurated Jan. 1, 1937. On Jan. 11, as other Michigan governors had done before him in response to labor strife, Murphy sent in the Michigan National Guard, but only to maintain order. He refused to use the guardsmen to eject the workers from the plants they occupied, even after they defied a court order to evacuate.

Murphy played a decisive role in mediating an end to the strike. But a wave of other sit-down strikes followed the settlement, leading to increased criticism of the governor for failing to enforce the court order in Flint.

The New York Times called Michigan "the uneasy place between the lakes, the place where all the trouble that affects the nation starts."[2]

In his broadcast speech, Murphy told the nation: "As a last resort government may properly use and was prepared to use whatever force might be required to maintain its authority. But the government of Michigan was unwilling to employ force unnecessarily to dignify the law.

"... Better and more lasting results are often achieved by the application of moral pressure and emphasis on moral and spiritual values than by resort to physical force."

Criticism of Murphy's handling of the Flint strike was but one among many factors contributing to his failure to win re-election two years later.

Frank Murphy was born April 13, 1893, at Harbor Beach near the tip of Michigan's Thumb. He attended public schools there before going to the University of Michigan, where he obtained his law degree in 1914. He practiced law for 30 months in Detroit. When the United States entered World War I, he entered the Army and served as a first lieutenant and then captain in the 4th and 85th divisions in France.

In 1919, Murphy became chief assistant U.S. attorney for the Eastern District of Michigan, assisting in the prosecution of war graft offenders. He re-entered private practice in 1922 and in that year won a close election to become a judge in Detroit Recorder's Court. He was easily re-elected in 1928.

When Detroit Mayor Charles Bowles was recalled in 1930 for his handling of the unemployment problem, Murphy resigned from the bench and defeated four opponents to become mayor. He easily was re-elected to a full term in 1931.

The mayor's job put Murphy in a career spotlight that blazed for most of the rest of his life. Murphy provided money for food programs, and used an abandoned warehouse to house the homeless. He also permitted mass meetings in Grand Circus Park that allowed those angry with the world, the nation or him to vent their feelings.

In 1933, Murphy was appointed governor-general of the Philippines by President Franklin D. Roosevelt, who had Murphy's strong support in the 1932 election. Murphy was named high commissioner when the Philippines gained commonwealth status in 1935.

In 1936, Roosevelt, worried about his re-election campaign, wanted Murphy back in Michigan. He wanted him to run for governor. Murphy had a strong following and he embraced Roosevelt's New Deal. By heading the state ticket, he could help hold Catholics who might be inclined to defect to a third party movement that included Royal Oak's Fr. Charles Coughlin, the radio priest who once, but no longer, supported Roosevelt.

As it turned out, noted Murphy

State Archives

biographer Sidney Fine, Roosevelt was "unnecessarily concerned. ... It was Roosevelt who carried Murphy to victory."[3] Roosevelt carried Michigan by 300,000 votes. Murphy was elected by a plurality of less than 50,000, defeating incumbent GOP Gov. Frank D. Fitzgerald 892,774-843,855.

Control of the Legislature switched from Republican to Democratic in the 1936 election so Murphy had little trouble enacting a series of "Little New Deal" programs. Among them: liberalized old-age assistance; expanded health care for the indigent; Michigan's first public child-guidance clinic; expanded mental health programs; and a broad range of labor legislation that included an occupational disease act and one of the nation's most liberal

The Detroit News

Murphy, soon-to-be President Franklin D. Roosevelt, and Horatio J. Abbott in 1932 Detroit parade

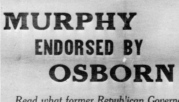

MURPHY
ENDORSED BY
OSBORN

Read what former Republican Governor Osborn has to say about the re-election of Frank Murphy

For Governor Of Michigan

"The President of the United States has promised personally and officially to build a bridge at the Straits of Mackinac.

A vote for Frank Murphy for Governor insures perfect co-operation for the bridge.

Vote for the clean, sober, brilliant statesman-- Michigan's wonderful industrial peace-maker...

FRANK MURPHY FOR GOVERNOR"

(Signed)
CHASE S. OSBORN

Political Advertisement, Inserted and Paid for by Chase S. Osborn

Iron Mountain News

unemployment insurance acts.

However, Murphy did not tend his political fences. Every so often, Michigan governors are zapped from within their own party. Murphy was such a governor.

"Many old-line Democrats were infuriated by Frank Murphy's unapproachableness, and his apparent complete disregard of the 'party machine,'" wrote author Frank McNaughton. "His appointments, frequently Republican and seldom with the approval of the party organization, were incitements to political rebellion."[4]

Murphy needed a united party behind him in his 1938 re-election bid. It was an off-year election in presidential politics. As a Democratic governor, Murphy was an exception to Michigan's tendency toward Republican governors ever since the Republican Party was founded in 1854.

In his campaign, Democrat Murphy had the opposition of former Democratic Gov. William A. Comstock — and the support of former Republican Gov. Chase S. Osborn.

Murphy lost to the man he had ousted in 1936, Republican Fitzgerald. The vote was 847,245 to 753,752.

After leaving the governorship, Murphy

was appointed U.S. attorney general by Roosevelt, and then, in 1940, to the U.S. Supreme Court.

According to biographer Fine, Murphy wanted to be secretary of war but came to the conclusion that the court would allow him to "evangelize for tolerance and all things that are just, that sweeten this life for men." And he could "thrust my lance at intolerance."[5]

Murphy served on the high court until his death on July 19, 1949, in Detroit. He was buried near Harbor Beach.

Among Murphy's legacies was a protege who later became governor — Democrat G. Mennen Williams. Murphy, an attorney for Williams' parents, helped inspire Williams to go into government service; steered and advised him toward jobs; hired him in Lansing and Washington; and was a pen pal when Williams was in the Navy during World War II.

When Williams wanted to return to Washington at one point, Justice Murphy advised him to take a job that Murphy earlier had arranged for Williams as deputy director of the Office of Price Administration in Detroit.

Murphy knew the job would help put Williams on a track toward the governor's job that Murphy held only briefly.

As it turned out, Williams carried the torch and lance of Murphy for 12 years in Lansing.

Dec. 31, 1938 — Murphy, who defeated Gov. Frank D. Fitzgerald in 1936, prepares to turn the office back to Fitzgerald, who won their 1938 rematch.

The Detroit News

State Archives

Luren D. Dickinson (1939-1940)

A pipeline to God. — **Dickinson's quest.**

He inherited the job upon the death of Gov. Frank D. Fitzgerald and he failed when he tried to win it on his own. But Republican Luren D. Dickinson set records as governor of Michigan. The office never had one like him before or since.

Dickinson was elected to a record seven terms as lieutenant governor; he was the only governor to succeed an incumbent who died in office; at 79 he was the oldest person to become Michigan's governor; and he appointed the first woman to become Michigan's lieutenant governor.

President of the Michigan Anti-Saloon League, he was an outspoken opponent of drinking, gambling and other "sins." When the Legislature passed a bill to legalize the clipping of horses' tails, Dickinson scrawled in a handwritten veto message: "Had God wanted horses' tails to be short, He would have made them short."[1]

Dickinson prayed every day for better government, saying prayer was "a spiritual pipeline between God and every state and every community in the nation."[2] In an article written for the Associated Press on his first year in office, Dickinson said that upon becoming governor: "My first act was to drop on my knees before Almighty God and tell him that he must steer me through. Jeers and insinuations from a number of our own papers, to say nothing of those outside the state, followed."[3] Later, in seeking help to reduce what he described as a $30-million budget deficit "thrown into our lap," Dickinson issued a call for all churches to seek Divine guidance for state officials involved in writing the budget. "The Christian and good people all over the state should not stop with me," he said.[4]

Luren Dudley Dickinson was born April 15, 1859, in Niagara County, N.Y., son of a farmer. Upon moving to Michigan, he attended Charlotte High School. For 19 years, he taught in rural schools and became principal of Potterville High School. He also engaged in farming, fruit growing and raising of stock on a 250-acre farm near Charlotte.

In 1888, Dickinson married Zora Della Cooley, a former student of his and soloist and organist in their neighborhood church. They adopted a daughter.

Dickinson said he considered "Mrs. Dickinson's advice far more valuable than that of the eminent leaders of the state."[5]

After serving in a number of local government positions, Dickinson was elected to the House of Representatives in 1886 and served four terms. He served a term in the Senate, following election in 1908.

Dickinson was first elected lieutenant governor in 1914 and served six terms before he was elected again to that office in 1938 along with Republican Frank D. Fitzgerald. (His terms, under four governors, were 1915-20, 1927-32, and 1939.) In those days, governors and lieutenant governors ran separately, not as a ticket as provided in the Constitution of 1963.

"Fitzgerald showed disdain" for Dickinson during the 1938 campaign, according to William Kulsea, a newsman who covered both of them for Booth Newspapers.[6] Kulsea, who became the Lansing bureau chief for Booth, recalled that Fitzgerald's distaste for Dickinson surfaced in Bay City at a joint appearance of Republican and

The Detroit News

Democratic candidates.

"If I die, you're going to be the new governor," said Fitzgerald, eying the incumbent lieutenant governor, Leo J. Nowicki. Democrat Nowicki had beaten Dickinson by a wider margin in the 1936 election than Democratic Gov. Frank Murphy's winning margin over Fitzgerald.

Kulsea recalled: "The remark caused consternation. Dickinson, the darling of the anti-prohibition and gambling constituency, demanded an explanation.

"It was said in the spirit of fun," Fitzgerald answered.

"Prove it," Dickinson challenged. Fitzgerald issued a formal statement declaring he was behind Dickinson all the way.

Said Kulsea of Dickinson: "In politics he was a loner; he never formed alliances. He traveled year after year around Michigan, a small, old-fashioned satchel in hand, talking to church groups, not about politics but about prohibition and religion. ... He distributed no political literature. He used no political signs, he quarreled with no one and never spoke ill of any opponents. He never spent great amounts of money to reach office."

Dickinson never reached the governorship on his own. He became governor March 16, 1939, upon Fitzgerald's death. In 1940, he lost by 131,281 votes to Democrat Murray D. Van Wagoner.

During Dickinson's administration and through a GOP-controlled Legislature, a Michigan civil service code was adopted, and schoolteachers were required to take an oath of allegiance to the government.

It was also during his term that Matilda Wilson, who was Mrs. Alfred G. Wilson and heiress to the Dodge auto fortune, became the first woman to be lieutenant

governor.* Dickinson appointed her to his vacancy Nov. 19, 1940. This meant she served less than two months since they both went out of office in January.

Dickinson was just a month short of his 80th birthday when he became governor, and was one of the nation's oldest governors ever. (Wisconsin Gov. Walter Goodland died in office at age 86 in 1947.)

Dickinson died April 22, 1943, in Charlotte, where he was buried.

* Former judge and congresswoman Martha Griffiths was the first woman elected lieutenant governor in Michigan. She was elected in 1982 and 1986, running as a team with Democratic Gov. James J. Blanchard, who selected her for his ticket.

The Detroit News

Left **Dickinson saw prayer as "a spiritual pipeline between God and every state..." Here, he prays in 1939 with the Rev. Frank Norris of Detroit's Temple Baptist Church.**

Right **On his Eaton County farm**

State Archives

Murray Van Wagoner (1941-1942)

This is a war of civilian production of guns and food. The farmer in the field and the worker at the lathe are giving battle. — **Report to Legislature on World War II mobilization, Jan. 19, 1942.**

Nothing made Murray D. Van Wagoner prouder than modernizing Michigan's roads and helping make it the "Arsenal of Democracy."

"Michigan did her part," Van Wagoner recalled of its mobilization for World War II. "Our own industrial front was the most vital theater in the war."[1]

Democrat Van Wagoner, one of the first governors to call a state legislature into special session after the bombing of Pearl Harbor, had a busy first year as governor directing war mobilization even before the Japanese attack.

He acted quickly when fighting broke out during an April 1941 UAW-CIO strike that interrupted production of Army vehicles at the Ford Motor Co. Rouge River plant. He mobilized state police, and

brought Ford and union officials together for a conference that led to an end of the strike. Ford agreed to an election that established the UAW-CIO as the bargaining agent for Ford workers.

"That was my biggest job as governor — keeping the factories going," said Van Wagoner.

In other mobilization action, Van Wagoner doubled the size of the Michigan State Troops, a home guard organized to replace the Michigan National Guard units that went to war. He also established a War Emergency Fund that financed civil defense and other war needs, provided for local firefighting facilities, and gave tax relief to enterprises whose stocks were frozen by federal rationing orders.

Van Wagoner also was among Michigan governors who took credit for wiping out an inherited financial deficit.

"A year ago, the financial report showed that Michigan had a $27-million operating deficit," he told the Legislature in 1942 as an improved economy boosted sales tax receipts. "Today, the entire deficit is wiped out, and we are operating in the black for the first time in many years."[2]

Murray Delos Van Wagoner was born March 18, 1898, on a farm in Michigan's Thumb, a mile east of Kingston in Tuscola County. His parents, both teachers, hoped for a girl and had no immediate name in mind for a boy. Since Van Wagoner was born five minutes after St. Patrick's Day, the family doctor said, "I'll name him Patrick. I don't care what you do later. Pat's the name he'll go by." And that's what he was called all of his life.

In 1900, the family moved to Pontiac, where Van Wagoner attended schools. In 1921, he received an engineering degree from the University of Michigan, where he played football. In his first game as a starting center during his sophomore year, he injured a knee that plagued him throughout his college career.

After graduation, he worked for two years for the state Highway Department, helping build bridges. He then worked for a private engineering company before starting his own firm. He failed in his first bid for public office, as Oakland County surveyor, in 1928, but in 1930, he was elected Oakland County drain commissioner.

In the spring race of 1933, Van Wagoner was elected state highway commissioner, a

Milton Brooks/The Detroit News

Left **"Picket Line" — for this picture of 1941 strike violence at Gate 4 of the Ford Rouge Plant, Milton "Pete" Brooks of The Detroit News in 1942 won the first Pulitzer Prize for spot news photography.**

Below **Highway builder Van Wagoner at a construction site**

State Archives

choice job for an ambitious politician because of the patronage dispensed and the local road funds dispersed. Van Wagoner used the job to advantage, building an organization that got him re-elected and in a good position to run for governor. He also did a good job building highways.

As commissioner, Van Wagoner strongly advocated building the Mackinac Bridge. The state actually started construction, but had to stop because of the war.

In 1940, Van Wagoner was elected governor when he defeated Republican Gov. Luren D. Dickinson, 1,077,065-945,784. He was the first governor to garner more than one million votes.

Van Wagoner's inaugural was symbolic of a nation struggling to arm itself for war. All of the modern guns of the National Guard, which fire the traditional 19-gun salute to an incoming governor, had gone to battle. An antique gun was pressed into service but failed to fire.

While Van Wagoner found the Legislature receptive on the war agenda, it rejected much of the rest of his program. He vetoed 33 of its bills.

In 1942, Van Wagoner lost a re-election bid to Republican Secretary of State Harry F. Kelly, 645,335-573,314.

He made a comeback attempt in 1946 as the Democratic nominee for governor, but lost to Republican Kim Sigler, 1,003,878-644,540.

In 1960, a biography of 1949-60 Gov. G. Mennen Williams asserted that Van Wagoner became governor by "riding in with Roosevelt in 1940."[3] The feisty Van Wagoner battled that image the rest of his life. On his 85th birthday in 1983, he told the Detroit Free Press: "It's just not true. I want you to print that. I carried the state and Roosevelt lost it."[4]

The truth was, as highway commissioner, Van Wagoner built a good foundation to oust an unpopular Republican governor. As governor, he didn't last long. But his reputation as road builder and war governor did.

For two postwar years, Van Wagoner was U.S. military governor of Bavaria by appointment of President Harry S Truman.

Van Wagoner died June 13, 1986, in Farmington Hills at age 88. He was buried in Troy. His wife, the former Helen Josephine Jossman of Clarkston, preceded him in death.

State Archives

Harry F. Kelly (1943-1946)

This war has been peculiarly Michigan's war. It is a war of wheels and wings. — **Message to Michigan Legislature, Jan. 4, 1945.**

Harry F. Kelly, who lost a leg in World War I, led Michigan's response to the final years of World War II and its aftermath. One-term Gov. Murray D. Van Wagoner, the man Republican Kelly defeated to become governor, mobilized Michigan in the first year of the war.

But two-term Kelly looked ahead and began postwar planning. He summoned the Legislature into emergency session in 1946 to help colleges and universities "desperately" trying to cope with an influx of returning veterans.

He said Michigan State College had "hundreds of veterans housed in the gymnasium, sleeping on double-decker beds, too often providing less comfort than the barracks of the Army camps they have left so recently."[1]

In his first year as governor, Kelly mobilized troops for an ugly conflict at home — the June 20-21, 1943, Detroit race riot that left 34 persons dead. He refused initially to issue the martial law declaration that would lead to the sending in of U.S. soldiers. Instead, he proclaimed "modified" martial law and ordered the State Police and the Michigan State Troops (the home guard replacement of the National Guard that had gone to war) to go to Detroit.

By the night of June 21, however, at the urging of Detroit Mayor Edward J. Jeffries, Kelly formally asked for federal help. A Military Police battalion restored order without firing a shot.

Kelly had one pleasant task in his first year: He announced that at the beginning of 1943, the state treasury had a surplus of more than $25 million. In 1945, he was able to declare: "The state is entirely out of debt."[2]

Harry Francis Kelly was born April 19, 1895, in Ottawa, Ill. After he graduated from Ottawa High School, he wanted to be a lawyer, like his father.

He interrupted study at the University of Notre Dame in 1917 to enlist, and went to France as a second lieutenant. He was in the historic charge at Chateau Thierry, where he suffered the wounds that cost him a leg. While governor, he refused to discuss his war record, saying, "I've got to stand or fall on what I am and do today." But the French citation for its award of the Croix de Guerre provided a glimpse of what he declined to discuss:

"Wounded in both legs and made prisoner by five Germans, this officer defended himself valiantly, and extricated himself with the aid of some men who came to his help. He was wounded a second time and spent the entire night at the end of a trench before he could be evacuated."[3]

Kelly returned to Illinois and was elected as state's attorney in LaSalle County in 1920. He moved to Michigan in 1924, and five years later married Anne V. O'Brien of Detroit. They had six children.

He was appointed an assistant Wayne County prosecutor and in 1930 was named special prosecutor of a 23-man grand jury investigation into the murder of radio commentator Jerry Buckley that year. Kelly was named Detroit supervisor of the state Liquor Control Commission in 1935, and was credited with cleaning up bootleg

Ford Motor Co. Archives

The Detroit News

Above left Building bombers at Willow Run

Above right Troops patrol riot-torn Detroit, 1943.

Left Kelly and Sen. Robert Taft visit the fort on Mackinac Island in 1943.

AP

activities.

In 1938, and then again in 1940, he was elected secretary of state. In 1942, he became governor when he defeated Van Wagoner, 645,335-573,314. Republicans took all administrative offices, and tightened control of the Legislature. In 1944, Kelly was re-elected, defeating Democrat Edward Fry, 1,208,859-989,307.

As governor, he had a reputation as a solid administrator. He established a trust fund to aid veterans, revamped mental health programs, and expanded postwar building at colleges and universities.

During Kelly's administration, the legislative branch was the focus of a corruption scandal. A grand jury investigation into reports of lobbyists buying off legislators resulted in more than 40 convictions. In 1945, Sen. Warren G. Hooper of Albion was murdered the day before he was to testify in the case. His killer was not found.

Kelly decided not to seek a third term and returned to law practice in 1946. However, he tried a comeback in 1950 and came within 1,154 votes of beating incumbent Democratic Gov. G. Mennen Williams. It was the closest gubernatorial race since Stevens T. Mason's 768-vote margin in 1837.

He was elected in 1953 as a justice of the Michigan Supreme Court, serving until 1971.

Kelly died Feb. 8, 1971, in West Palm Beach, Fla. He was buried in Southfield.

State Archives

Kim Sigler (1947-1948)

Michigan, a state which has led the world in modern management techniques in industry, lags behind many of her sister states in the administration of government.

— Message to the Legislature, March 16, 1948.

Republican "Hollywood Kim" was best remembered as a flamboyant corruption fighter whose brief act as governor ended with the rise of Democrat G. Mennen Williams.

Kim Sigler punched cattle and prize-fighters in Nebraska, and then came to Michigan with $40 sewn in his vest. He became a colorful prosecutor, governor — and dandy dresser.

Sigler's showmanship obscured the fact that he advanced ideas that led to major improvements in management of state government. Among his best proposals ultimately adopted: Four-year terms for governors, and consolidating scattered management and budget functions in a single department.

In urging the Legislature to submit a constitutional amendment to the electorate to provide for four-year instead of two-year terms, Sigler said:

"Looking at it from a realistic standpoint, we all understand that it takes any man, whoever he may be, a certain length of time to get his feet on the ground. Yet in Michigan, he is barely in office when he must start running for re-election."[1]

Creation of a Department of Administration was approved but the four-year term did not come until the Constitution of 1963.

Also of significance about Sigler was that he was among a long line of governors who saw a surplus become a deficit through no fault of his own. Sigler inherited a surplus of about $25 million and left with a general fund deficit of about $20 million. This was largely because of a decision by voters diverting a share of all sales tax collections to schools, cities and townships.

After his defeat by Williams in the 1948 election, Sigler said with characteristic flair:

"I am very grateful to the voters of Michigan who kicked me out of office. It is so pleasant to be able to talk only with the people you enjoy, instead of all kinds of fatheads. ... I am having the happiest time of my life watching all the political gyrations without being a part of them."[2]

Also characteristic was the way he died — in a blaze. A pilot who often would swoop in on surprised citizens, he died in the flaming crash of his private plane.

Kimber Sigler was born May 2, 1894, in Schuyler, Neb., a son of ranchers. In Nebraska, he played football and had his nose broken while boxing for his meals.

He came to Michigan in 1913 to study at the University of Michigan, working part-time as a brick carrier for a mason. He then latched onto a $5-a-day job cutting gears at the Highland Park plant of the Ford Motor Co., and attended the University of Detroit, obtaining his law degree in 1918. A year earlier, he married Mae Louise Pierson of Goodrich, whom he met when he rescued her from a canoe that overturned on the Huron River.

Sigler was a lawyer in Detroit before he decided on a country law practice in Hastings in 1922. His first case involved the theft of a team of horses.

In Hastings, southeast of Grand Rapids in Barry County, he was elected prosecutor, as a Democrat, and served three terms. He ran for attorney general on the Democratic ticket in 1928 against Wilber M. Brucker, who won and later became governor. In 1942, Sigler ran unsuccessfully for a Republican nomination to the state Senate.

His big break came with the Carr-Sigler grand jury investigation of legislative corruption involving payoffs from lobbyists. Ingham County Judge Leland W. Carr was named a one-man grand juror and Sigler was appointed special prosecutor. Many cases were dropped after one witness refused to testify and another — a state senator — met a mysterious death.

Sigler was replaced when a new judge took over the cases, but there were enough indictments and convictions to put Sigler on the road to the statehouse.

In 1946, Sigler beat Lt. Gov. Vernon J. Brown, the GOP establishment's choice, in a four-man race for the Republican nomination for governor. He was elected when he defeated former Democratic Gov. Murray D. Van Wagoner, 1,003,878-644,540.

Sigler quickly ran into trouble with the Republican-dominated Legislature.

"Political malcontents, factional leaders, lobbyists who he had attacked, supporters of the old regime, fought his every proposal," observed Detroit News political writer Will Muller.[3]

He was, however, able to revamp the Michigan State Police and administration of the unemployment compensation program. Before his term was over, he won legislative support for other reforms that included a lobbyist registration law and a revamped Public Service Commission. A cigarette tax also was enacted.

"As governor, (Sigler) had a weakness," recalled Booth Newspaper writer William Kulsea. "He was a better golfer than administrator and left the heavy work to advisers and staff."[4]

As to the lobbyist law Sigler moved through the Legislature, Kulsea said "it proved to be as full of holes as Swiss cheese and unenforceable."

In 1948, Sigler faced the juggernaut of "Soapy" Williams, who put together a coalition of dissident Democrats, organized labor, Republican defectors, veterans, ethnic groups and others. He upset Sigler, 1,128,664-964,810.

After leaving office, Sigler practiced law. On Nov. 30, 1953, while flying home from a business trip to New Orleans, Sigler and three passengers were killed when his plane

AP

Milton Brooks/The Detroit News

hit the fog-shrouded guy wire of a newly built TV tower near Battle Creek. He was buried in Hastings.

State Archives

G. Mennen Williams (1949-1960)

Already we have suffered some of the preliminary symptoms of financial collapse. Our treasury has been unable to meet in an orderly manner the obligations imposed by the Constitution for the support of our public schools. ... The situation we face is indeed a desperate one.

— Message to the Legislature, Jan. 15, 1953.

This politician-diplomat-jurist was elected to an unprecedented six terms as governor in an extraordinary public career that spanned the last third of Michigan's first 150 years as a state.

More than any other governor, Democrat G. Mennen Williams bore the brunt of the financial pendulum and the political polarization that were the twin plagues of the Michigan governorship long before he became chief executive.

But Williams, who was thwarted on funding plans and other issues by recalcitrant Republican legislators for much of his 12 years as governor, brought on some of the problems by his own stubbornness.

Compromise, he recalled a quarter century after leaving the governorship, was "a word that didn't fit into my vocabulary very well." Of course, he quickly added, "that was the young Williams."[1]

For years, Williams struggled to match revenue expenditures. In calling for a corporate income tax in 1951, Williams reported the previous year's operating deficit was $45.7 million. He said Michigan could not sustain its obligations to the national defense effort required by the Korean War "with an unbalanced budget and a crippled treasury." He said, "Our nation is in deadly peril. Our troops are already in battle in Korea, and we do not know at what moment we may be subjected to all-out attack."[2]

In 1953, he warned the Legislature that the state faced a two-year cumulative deficit of about $90 million and could no longer delay enacting new taxes. "Soon we shall find delay turning into default, and actual bankruptcy will be upon us."[3]

Stop-gap measures failed to do the job. In 1959, Michigan had a payless payday for state workers when the Republican Senate and the Democratic governor failed to reach agreement on a funding plan. At the height of the cash crisis, lobbyist Joe Creighton of the Michigan Manufacturers Association wired GOP senators, who had been branded "Neanderthals" by Williams: "You have Soapy over a barrel. ... Keep him there till he screams 'Uncle.'"[4]

(It was not the first time boom-and-bust Michigan had a payless payday. In 1908, a cash crisis during Republican Gov. Fred M. Warner's administration prompted a two-month delay in payment of state obligations, and state employees were a few weeks late in getting their pay. Also, when Michigan reeled from a downturn in the national economy in the late 1970s, state workers participated in a deferred pay plan to help Republican Gov. William G. Milliken's administration meet state obligations.)

The 1959 cash crisis that could have been avoided with bipartisan cooperation gave Michigan and Williams a black eye in the national press. Picking up on headlines of the day, a mock cocktail order was "Michigan on the rocks."

The episode did little to enhance Williams' already-lagging presidential ambitions. But his six unprecedented terms as governor and his 50-year public career ranked "Soapy" Williams, the Democrat with the trademark green and white polka-dot bow tie, as Michigan's Politician of the Century.

Gerhard Mennen Williams was born Feb. 23, 1911, in Detroit. His nickname derived from his family background. His mother was Elma Mennen, daughter of Gerhardt Mennen, who went from a tiny drugstore in Newark, N.J., to fame as founder of the Mennen line of shaving lotions and other skin preparations.

Williams attended the Liggett School in Detroit, then Detroit University School before going on at age 14 to the Salisbury School in Connecticut. An Episcopal school, Salisbury emphasized the classics and oratory. Every Sunday, its students dressed in tuxedoes and gathered in the auditorium to give speeches. It was there that the young Williams got his first taste of politics.

After graduating from Salisbury, Williams went on to Princeton, where he became president of the Young Republicans Club. His family had a history of Republicanism, and some members considered it political heresy when Williams later became a Democrat. Williams liked to recall one moment during his gubernatorial campaign against Republican Fred M. Alger in 1952, when his opponent pointed at him during a joint appearance at the Olds Hotel in Lansing and said: "He's a traitor to his class."

Reflecting later on his evolving political interest during school days, Williams said: "As a sophomore in prep school, I decided to make my career one of public service so as to help the underdogs. In college, I decided to be governor. In law school, I decided to be a Democrat rather than a Republican."

After graduating from Princeton in 1933, Williams attended the University of Michigan, where he received his law degree in 1936. In 1937, he married Nancy Quirk of Ypsilanti. They had three children.

Williams embarked on an early governmental career that was aided by a family lawyer who became governor — Frank Murphy. He helped Williams land jobs and plan his political career. In the 1936-38 period, Williams was an attorney for the Social Security Board in Washington, and then an assistant state attorney general. After that, he worked for the U.S. attorney general, and then, in the 1941-42 period, was in the general counsel's unit of the

Charles T. Martin/The Detroit News

Edwin C. Lombardo/The Detroit News

AP

Top In 1950, "tired but confident" on election night

Middle In 1956, on the campaign trail

Bottom In 1960, at the Georgetown home of President-elect John F. Kennedy, where he was announced as Kennedy's choice to be assistant secretary of state for African affairs

111

Bentley

With Nancy and the DeSoto convertible that carried them on the 1948 campaign trail

Office of Price Administration (OPA).

From 1942-46, Williams was in the U.S. Navy and served as an air combat intelligence and legal officer on four aircraft carriers. He was awarded 10 battle stars. After the Navy, Williams took a job that Murphy had arranged as deputy OPA director in Michigan.

In 1947, GOP Gov. Kim Sigler appointed him to the Liquor Control Commission. That was Sigler's mistake because, even before that, Williams had decided to run for governor. The job gave him an opportunity to win friends, travel throughout the state and develop a name and contacts.

In 1948, conditions were ripe for a bold move to seize control of a weak party and win the nomination for governor. Williams took on Sigler, a chief executive with waning popularity. Organized labor was considering forming a third party that year because it was unhappy with both Republicans and Democrats over the workers' compensation program. Instead, it threw in

with Williams in an alliance that helped change the face of the Michigan Democratic Party. "We wouldn't have won the campaign without the UAW and the AFL and the CIO, which were three separate groups then," Williams said. "But if that had been all we had, we wouldn't have won, either."

In fact, Williams had much more than that going for him. He had the support of such Wayne County officials as Sheriff Andrew Baird, "who would post my posters when he was out posting his," and a pair of Detroit lawyers — Hicks and Martha Griffiths who later became party chairman and lieutenant governor, respectively. They opened doors to labor and helped organize the Democratic clubs that sprouted up around the state to counter anti-Williams leaders of the state party establishment.

Williams also had the quiet support of former Republican Gov. Alexander J. Groesbeck, who was anti-Sigler. Thus, Williams, in one way or another, got a boost from two ex-governors — Murphy and Groesbeck.

Veterans, conservationists and ethnic and other groups helped, but labor was of special importance. Early in 1948, Williams invited Michigan CIO President August Scholle to ride with him to Bay City, where both were scheduled to address brewery workers. They had not met previously, but Scholle liked what he had heard about Williams' record and liberal philosophy. After that day, Scholle later would say, "I liked him even more."[5]

Scholle helped set up contacts for Williams with Frank X. Martel, head of the Detroit-Wayne County Federation of Labor, and Harry Southwell, president of the 35,000-member CIO Local 174 in Detroit. Before long, Williams was a welcome man at union picnics and plant gates.

There were other dissident Republicans besides Groesbeck unhappy with Sigler. "They didn't particularly like me, but thought they could throw me out later," Williams said. They never did.

Despite all the political help, Williams faced some serious obstacles. Chief among them was money. He had not yet inherited his fortune, and was so worried about finances, he said, that he'd wake up in the morning "sweating and wound up in the sheets." He mortgaged his home to get the $16,000 he needed for his first step — a primary campaign to get the Democratic nomination. His chief opponent was Victor

Bucknell of Kalamazoo, who had the backing of Teamsters President James R. Hoffa. Williams was helped by the fact that Burnett J. Abbott of Albion got in the race and split the anti-Williams vote. Williams won by a plurality of 8,000 out of a total vote of 285,113.

Williams went on to beat Sigler, 1,128,664-964,810. But he then had two squeaker elections. In 1950, he defeated ex-Gov. Harry F. Kelly by just 1,154 votes — 935,152-933,998. In 1952, he beat Republican Fred M. Alger by only 8,618 votes — 1,431,893-1,423,275. Williams' other Republican victims were Donald S. Leonard in 1954, 1,216,308-963,300;

Albert E. Cobo in 1956, 1,666,689-1,376,376; and Paul Bagwell in 1958, 1,225,533-1,078,089.

All of the campaigns were difficult but the first one — 1948 — was the breakthrough. It was the one where Williams took control of a splintered Democratic Party and began the longest Democratic control of the governor's office since the Republican Party was founded in 1854.

In that first campaign, Williams' wife, Nancy, drove their battered gray DeSoto convertible — a job for which she was well trained. She was a driver for the Red Cross Motor Corps while he was in the Navy. She

With former President Harry S. Truman and Sen. Hubert H. Humphrey in 1959

AP

113

AP

He called it "miserable, inadequate and unfair," but said he had no choice but to sign the 1959 tax package.

accelerated work on Michigan's network of four-lane divided freeways. He called it a "Little New Deal" — a description as well of the program of his mentor, Frank Murphy.

Williams' greatest frustration was his failure to get an income tax enacted, something he commended Republican Gov. George Romney for accomplishing. "We would not have survived" without it, he said. Williams, as Republican Sigler before him, warned that the state was in financial trouble because the 1946 constitutional amendment, voted by the people, earmarked a large share of the sales tax for schools and local government.

On March 3, 1960, Williams said he would forgo seeking a seventh term in order to "work for the cause of peace in some public office where I could be effective." By the end of the year, Williams appeared to be headed for such a job because he had been an important supporter of President-elect John F. Kennedy's bid for the Democratic nomination. They had met on Mackinac Island, and Williams made his pledge then.

After the November election, Kennedy called reporters to the front steps of his Georgetown home and — with Soapy at his side — announced what he said was the first major appointment of his administration-to-be. He said Williams would be his assistant secretary of state for African affairs — "a job second to none" in importance. Williams said later: "It wasn't anything I had in mind," but "as it turned out, it was an exceedingly significant thing."

Williams established remarkable goodwill in black Africa. He was on a first-name basis with Cabinet ministers throughout the continent. One night in the early 1960s, a startled Secretary of State Dean Rusk nearly choked on a cookie when he entered the State Department's rooftop dining room and saw robed African diplomats swirling around Williams as he called square dances. Rusk beat a hasty retreat, but later called Williams "one of the best appointments that President Kennedy ever made." Williams said square dancing "helps break the ice" in diplomacy and politics — where he started using it in his first campaign.

Williams angered many white Africans when, in Kenya in 1961, he declared that he favored "Africa for the Africans." He was banned from visiting South Africa ... there was a fuss in the British Parliament ... and a white Rhodesian was so angry he punched

also was at his side for many of his political powwows. She recalled, for example, being within earshot when Teamsters boss Hoffa threatened to have Williams' campaign manager, Larry Farrell, "rubbed out" if Williams refused to back Hoffa's choice for attorney general. Williams refused, and Farrell went on for a lengthy tenure in the Williams administration.

Reflecting on his six terms, Williams quipped, "I made myself a failure by not having two or three headline achievements, outside of maybe the Mackinac Bridge." But he was proud to have brought Michigan "a real two-party system" and "into the 20th century" in social service, civil rights and other areas. He improved staffing of schools and mental hospitals and

Williams in the jaw. (It was not the first time Williams had been attacked. While governor, the 6-foot, 3-inch Williams fought off a knife-wielding inmate in the dining room of Marquette State Prison, where he went to check on complaints about food. While Williams held the attacker's wrist in the air, his State Police bodyguard shot and killed another attacking inmate, thus foiling their attempt to take the governor hostage.)

When Kennedy was assassinated and Vice-President Lyndon B. Johnson became president, there was some reason to believe that Williams' diplomatic career would end. In 1960, Williams — who was among northern liberals opposed to having the more conservative Texan on the ticket — had shouted, "No, no!" from the floor of the Democratic National Convention at a request for nomination by acclamation for Johnson to be the vice-presidential nominee. But Johnson retained Williams, and told him he was as welcome at the White House as he was during the Kennedy years.

In 1968, after Williams' unsuccessful 1966 campaign for the U.S. Senate against Republican Robert P. Griffin, Johnson named him U.S. ambassador to the Philippines. He was as unorthodox there as he was in Africa. He participated in native dances and once, while wearing a bathing suit, rode a water buffalo. In the Philippines, Williams once again was following the path of his mentor Murphy. As U.S. high commissioner in commonwealth days, Murphy had been the top American diplomat there.

In 1970, Williams was elected to the Michigan Supreme Court. In 1983, he became chief justice and remained in that capacity until he retired from the bench at the end of 1986 at age 75.

But even as he approached retirement, Williams was still remembered beyond Michigan's borders as "Soapy."

On one brisk January day in 1985 at Detroit's Cathedral Church of St. Paul, Williams turned to visiting South African Bishop Desmond Tutu and mentioned that he had once been assistant secretary of state for African affairs. The diminutive Anglican leader nodded, but didn't appear particularly impressed. That means "ambassador to Africa," Williams added. Tutu smiled but still did not register much reaction. Then Nancy Williams leaned forward. "Bishop Tutu," she said, "this is Soapy Williams."

"Oh!" Tutu beamed. "*Soapy* Williams! ... You're a great man."

Bottom **On Mackinac Island in 1960, Sen. John F. Kennedy got a carriage ride and Williams' pledge of support for Kennedy's bid for the Democratic presidential nomination.**

Below **A button distributed by the UAW in 1987 when Williams retired after 50 years of public service**

Thanks!

Cottage Book Shop, Glen Arbor

George Weeks

Chase Photo

John B. Swainson (1961-1962)

Tax revision is one of our great unmet needs. ... Michigan's patchwork tax structure of today ... does not meet the reasonable tests of adequacy, permanency and equity. It has, usually, been conceived in crisis.

— Message to the Legislature, Feb. 1, 1962.

The story of John B. Swainson was one of political triumphs between personal tragedies: He lost both legs in World War II, but went on to become the second youngest man elected governor of Michigan.* Years later, he resigned in disgrace from the Michigan Supreme Court, convicted of perjury.

But it was as a young governor that Swainson grappled with one of the oldest dilemmas of the Michigan governorship — taxes.

He failed, as governors before him, to win legislative support for a more equitable and stable tax structure. But his biggest political problem on taxes was his veto of a bill that would have exempted suburbanites who worked in Detroit from that city's income tax.

"I think it was the right approach, but it was certainly a costly one," Democrat Swainson said later of the veto that was so unpopular in Detroit's suburbs.[1]

The biggest political undoing of all for Swainson was his Republican challenger — George Romney, the former American Motors Corp. president, who led a successful drive to rewrite Michigan's Constitution. Romney was on the rise and Swainson was a vulnerable incumbent.

Ironically, it was Romney who — after defeating Swainson — was able to win passage of what Democrats Swainson and former Gov. G. Mennen Williams had said was essential to Michigan — a state income tax.

As he began his first year in office, Swainson warned the Legislature:

"The Michigan state and local tax systems produce grave inequities. Because they place heavy emphasis on consumption and property taxes, they place a heavier tax burden on persons on the lower end of the income scale than they do on those with higher incomes. It is also a structure that imposes heavy, fixed costs on industry. ... Our fiscal structure has been rigid and inflexible and one not reflecting economic advancement."[2]

Upon taking office, Swainson also addressed his inherited economic problems: "These are perilous and troubled times for our state as they are for the nation and, indeed, the world. ... Economic growth is the single most important area of concern that faces us. Michigan is dotted with deep pockets of economic distress."[3]

In that he inherited financial woes and failed to get the Legislature to buy his tax plans, Swainson was like many governors before him. But what made Swainson a phenomenon of Michigan politics was more personal than political. He was the youngest man in Michigan history to serve in all three branches of state government — senator at 29; lieutenant governor at 33; governor at 35; Supreme Court justice at 45. And then, at 50, a convicted felon.

* Swainson was 35 when elected governor in 1960. Stevens T. Mason was 24 when elected and was 25 when Michigan gained statehood in 1837. Michigan's second youngest governor was James Wright Gordon who was 32 when, as lieutenant governor, he became governor in 1841 upon the resignation of Gov. William Woodbridge.

John Burley Swainson was born July 31, 1925, in Windsor, Ontario, and moved two years later with his parents to Port Huron at the base of Michigan's Thumb. He attended public schools there, participating in various sports and serving as captain of the Port Huron High School football team. He also became an Eagle Scout, the highest rank in scouting.

Swainson became a U.S. citizen, enlisted in the Army at 18 during World War II and went overseas with the 95th Infantry Division under Gen. George S. Patton. In November 1944, Swainson volunteered to go with three others in a Jeep to deliver ammunition and other supplies near Metz, France. The Jeep hit a land mine and its load of ammunition exploded. In a letter home, Swainson explained what happened:

"I caught the full force of that blast, and three days later I woke up in a hospital. ... Both my legs had been blown off below the knee, I had a broken jaw, a broken rib, a badly lacerated tongue, and shrapnel in both hands. ... The pain is quite bad, but there are guys here worse off than me." He apologized for the "terrible" writing but said "my hand is still numb." The letter was signed "Your son, Goad" — a family name by which he was known as a youth.[4] Swainson later learned that only one leg was lost in the blast. The other one, severely mangled, was amputated at a field hospital.

There were more operations to even the length of the bones, and Swainson was sent to Percy Jones Army Hospital in Battle Creek for recuperation and adjustment to his artificial legs. In 1946, he entered Olivet College, where he met and married Alice Nielsen of Detroit. They had three children. Adversity soon struck again when he reinjured his legs in a tobogganing accident, requiring further surgery.

In 1951, Swainson received a law degree from the University of North Carolina and began practicing in Detroit. In 1954, he was elected to the state Senate. Two years later, he was chosen Senate minority leader, and was named "Mr. Success" by the American Federation of the Physically Handicapped.

In 1958, Swainson was elected lieutenant governor. In 1960, with the help of organized labor, he defeated Secretary of State James M. Hare to win the Democratic nomination for governor after Williams decided not to run for a seventh term. Swainson was elected governor when he defeated Republican Paul Bagwell in a tight race, 1,643,634-1,602,022 — a plurality of 41,612.

Swainson faced a Legislature where Republicans had solid Senate control and a narrow 56-54 edge in the House. Williams-era polarization continued. Nevertheless, a patchwork tax package was enacted, as was court reform and expansion of

Young entertainer Stevie Wonder waits as Swainson signs an autograph. Alice Swainson is seated at right.

Motown Museum at Hitsville USA, Detroit

117

State Archives

Swainson presides in his office at a 1961 meeting of the State Administrative Board. From left to right are: State Treasurer Sanford A. Brown, Superintendent of Public Instruction Lynn M. Bartlett, Auditor General Billie S. Farnum, Attorney General Frank J. Kelley, Lt. Gov. T. John Lesinski, Swainson, Secretary Doris Barber, Budget Director Ira Polley, Secretary of State James M. Hare, and Highway Commissioner John C. Mackie

community colleges.

By a margin of 80,573 votes in 1962, Swainson lost his re-election bid to Romney. After practicing law in Detroit, Swainson was elected to a Wayne County Circuit Court judgeship in 1965. In 1970, Swainson was elected to the Michigan Supreme Court, leading the field that included former Gov. Williams. Swainson, who was still in his 30s when he became an ex-governor, had undergone a political rehabilitation of sorts.

But it all came tumbling down in 1975. He was convicted by a federal jury of perjury during an investigation into a charge that as a Supreme Court justice he had accepted a bribe to arrange a new trial for a convicted burglar. He was acquitted of the bribery charge. But he served 60 days in a Detroit halfway house on the perjury conviction.

Because of the conviction, he resigned from the Supreme Court, and had his license to practice law suspended.* Twice during his suspension, he pleaded guilty to drunken driving charges.

Once again, Swainson set out to rehabilitate himself. He enrolled in an alcoholism treatment program. His license to practice law was restored. He became a respected mediator and arbitrator. In 1982, the Supreme Court on which he had once served assigned him to hear a medical malpractice case that had long been pending in a circuit court.

One night in 1987, in the den above the garage at his 165-acre farm (that he called "The Hustings") outside Manchester southwest of Ann Arbor, Swainson talked about

his long road back.[5] "I couldn't do this before," he said in regard to talking about his personal problems. "It was too painful." What went wrong?

"Obviously, I got into the sauce," said the Eagle scout who went astray.

Swainson, who long had worked quietly with amputees who were trying to rehabilitate their lives, wanted alcoholics to know that they, too, could come back.

In 1977, Swainson told Detroit Free Press writer Remer Tyson: "I'll probably go down in the history of Michigan as an asterisk. An asterisk that says: John Swainson, governor, convicted and died."[6] In 1987, Swainson, then president of the Michigan Historical Commission, was asked for a personal historical footnote to go with the asterisk. He responded:

"The recovery from my trial in 1975 was much more difficult for me than the recovery from the loss of my legs in 1944. In 1945, I was young and looking forward to my life and couldn't wait to get started on my career. The world was warm and accepting of my wounds and, like all who served, I was treated as a hero.

"In 1975, exactly 30 years later, I was 50 years of age and had been stripped of my career. I found myself unemployed in what I felt was a hostile world. I had been

* Swainson chartered a plane to fly to Traverse City to personally deliver his resignation to Gov. William G. Milliken. "It was a tragic moment in history," Republican Milliken recalled. "It was very difficult for me, and obviously for him. I liked and respected him, and had no reason to change my view. I always had grave misgivings about the charge against him — that he was kind of set up on it. I had no firm basis for this, I just instinctively felt it."

humiliated, and my license to practice law suspended. I was unemployed and could not, because of the physical limitations connected with my war injuries, do many ordinary things that required walking or standing. I was psychologically unable, as a former governor and Supreme Court justice, to even bring myself to seek ordinary employment.

"I wanted at least to preserve my self-respect and this, too, got in my way. I sought refuge and escape — and escape came in a bottle. At least you could blot things out of your mind. That was a mistake that has victimized many. I was no exception. I was depressed and became withdrawn. I didn't want to face people.

"This was a complete reversal of my nature, and my life of the past 30 years in the political arena of Michigan. It is a terrible thing to be unemployed when you have worked every day of your life, and there was nothing for me to do, or at least that is the way I felt.

"The trial itself nagged at me. I was acquitted of all of the substantive charges, but convicted of perjury before the grand jury. I had denied receiving anything of value from anyone in connection with the charges upon which I was tried, and had stated so before the grand jury. But the petit jury thought I had not been candid in this regard, or in stating that I did not remember two telephone calls of 18 and 22

seconds made some 33 months before my appearance before the grand jury.

"I had been convicted by a jury, and although I felt they were misled by the prosecution, as a judge I knew there has never been a perfect trial, and I could not say that I was denied a fair trial, nor a review by an appellate court.

"I felt terribly alone, but now realize I was supported by a loving, caring family, and supported by my friends and the people of my community. It was the most dismal time of my life, but I survived, and I hope have become a better person for the experience. I became an antique dealer, and enjoyed the challenge of following history through the discovery of the furnishings and artifacts of earlier times.

"I was subsequently reinstated to the practice of law and my life has been both satisfying and rewarding for the past five years, but I will never forget the pain and frustrations of those five years of suspension.

"Upon reflection, I feel that as hurtful as all this was for me personally, it enabled me to learn who were my true friends, and who were friendly as long as I represented power. Not many persons in political life have such an opportunity. Political friends can best be described as allies whose loyalties constantly change as circumstances dictate. True friends are beside you in prosperity and in adversity, and mine have been identified, and I am richer for it."

Swainson in 1962 with President Kennedy and, on right, longtime Democratic State Chairman Neil Staebler, who became a congressman-at-large and was the 1964 Democratic nominee for governor

Jim Yardley

George W. Romney (1963-1969)

The inequities and weaknesses of Michigan's tax structure have been documented time and again. Corrective action has been sought, year after year. ... The stark fact is that the cost of state services demanded by the public is outrunning the revenues produced by present taxes.

— State of the State Address, Jan. 12, 1967.

As head of American Motors Corp., George Romney brought profound change to the auto industry, championing the compact car as an alternative to "gas-guzzling dinosaurs." Then, in his first venture into politics, he successfully championed profound change in Michigan's outmoded Constitution and tax structure.

Controversies surrounding his public career — including the abrupt end of his 1968 presidential bid — obscured the fact that Romney, as governor, presided over some of the biggest changes in state government since Stevens T. Mason led Michigan to statehood.

Few Michigan governors showed as much

grit as this blunt-speaking Republican. Double-amputee John B. Swainson, the Democrat Romney defeated to become governor, had to overcome greater personal adversity. But Romney slew more dragons.

As a flame-throwing governor, he was in the tradition of two progressive Republicans of the early 20th century, Hazen S. Pingree and Chase S. Osborn.

A single word best described the public and private Romney: Intense. As governor, he would tug at a legislator's lapels, jab a menacing finger for emphasis, and begin his pitch by saying: "Look!" He crashed a Labor Day rally to which only Democratic candidates were invited. Romney's intensity in sports carried late into life. Once, in his 70s, he injured his ribs when he tumbled into some sideline chairs while lunging after a ball in a tennis game on Mackinac Island.

Even as Romney approached his 80th birthday in 1987, he still would get up every morning at 5, and walk for eight or 10 miles, or jog, or, weather permitting, play a fast-paced round of golf with only a 2-iron. On occasion, he would keep as many as four balls in play between holes.

Nowhere was the Romney intensity more evident than in his pursuit of, and relationship with, his wife, Lenore. He moved from Washington, D.C., to California to court her. "I crossed the continent six times just to be in her dust. It was the best sale of my life when I convinced her to become my wife."[1] He gave her a rose virtually every day thereafter. One Easter, he gave her an entire rose garden, having it planted at their Bloomfield Hills home as a surprise. When he was a Cabinet officer in Washington, the Shoreham Hotel allowed Romney to snip a rose from its garden every morning.

And then there were the constant love notes — slipped under a door, or left under a pillow. Read one: *"Darling, Have gone to the grocery store. I will love you eternally. George."* A Romney-composed poem concluded, *"I love you for the part of me that you bring out."* Once, on a vacation trip to Mexico when both of them were in their 70s, Romney steamed when he thought she danced too long with another man, and he told her so when she left the dance floor. At least he didn't do what he did during their high school days. According to one Romney biographer, "At one dance, when he thought she had danced too long with another boy, he pulled her away and literally carried her off the floor."[2]

George Wilcken Romney was born July 8, 1907, in Colonia Dublan in the Mexican state of Chihuahua. His Mormon grandparents had gone there in the 19th century about the time the U.S. government outlawed the practice of polygamy. In 1912, when he was 5-years-old, Romney's parents moved the family to California, and then to Idaho and Utah.

When Romney first went out for high school football in Salt Lake City, there was no uniform small enough for him. He took the smallest one, and used shoelaces to tie up the legs and sleeves. Coach Vadal Peterson recalled: "It was just plain grit."[3] As he grew, Romney became an accomplished all-around athlete.

In the 1926-28 period, Romney was a missionary in the British Isles for the Church of Jesus Christ of Latter-Day Saints. For his future in industry and politics, the assertiveness developed in his Mormon missionary days proved to be better training than that he received during his subsequent college years — one at the University of Utah and two at George Washington University.

In 1929, Romney served as a tariff specialist for U.S. Sen. David I. Walsh of Massachusetts. Remaining in Washington, he began in 1930 to work with the Aluminum Company of America in Washington. He sought and received a transfer to California, saying he needed to be with relatives. "Of course, he was talking about a future relative," said Lenore LaFount, whom he married in 1931. They had four children.

The Romneys financially were strapped early in their marriage. She had turned down a three-year contract as an actress with Metro-Goldwyn-Mayer and he was earning only $125 a month. They lived in Santa Monica in a one-room apartment with a pull-down bed. But Romney moved up fast. He left his lobbyist job with Alcoa and moved to Michigan as Detroit manager of the Automobile Manufacturers Association.

In 1948, Romney went to work for Nash-Kelvinator Corp. and helped arrange its 1954 merger with Hudson Motor Car Co. to form American Motors Corp. (AMC). That fall, he became president and chairman of AMC. At the time, the firm had a debt of $70 million. Within four years, it became profitable, its down-sized Rambler helped make Romney a folk hero of sorts, and the dinosaur became a Romney trademark.[*] He said the main factor in extinction of dinosaurs "was the fact that they kept getting bigger and bigger and finally got so big they were unable to live."[4]

While at AMC, Romney assumed leadership of nonpartisan "citizen action" groups. He was 1957-58 chairman of the Detroit Citizens Advisory Committee on

[*] Biographer D. Duane Angel, in his 1967 book *Romney*, said Romney picked up on the theme after reading a Detroit News editorial concluding that "bigger bodies and bigger engines must stop or the private automobile will go the way of the dinosaur."

In 8-below-zero weather, Romney jogs near his Bloomfield Hills home in 1962.

AP

UPI

UPI

Above left **At the 1964 Upper Peninsula State Fair in Escanaba**

Above right **It's a tradition for Michigan governors to scrub the streets at the Holland Tulip Festival, as Romney does here with First Lady Lenore Romney.**

Right **Wayne County Sheriff Peter Buback swears in 1961-62 Constitutional Convention delegates: the Rev. Malcolm Gray Dade, Sr., Daisy Elliott, and Tom Downs.**

Al Deneau/The Detroit News

School Needs. In 1959, he founded Citizens for Michigan, which became the driving force behind convening the convention that produced Michigan's Constitution of 1963. His first partisan political undertaking was to run in 1961 as a Republican candidate from Oakland County to be a delegate at the Constitutional Convention. He sought to become its president, but a deadlock developed as Romney had his first in a long career of clashes with GOP conservatives. He had to settle for one of three convention vice-presidencies.

In 1962, Romney resigned from American Motors to run for governor, his first bid at statewide office. He ended 14 years of Democratic rule by defeating one-term Gov. John B. Swainson, 1,420,086-1,339,513

— a relatively narrow plurality of 80,573. In 1964, Romney was re-elected by a plurality of 382,913, defeating Congressman-at-large Neil Staebler, a former Democratic state chairman, 1,764,355-1,381,442. This was in the face of a state and national Democratic landslide led by Lyndon B. Johnson's trouncing of Republican presidential nominee Barry Goldwater. (Romney virtually shunned Goldwater, saying, "I accept but do not endorse" him.)

In 1966, Romney was elected to a third term with a plurality of 527,047, defeating Democratic State Chairman Zolton Ferency, 1,490,430-963,383. It was the first election of a Michigan governor for the four-year term specified in the new Constitution. Republicans also narrowly won control of both houses of the Legislature.

In his first State of the State address as governor, with auto sales booming, Romney said state government's income would equal expenditures for the first time in seven years. He called for "genuine total fiscal reform," and said: "In economic expansion, Michigan simply has not kept pace either with the nation or with directly competing industrial states."[5] Romney later said he had inherited a 1962 fiscal year general fund deficit of $85 million.

In subsequent State of the State addresses, Romney was more upbeat. In 1964, he said, "The negative attitude toward Michigan has been replaced by a confidence that this state is going places, that Michigan is no longer a problem state."[6] In 1965: "Michigan is booming economically. ... A sizable deficit has been replaced by a sizable surplus."[7] In 1966: Michigan's "recession has been replaced by an unprecedented boom," and the general fund surplus had hit $136 million.[8]

In 1967, after four years of trying — and even more years of efforts by earlier governors — Romney won legislative approval to have Michigan join the majority of states that imposed an income tax. Romney presented Michigan's first billion-dollar budget, using income tax revenues for what he said were unmet needs in education

Romney called the 1967 riots "seven days of terror and trouble and tension."

The Detroit News

UPI

AP

The Michigan delegation to the 1968 Republican National Convention in Miami Beach marches past Romney after his name was placed in nomination for the presidency. Leaning over the rail at the left is UPI reporter Helen Thomas, a Detroiter who became dean of the White House correspondents.

and mental health.

It also was 1967 that brought what Romney later would call the "low point" of his governorship — race riots.[9]

In a statewide radio-TV address on July 31, Romney said Detroit "and much of Michigan" had "just lived through seven days of terror and trouble and tension ... at least 40 persons have died ... Detroit was rocked with about 1,607 fires." Amazingly, the same kind of misunderstandings that delayed use of federal troops in Detroit's 1943 riot delayed deployment of federal forces in the 1967 strife. Federal authorities wanted a formal declaration that state and local authorities could not handle the situation. Romney initially balked, as Gov. Harry F. Kelly did in 1943. Finally, as Romney recalled later, he told federal authorities: "Look, you can blame me if you

want to, but let's get the troops out on the streets."

When he finally dispatched U.S. airborne soldiers to Detroit, President Johnson was critical of Romney, and Romney accused Johnson of "playing politics" with the situation. "I was ahead in presidential polls at the time," Romney said in recalling his 1967 status as a potential 1968 Republican presidential nominee.

Romney contended a major cause of the national epidemic of riots stemmed from Washington, where "self-serving leaders ... led the people to believe that passing a law and spending a little money would put everything right." He said Johnson's Great Society "treated Detroit more generously" than other cities but that did not ease conditions and did not "prevent the raising of false hopes and false expectations." In

124

fact, he contended, blacks were being bulldozed out of their homes by urban renewal projects.

On Nov. 18, 1967, Romney announced as a candidate for president, vowing "to build a new America." But he was haunted — or, as he put it, "cut to pieces" — by his remarks two months earlier on a television talk show about the "brainwashing" he received from U.S. military-diplomatic briefings in Vietnam. Two months into the election year, polls showed Romney badly trailing Richard M. Nixon for the nomination.

When New York Gov. Nelson Rockefeller, who had been supporting Romney, refused to flatly rule himself out as a candidate, Romney made an abrupt and surprise withdrawal. He conceded he had not won broad enough acceptance of rank and file Republicans. Later, he recalled, "I got caught between two men who were absolutely determined to be president of the United States, regardless of what it took." He accused Nixon "or those associated with him" of using "dirty tricks" against him by spreading "distortions" during the early presidential primary campaigning about Romney spending increases as governor.

Said Romney: "The dirty tricks didn't start with Watergate. ... The most tragic figure in American life, in my view, is Richard Nixon, who destroyed himself. A split personality, who couldn't resist from resorting to indefensible political manipulation and tricks."[10] Such sentiments were not at all evident in Romney's public statements in 1968. In the closing days of the presidential campaign, Romney signed a "Fellow Citizens" letter on Office of the Governor letterhead which was published as a campaign ad and said Nixon, running-mate Spiro Agnew and the Republican Party "offer a politics so old it seems new: a politics of principle, personal responsibility, and reconciliation ..."[11]

After Nixon's election, Romney was named secretary of housing and urban development. He continued an intense interest in Michigan politics, especially when Lenore Romney became the Michigan GOP's 1970 "consensus" candidate for the U.S. Senate. Romney said the original idea for Lenore running was suggested by Grand Rapids Congressman Gerald R. Ford, who then was House minority leader, and

AP

Romney laughs at the 1968 Republican National Convention when, to his surprise, he hears a vote cast for him to be the vice-presidential nominee. At top of picture is U.S. Sen. Robert P. Griffin, who in 1987 became a justice of the Michigan Supreme Court.

embraced by Gov. William G. Milliken, the lieutenant governor who had stepped up when Romney resigned to go to Washington. But some Republican leaders balked at the idea, and the initial consensus meeting did not produce a clear-cut choice. Romney said Milliken "weaseled, and frankly destroyed my wife as a candidate."

Lenore, with George playing a forceful role behind the scenes, ultimately emerged as the preferred choice of GOP leaders. She won the primary, but then was a big loser to Democrat Philip A. Hart. Consensus became a scorned word in much of the Michigan GOP. But George Romney, never half-hearted about anything, continued into the 1980s to urge the GOP to unite behind consensus candidates rather than go through brawling primaries. His advice was largely ignored, and Republicans were largely winless in statewide races where they had brawling primaries.

125

State Archives

William G. Milliken (1969-1982)

Since I have been governor, there have been four national recessions. But Michigan has not been hurt as much as it hurts now. — **Televised economic report to the people, March 10, 1982.**

William G. Milliken was a third generation state senator who inherited both his zest for public service — and the governorship. But this outstate Republican, with the help of a coalition that included big city Democrats, was elected enough times in his own right to become Michigan's longest-serving governor.

As lieutenant governor, he became Michigan's chief executive in 1969 when Gov. George Romney resigned to become U.S. secretary of housing and urban development. Milliken went on to build a progressive record on environmental, transportation, urban, civil rights, women's rights and other programs. He also served as chairman of the Republican Governors' Association, the Midwestern Governors'

Conference and the National Governors' Association and was selected by his peers in 1976 as the nation's most effective governor.*

But Milliken's 14-year governorship was not without its failures. A notable one was the state's bungled response in 1973 when cattle feed accidentally was mixed with PBB, a toxic chemical flame retardant. Traces of PBB got into the food chain and farmers had to destroy thousands of head of livestock. Also during his tenure, Michigan's economy took two of its biggest nose-dives. One came during the 1974 Arab oil embargo, which hit Michigan harder than any other state; the other, the 1981-82 national recessions that forced about 40 states to slash budgets, none more severely than Michigan. During the year that ended Sept. 30, 1981, cuts in state spending totaled more than $1 billion. Democrats controlled the Legislature throughout Milliken's 14 years — except for the 1969-74 GOP rule in the Senate — but he was able to maintain an essentially cooperative relationship.

Unlike many earlier Michigan governors who had attained national prominence, Milliken shunned suggestions that he run for national office or the U.S. Senate. Nor did he express interest in a Cabinet position.

William Grawn Milliken was born March 26, 1922, in Traverse City, and developed a boyhood interest in politics. His father and grandfather had been state senators. Milliken was elected freshman class president and then governor of the Traverse City High School, where he played on the 1940 Class B championship basketball team. It was in high school that he first thought of someday becoming governor of Michigan, an ambition fanned by correspondence with former Gov. Chase S. Osborn, who would include a $1 bill when he wrote Milliken.

Milliken interrupted his studies at Yale University in 1942 to enlist in the Army Air Force. During one of his 50 combat missions as a B-24 waist-gunner, he survived a crash on takeoff with a full bomb load; on another, a crash landing in a field. On one mission over Austria, he was wounded in the stomach by flak. On another, he bailed out over Italy when his

* Based on responses by governors to a survey conducted by U.S. News & World Report.

JAPAN-U.S. GOVERNORS' CONFERENCE
日 米 知 事 会 議

UPI

Promoting Michigan's role in foreign trade at the 1977 U.S. Japan Governors' Conference in Tokyo

crippled plane, its hydraulic system shot out, ran out of gas 50 miles from its base. He once was demoted temporarily from staff sergeant to private when he accepted blame for a mess some departing crew members left behind in the crew's tent.

In contrast to his "Mr. Nice Guy" image as a straight-arrow governor who never smoked and seldom drank, Milliken at one point in his early life smoked two packs of cigarettes a day. He confessed taking an occasional whiskey after a harrowing mission, and once broke the leg of a fellow airman in a wrestling match.

Milliken married Helen Wallbank of Denver in 1945 (they had two children) and resumed his studies at Yale. After his graduation in 1946, he returned to Traverse City, where he became president of J.W. Milliken, Inc., a department store founded by his grandfather and run by his father.

In 1947, Milliken was appointed by Republican Gov. Kim Sigler to the Michigan Waterways Commission. In 1960, he was elected to the state Senate where he joined a group of moderate Republicans at odds with conservative Republican Old Guard senators. It was the Old Guard conservatives whose deadlock with Democratic Gov. G. Mennen Williams brought on Michigan's 1959 cash crisis. In 1961, the moderates gathered in Traverse City and drafted a 20-page document proposing a liberal agenda for mental health, civil rights, education and other fields. Much of the agenda later was written into the Michigan GOP platform. Milliken emerged as a leader among moderate Republicans, became Senate majority floor leader and was ready in 1964 to make a bid for the Republican nomination for lieutenant governor. He won it by an 834-to-636 convention vote over House Speaker Allison Green. Milliken thus became the 1964 running mate of Romney, who appeared to lean toward the more conservative Green, but officially was neutral in the Milliken-Green battle. "What I got, I fought for," Milliken recalled. "... nobody put his hand on my shoulder and said, 'You're my boy.'"[1]

In 1966, governor and lieutenant gover-

127

Cows that were killed because they had traces of PBB are buried at Mio in 1978.

family trees of Michigan politics.** The vote was 1,339,074-to-1,294,638. In 1974, Milliken again defeated Levin, this time 1,356,865-1,242,247 — a plurality of 114,618.

In 1978, Milliken became the first Republican gubernatorial candidate to carry Wayne County since Sigler in 1946, and won re-election by a plurality of 391,229, a margin that had been exceeded by only three other Michigan governors. He defeated former state Senate Democratic Leader William Fitzgerald 1,628,485-to-1,237,256. Polling by Detroit's Market Opinion Research showed that a turning point of the campaign came in early October when Fitzgerald broadcast, but then canceled, commercials on the PBB episode that included such phrases as "brains growing on the outside of the head." The reference was to laboratory rats fed high doses of PBB, but the impression created was one of a human health threat. The excess helped minimize a political vulnerability for Milliken.

The governor blamed much of the state's PBB problem on the Michigan Department of Agriculture's rejection of his request that it lower the tolerance limit on the trace amounts of PBB allowed in food products.

(The fact that the department director was appointed by a commission rather than the governor was cited by Milliken and later by his successor, Gov. James J. Blanchard, as an example of why accountability would

nor candidates ran in tandem for the first time. Milliken was part of Romney's successful "Action Team" that included Robert P. Griffin, the U.S. Senate candidate who defeated former Gov. G. Mennen Williams.*

Milliken became governor Jan. 22, 1969, upon Romney's resignation. He got into immediate political trouble outstate when he urged that a third of the state's recreation bonding money be devoted to urban areas. He was branded the "ghetto governor" by some of his opponents. In 1970, he won a narrow 44,409-vote victory over Senate Democratic Leader Sander Levin who, like Milliken, had sprouted from one of the

* The Milliken-Romney relationship was sometimes chilly, always fascinating. Milliken labored long in Romney's dominating shadow. He was given some important assignments as lieutenant governor, and became governor upon Romney's resignation. In his early years as governor, the mild-mannered Milliken often was compared, not always favorably, with the hard-charging Romney.

In a 1981 oral history interview Romney had with University of Michigan Professor David L. Lewis, Romney was asked if he had walked across the Mackinac Bridge, a tradition for latter-day Michigan governors. Romney replied: "Sure, I walked across, many times. I set the record until Milliken ran across — and accused me of having run across." In 1971, Milliken set a gubernatorial record of 46 minutes, 50 seconds in the annual five-mile Labor Day Bridge Walk. The author was the timekeeper and can attest that Milliken broke into a near-run after being told by his State Police bodyguards that Romney also used a pace faster than a walk in setting the previous record in 1967. Wire service accounts of Romney's time varied. UPI said it was 47 minutes. AP reported it was 47 minutes, 30 seconds. Gov. G. Mennen Williams made the first bridge walk — a leisurely one — in 1958.

** Levin went on to become a U.S. congressman. His brother, Carl, was a Detroit city councilman who became a Democratic U.S. senator. A cousin, Charles Levin, became a justice of the Michigan Supreme Court.

The Detroit News

Deb Borin/UPI

AP

A workout at Michigan State University's Jenison Field House

be improved if Michigan governors could appoint more departmental directors.)

One action that contributed to Milliken's strong 1978 showing in the Metro Detroit area was his decision to order state police to patrol Detroit freeways, where crime was high and local patrol scant. The move was not popular in some outstate areas where state police posts gave up troopers to provide the added manpower in Detroit. Another factor in his strong Wayne County showing was behind-the-scenes support from Democratic Mayor Coleman A. Young of Detroit. Milliken carried about 40 percent of the black vote.

In his first State of the State address, delivered while he was still lieutenant governor and awaiting the formal changing of the guard, Milliken said, "It is my greatest hope that this administration will be known for its compassion, its idealism, its candor and its toughness in the pursuit of public ends."[2]

There was considerable parental influence in the shaping of Milliken's idealism and politics. His mother, Hildegarde, was an advocate of wilderness preservation. Like Milliken, his father, James T. Milliken, known around the state Senate as "Gentleman Jim," was far more liberal than the constituents he represented in northwestern Lower Michigan. "My father was a great progressive liberal," said Milliken. "He took positions that were considered to be quite un-Republican. And I guess I tend to do the same."[3]

This idealism was reflected in the heavy emphasis on "quality of life" initiatives on

George Weeks

When the 1980 presidential campaign came to Detroit, Milliken enjoyed a light moment with, left to right: James A. Baker III, who later became secretary of the U.S. Treasury; presidential candidate Ronald Reagan, and vice-presidential candidate George Bush.

environmental, consumer protection and other fronts. The Environmental Protection Act of 1970 made it easier for individuals to sue businesses over pollution. After failing to get legislative action, Milliken joined with the Michigan United Conservation Clubs, the United Auto Workers and others in a successful referendum that established deposits on bottles and cans as an anti-litter device. The Consumer Protection Act of 1976 prohibited unfair or deceptive practices in many areas. He also proposed a number of tax relief programs and at one point during the Milliken years, Michigan had the nation's biggest property tax cut program.

Milliken opened trade and investment promotion offices in Tokyo and Brussels, worked out a bipartisan program to ease Michigan's excessive workers' compensation costs, and initiated efforts to attract high technology firms to Michigan. But other Milliken programs, including environmental protection and consolidation of several taxes into the single business tax, stirred opposition in some business circles.

The ambitious agendas of Milliken and other U.S. governors of his era were moderated in the late 1970s by realization that the nation was in an Age of Limits.

"This pragmatism was to be further tempered ... by a souring economy," observed Detroit News writer John Broder.[4] Just how sour was spelled out in March 1982 when Milliken asked for an increase of seven-tenths of 1 percent in the personal income tax and announced a $450-million budget cut on top of more than $1 billion in cuts the previous year:

"We are tonight in the midst of the second of two back-to-back national recessions. They have left depression conditions in Michigan.

"The effects of the recession have included slumping auto sales that last month fell to the lowest level in 32 years, record high unemployment and welfare cases, record high interest rates which have increased state costs and jeopardized our economic recovery efforts, declining retail sales and other factors that have resulted in a sharp drop in anticipated revenue, and federal actions that have meant massive cuts in federal funds for Michigan."[5]

At the time, Michigan had a 16 percent unemployment rate, the highest in the nation. Retail sales were at the lowest-ever level. Construction was in a slump. This was dramatically illustrated in 1982 when, in a state of more than nine million people, construction was started on only 136 homes in the entire month of January.

In announcing in December 1981 that he would not seek re-election or any other office, Milliken said, "Michigan's problems in these extraordinary times are too serious to have a governor unable to devote full energies to them ... a governor preoccupied with months of campaigning."[6] It was a decision he had been leaning toward throughout the year.

Historian George S. May wrote: "Despite his perennially boyish appearance and his low-key style, Milliken would prove even more adept than (Romney) in building and maintaining an effective coalition of moderates from both parties that could deal with the problems of the succeeding decade."[7] William Kulsea, whose 50-year coverage of Michigan governors for Booth Newspapers went back to Frank Murphy, wrote:

"Skeptics smirked when Milliken took over as governor. Many suggested he was too nice, in manner and speech, to last. ... No threats to punch noses, no desk-pounding, just a firm approach by a man who was learning that good politics was good government. His easy style paid off at the ballot box."[8]

City of Detroit

In 1978, with Detroit Mayor Coleman A. Young, who said, "Bill Milliken proved that you can appeal to people's best instincts and be a very successful politician in Michigan. His administration understood the importance of Detroit to the rest of Michigan and carried out policies which recognized the interdependence of the city and the state.

"A lot of people argued he was committing political suicide in dealing with Detroit's needs so effectively. Yet, the last time he ran for re-election he piled up his biggest margin of any time ... while being the first Republican to carry Wayne County since 1946."

For the nine years that their terms overlapped, Young and Milliken were the odd couple of Michigan politics. Democrat Young grew up on the streets of Detroit, and Republican Milliken grew up in wealth along the placid shores of Grand Traverse Bay. The white governor and the black mayor used to battle, and on occasion, swear at each other (Young was better at this), but they became friends. Among things they shared: after Milliken left office, Bob Berg, who had been communications chief for Michigan's longest-serving governor, became press secretary to Young, Detroit's longest-serving mayor.

Executive Office

James J. Blanchard (1983-)

Four years ago, our state budget showed a $1.7-billion deficit. Our credit rating was the worst in the nation. Today, our budget is balanced. Our tax rate is below where it was four years ago. Our credit rating is the best in the nation.

— State of the State Address, Feb. 5, 1987.

Michigan's economic recovery propelled James J. Blanchard, a political junkie at age 10, into the biggest victory margin of the first 150 years of the Michigan governorship.

A major force propelling Blanchard into politics and toward his first big election victory was his mother, Rosalie Webb, who raised him and his sister after their father abruptly abandoned the family when Blanchard was 9-years-old. Her family of Ohio politicians had a strong influence on young Jamie. She encouraged him to make a successful 1959 bid for president of the Ferndale High School Student Council, and she financed more than one-third of the $40,000 cost of his 1974 congressional primary campaign that was his breakthrough into elective politics.

His mother minimized her role in Blanchard's political development, emphasizing, "he was a great self-starter."[1] Blanchard insisted she was being typically modest, and said, "My mother encouraged me to run for president of the student council. She said, 'If you run, you'll win. You just watch.'"[2]

Blanchard, whose gubernatorial salary was scheduled to reach $100,000 in 1988, earned 50 cents an hour at age 10 by hanging Democratic Party leaflets on neighborhood doorknobs. "I'd do it all for nothing," Blanchard quipped in 1987. "I'm still being paid for my hobby (politics). I'm like a professional golfer or baseball player — getting paid for what I love to do."

In his youth, Jamie Blanchard wanted to be a baseball player. Growing up, his loves were "the Detroit Tigers and the Democratic Party, in that order. At some point, the order shifted." He would hang around Tiger Stadium and ride his bike past the home of Tiger outfielder Al Kaline in hopes of seeing him mow his lawn. Soon Blanchard passed the time at the local Democratic headquarters. Blanchard knew he was hooked on politics when, as a page at the Democratic National Convention, it was as much of a thrill to stroll along the boardwalk in Atlantic City with former Democratic presidential candidate Adlai Stevenson as it was to catch a glimpse of Kaline.

As a boy, Blanchard treasured his chewing gum card collections on ballplayers, but who but a political nut would squirrel away scrapbooks on politicians as a kid — and still treasure them when he became governor? What made Blanchard tick was the pure excitement of politics learned at his mother's knee and hearth. A busy childhood helped block out the hurt of not having a father around. More than Michigan's cycle of boom and bust, more than the luck he admitted he had ("I'm about as lucky as they come in politics"), it was Blanchard's zest for politics that pushed him to the top of the ladder.

James Johnston Blanchard was born Aug. 8, 1942, in Detroit. The family enjoyed travel. Blanchard and his sister, Suzanne, visited 36 states as youngsters. Upon returning from a trip with their mother, they found that their father had moved out of the home. He was "a very fine person, very intelligent and very loving and a very fine father till he just decided he'd had enough, I guess," said Mrs. Webb.[3] Later, when Blanchard was a high school sophomore, she remarried, but her second husband died of a heart attack. By the time Blanchard was governor, she was living in South Lyon in Oakland County and Clearwater, Fla., with her third husband. Blanchard seldom saw his father while he was a youth. When the senior James Blanchard once stayed over at the governor's residence in Lansing, it was the first time father and son had slept under the same roof since Blanchard was 9-years-old.

Mrs. Webb said Blanchard as a youngster had "a lot of drive and energy. And he was very outgoing, very diplomatic from a very young age. ... He could just come out with the right thing and you'd think, 'Where'd he know enough to say that?'"[4] Her family, the Johnstons, had been active in Ohio politics. Her mother, a crusader for women's rights, was successful in school board politics, and her brother ran unsuccessfully for lieutenant governor of Ohio.

In high school, Blanchard was elected freshman class president before his successful bid in his senior year to become student council president. At Michigan State University, Blanchard was elected president of the sophomore class after "the best campaign I ever ran." He also was elected president of the senior class. He received both a bachelor's and master's degree from MSU, writing his thesis on "Marketing and Politics."

It was at the university that he met Paula Parker of Clarkston, Mich. They were married in 1965, and had a son, Jay. After leaving MSU, Blanchard went to the University of Minnesota, where he earned a law degree.

In 1969, Blanchard began five years of service as an assistant attorney general under Atty. Gen. Frank J. Kelley, Michigan's longest-serving attorney general and a political mentor to Blanchard.

While representing the state in courthouses across Michigan, Blanchard was able to work toward his life's ambition — to be a U.S. congressman. His uncle, Ohio politician Kenneth Johnston, had told Blanchard's mother at one point, "That boy is going to be governor of Michigan someday." Blanchard, however, said, "My lifelong goal was to be a U.S. congressman, not a senator, and certainly not a governor."

In 1974, Blanchard defeated three primary opponents to win the Democratic nomination and the right to challenge Republican Rep. Robert J. Huber in the 18th Congressional District, which at that time covered portions of Macomb and Oakland counties. Blanchard didn't have much organized support, but he had a wizard of a fund-raiser in Ron Thayer and an intense band of supporters who helped him pull it off. Blanchard defeated Huber, 83,523-57,133, and was re-elected three

In Trenton with six 1982 gubernatorial primary opponents, left to right: Zolton Ferency, William Fitzgerald, Kerry Kammer, Edward Pierce, David Plawecki and John Safran

Harold Robinson/The Detroit News

William T. Anderson/The Detroit News

Ivory Photo

Top At a 1986 meeting of the Governor's Task Force on Jobs and Economic Development are, left to right, Chrysler Chairman Lee Iacocca, Blanchard, former UAW President Doug Fraser, and State Commerce Director Doug Ross.

Bottom A recall campaign started in 1983 after passage of a temporary increase in the income tax.

times.

In Congress, Blanchard wrote the Chrysler (Corp.) Loan Guarantee Act and was otherwise instrumental in winning adoption of the federal portion of a financial rescue plan for the ailing automaker. He planned to write a book about the episode but never got around to it because he ran for governor instead. "I never had fire in my belly to be governor ... but fate has its way," Blanchard later recalled.

Blanchard became convinced in 1981 that Republican Gov. William G. Milliken would not seek re-election in 1982. He heard Milliken speak in May 1981 and "all but hype Ronald Reagan's economic programs. I said to myself he can't be running for re-election." He became more convinced when Kelley, who had been appoached by Milliken about the legalities involved in leasing property on Mackinac Island, confided to Blanchard that he was certain this meant Milliken would not run. Blanchard said he didn't want to run against Milliken, but "I would have been prepared to do it."

He became the 1982 Democratic nominee by receiving 406,941 votes and defeating six other candidates, including 1978 Democratic nominee William Fitzgerald, who polled 139,453 votes, and 1966

nominee Zolton Ferency, who garnered 85,088. When Republicans failed to unite behind Republican nominee Richard H. Headlee, Blanchard was elected governor by a vote of 1,561,291-1,369,582 — a plurality of 191,709. Headlee, an Oakland County insurance executive, had solid conservative backing but lost moderate votes, in part because he criticized feminists, including Milliken's wife.

In 1986, Blanchard was re-elected by defeating Wayne County Executive William Lucas, an ex-Democrat who sought as a Republican to be the nation's first elected black governor.[*] The vote was 1,632,138-753,647. The plurality of 878,091 was the largest ever for a Michigan governor, surpassing the previous record of 556,633 of Republican Fred M. Green in 1928. However, Green's winning percentage of 69.9 topped Blanchard's 68.1 percent. In 1928 and 1986, minority candidates collected a scattering of votes.

When first elected governor in 1983, Blanchard and the Democrat-controlled Legislature enacted a 38-percent temporary

[*] The nation's first black governor was Pinckney Benton Stewart Pinchback, an elected member and president pro tem of the Lousiana Senate who served out the final month of the term of Gov. Henry Clay Warmoth, who had been suspended because of impeachment proceedings in 1872.

increase in the income tax. As a result, two Democratic senators were recalled and replaced by Republicans, enabling the GOP to take Senate control. An effort was undertaken to recall Blanchard, and his approval rating plunged to about 30 percent, a record low for the era of public opinion surveys.

Blanchard undoubtedly would have failed to be re-elected if Michigan had still had two-year terms for its governors, making it necessary for him to run again in 1984. (Blanchard said he never would have given up his congressional seat to run for governor in the first place if Michigan still had two-year terms). However, by staking out the political middle and promoting himself as the "comeback governor of a comeback state," he was able to capitalize on Michigan's economic recovery.

He credited fast action on increasing the income tax and his economic expansion and other programs for speeding the state's comeback. Republicans maintained the credit belonged to President Reagan for leading the national economic recovery. They accused Blanchard of designing a taxpayer-financed state promotion program to promote himself more than Michigan. In the closing days of the 1986 campaign, GOP candidate Lucas tried to make an issue of threatened plant closings and layoffs by General Motors Corp. Blanchard minimized the likelihood of that happening. Two days after the election, GM announced extensive closings. "Now, the governor is singing a different tune," the Detroit Free Press

reported under a headline that said "Blanchard faces a tough 2nd term."[5]

Senate Majority Leader John Engler, the chief opposition leader during Blanchard's first term, said by that by taking credit for Michigan's comeback, Blanchard was "very much on the spot" in his second term because he would have to take responsibility for any economic downturn. In that sense, Blanchard was no different than the 42 governors who had served before him.

David Coates/The Detroit News

Above **Thumbs up for the 1986 landslide**

Bottom left **Blanchard is sworn in at his 1987 inaugural by Michigan Supreme Court justice Dennis Archer. Looking on are Blanchard's son Jay and former governor and Supreme Court Chief Justice G. Mennen Williams.**

Bottom right **Bad news follows election day**

Duane E. Belanger/The Detroit News

Michigan's first ladies
From parlors to podiums

Cottage Book Shop, Glen Arbor

George Gryzenia/The Detroit News

Left **Helen Ferris, circa 1913**

Right **Paula Blanchard, 1987**

Today's first lady is more than the belle of the inaugural ball. This account of the changing role of Michigan's first ladies is written by a woman with firsthand knowledge of the changes. Paula L. Blanchard, who researched the roles of her predecessors, writes from the perspective of a first lady whose state promotional activities expanded the traditional role of the spouse of a governor — and one who pursued her own professional career.

Since its admission to statehood 150 years ago, Michigan has been ably served by more than 40 first ladies, beginning with Gov. Stevens T. Mason's sister, Emily Virginia Mason, who "entertained her brother's guests and did the honors of the home," thus establishing her as Michigan's first first lady.[1] The day my husband was inaugurated as Michigan's 45th governor,* that title was conferred upon me. Although I didn't receive a single vote in the elections of 1982 and 1986, I have had the best job — albeit nonpaying — in state government. As Michigan's first lady, I had a blank page on which to write a job description, and a world of choices.

While the role of first lady is an important one, there is no definitive description of that role. Is a first lady a hostess and a social director? Yes. Is a first lady a nurturer, anchoring the home and the family while her husband serves the state's citizens? Yes. Is the first lady a confidant and trusted adviser? Yes. Is the first lady an advocate for causes — her own or her husband's? Yes!

Like every first lady before me, I adopted some of those conventional roles while at the same time developing my own unique role. No two first ladies have chosen the same path; no two first ladies have pursued the

* Blanchard was the 43rd individual to serve as governor but two of them, John S. Barry and Frank D. Fitzgerald, served, were out of office and then returned.

same goals and activities. History sheds some light on the different roles that each first lady has pursued, but, unfortunately, very little is known about most of Michigan's first ladies.

Many stood in their husbands' shadows and few records of their activities existed. This became clear when I learned in researching this chapter that another first lady — Helen Jossman Van Wagoner — was from my hometown of Clarkston! Although we both grew up in that small village, I had never heard of my sister first lady.

For years Michigan's first ladies have served primarily as hostesses for their husbands — or brothers. So integral was this role that two bachelor governors called upon the talents and contributions of their sisters. Emily Mason, sister of Michigan's first elected governor, Stevens T. Mason (1835-40), and Marguerite Murphy Teahan, sister of Gov. Frank Murphy (1937-38), proved to be excellent hostesses. In fact, Emily was so effective that she often was given credit for her brother's popularity

during his first term in office.[2] In 1838 Mason married Julia Elizabeth Phelps of New York City. Juliana Trumbull Woodbridge (1840-41) was well known for her ability to host events and Angeolina Hascall Wisner (1859-60) even entertained the Prince of Wales.[3] Mary Kidder Barry (1842-46, 1850-51) took this role to the extreme:

"She brewed and stewed and boiled and baked and washed and ironed and when not hard at work in the duties of the kitchen, she busied herself in making ruffled shirts for the governor out of the finest linen."[4]

Thank goodness times have changed!

And yet, the roles of Michigan's first ladies often mirrored our times. During the Civil War, Sarah Horton Blair (1861-64) spent much of her time "helping young soldiers camped in Jackson as well as throughout the state. Her work for the relief of the sick and wounded ... was constant and great."[5] But when times changed and the war ended, Sarah's successor, Mary Ann Slocum Crapo (1865-68), spent her years as a governor's spouse managing the family

Alpheus and Lucretia Lawrence Felch, circa 1849, shortly after he left the governorship

Catlin

138

home in Flint and their Swartz Creek farm.

Frances Newberry Bagley (1873-76) may have tended to the home fires like her predecessor, but she was one of the first of us to go beyond the hearth and into the community, organizing the Women's Club in Detroit, in Lansing and throughout the state.[6]

Harriet Miles Begole (1883-84) was immensely important to her husband during his years as governor. A suffrage advocate, Gov. Josiah W. Begole said, "The success in (my) life is largely due to the faithful wife of (my) youth."[7] Helen Gillespie Ferris (1913-16), who remained at home in Big Rapids while her husband served in Lansing, had a great influence on the governor, who said, she deserved a large part of the credit for the best service he rendered Michigan.[8]

Clara Hantel Brucker (1931-32) ushered in the modern era with her own goals and objectives, closely resembling her counterparts of later years. Clara worked on her master's degree in political science at Michigan State University while first lady and may well have been the first governor's spouse in Michigan who actively campaigned for her husband. She also founded the School of Government, a nonpartisan group of the Federation of Women's Clubs in Detroit, and wrote her own book, *To Have Your Cake and Eat It,* a compilation of notes and photographs taken during her husband's years of service as secretary of the Army.[9]

The women who followed Clara Brucker as first lady were more visible than their predecessors, but they balanced their public life with the demands of home and family. Anne O'Brien Kelly (1943-46) raised six children and maintained the family home in Lansing. She once supervised a staff of prison inmates who renovated the newly acquired Mackinac Island governor's residence for the 1945 National Governors' Association meeting there. Anne even sewed the curtains for the residence herself so that they would be done in time for the conference.[10]

When Nancy Quirk Williams (1949-60) came to Lansing as first lady, she was fully prepared to be a part of the team that she and her husband had formed during their vigorous run for office. Like Clara Brucker, she actively campaigned for her husband's candidacy, with and without him. During his six gubernatorial elections, Nancy probably set the record for miles logged,

World Wide

This 1939 photo catches Gov. Luren Dickinson and First Lady Zora Cooley Dickinson at home. He's wearing his favorite boots.

and in 1948 drove herself and her husband in an old DeSoto as they criss-crossed the state. With no staff, no official Lansing residence and no budget, Nancy almost singlehandedly balanced her private life with a public life that included speaking, traveling, hosting her own TV show, Nancy's Scrap Book, and arranging countless meetings and functions.

Michigan's first lady was still chief cook and bottle washer as recently as 1961, when Alice Nielson Swainson (1961-62) came to Lansing. "When we had visiting dignitaries, we put them up in our home; I did all the grocery shopping and cooking, but we were fortunate to have a housekeeper."[11] Alice, too, actively campaigned for her husband by making public appearances and giving speeches across the state. But as the mother of a young family, she devoted much of her time to her children.

Lenore LaFount Romney (1963-69) was

Edwin C. Lombardo/The Detroit News

Above left **Gov. Wilber Brucker at 1931 inaugural with First Lady Clara and son, Wilber, Jr.**

Above right **Nancy Williams in 1961, with the scrapbook she kept of Gov. G. Mennen William's career and used on her *Nancy's Scrapbook* TV show**

Barnard Nagel/The Detroit News

the mother of grown children when she became Michigan's first lady. She had been a corporate wife and even an actress on contract with MGM before tackling her new role as a governor's spouse. Her years as first lady prepared her well for her 1970 United States Senate campaign. There was no doubt that Lenore Romney's candidacy was a direct result of her position as former first lady. Her name recognition, however, was derived from her husband's position. At a time when Michigan Republican leaders were discussing her possible candidacy, she said, "I am hoping desperately that they find another candidate. Nothing would please me more."[12]

My predecessor, Helen Wallbank Milliken (1969-82), visibly directed her influence and access as first lady, fighting for policies and issues that she personally believed in. During her tenure as Michigan's longest-serving first lady, Helen Milliken was a strong environmentalist, publicly supporting the passage of legislation to prohibit throwaway bottles and to limit oil drilling in the Pigeon River Country State Forest. She was an outstanding advocate for women's rights, serving as

a national spokeswoman for the Equal Rights Amendment and as a delegate to the International Women's Year Conference. Recognizing that her role provided a public forum, Helen has said, "My beliefs are not particularly unique. It's just that I'm now in a position to do something about them."[13]

Like all the first ladies before me, I was in a unique position, one held by only about 50 individuals in this country at one time. Simply because I was married to someone who happened to be our state's governor, I had the privilege and the advantage of a very valuable tool: Derivative power. In other words, I derived power from my husband's position.

Using this new-found influence required a whole new approach. Before and during my husband's career as a public official, I was a teacher, a member of civic organizations and an administrative assistant in an office in Washington, D.C. In all of those positions, my influence was based on my own experience and expertise. Suddenly, however, my opinions were important, not because they were particularly informed or any more significant than anyone else's. Instead, my views were noteworthy because I was first lady.

Using derivative power was both exciting and challenging, but there were no guidelines for its use. Together, my husband and I developed our approach: Exercise it for the good of this state and the citizens who live in it but be always mindful that whatever was done with it would reflect upon its source, the governor.

Motivating my decision about the best use of my position was my deep love for the beauty and bounty of this state and its people. I wanted to share my pride in Michigan with others, in an effort to generate pride among all her citizens. I wanted to prove to all, skeptics and supporters alike, that pride was an integral component in economic development essential to Michigan's future. In short, I wanted to market Michigan, her people, places, products and pride.

At first it was viewed as a bit unorthodox when I opened an office in the Michigan Department of Commerce, becoming the only governor's spouse in the nation who had an office in a state department and who worked directly on departmental goals and initiatives. In this capacity, I co-chaired four governor's conferences on tourism and established the Office of Michigan Products Promotion, the only one of its kind in state government. People were intrigued by this public policy-making role and expressed great support and appreciation for the work I did on their behalf.

Like millions of other working women, I found myself balancing the demands of work and home as I fulfilled the role of first lady.

Making the most of my position meant that I had to be a tightrope walker and a juggler, all at the same time, trying to use my role to its fullest advantage without stepping over the line. Like other governors' spouses, I walked that tightrope in public before a full house. So while I tried to keep my private life separate from my public life, it was really not possible because I lived in a glass house and the curtains were always open.

While the most compelling aspect of my private life was my family, I pursued another goal — completely for myself. In an effort to keep in touch with the "real world" and prepare for a career beyond public service, I worked on a master's degree in telecommunication at Michigan State University, my alma mater. This offered me much relief from the demands of public life. At the university, I knew I would be judged on my own merits and no amount of derivative power would help me pass a final! My studies were a great equalizer for me and a wise investment in my mental health.

While my role as Michigan's first lady evolved over the years, so too had the roles of my colleagues in other states. In fact, the term "first lady" could not be universally applied to all governors' spouses since there were three male spouses whom we affectionately called "first mates."

Spouses of governors across the nation moved into nontraditional areas as they defined their public roles. Traditionally, they were hostesses, private advisers to the governor and supporters of the arts. Many still fulfilled those responsibilities, but most were doing that and more, asserting

Lenore Romney in 1964

Robert Jacobs/The Detroit News

Duane E. Belanger/The Detroit News

Helen Milliken speaks at a rally for the Equal Rights Amendment outside the Republican National Convention in Detroit, 1980.

themselves by contributing to areas of economic development, arms control, human services, public safety, refugees, prisons and illiteracy. A small but increasing number of first spouses were gainfully employed in a profession of their own choosing, while maintaining a public role. They were doctors, lawyers, authors, TV personalities and social workers, to name just a few.

I, too, branched out in pursuit of my own professional goals as a staff member of the Department of Telecommunication at MSU. Also, I continued to market Michigan, devote time to human services and finish my master's degree. People changed, roles changed, expectations changed and the highwire juggling act performed by governors' spouses reflected the precarious balance we all had to strike to meet our own needs,

our families' needs and the needs of the society we tried to serve.

I was tremendously grateful that I was given the opportunity. I felt I had a responsibility to use my position and its power to help make Michigan the best place in the world to live, work and raise a family. To let an opportunity like that slip by without grabbing hold of it and putting it to good use would be regrettable, and no one would regret it more than I.

I would like to express my appreciation to Michigan author Willah Weddon, whose book, *First Ladies of Michigan,* was extremely helpful in preparing this chapter; and, to Kelly Rossman, whose assistance in research and editing was invaluable to me.

— *Paula L. Blanchard*

MICHIGAN'S FIRST LADIES

Emily Virginia Mason (sister)	Stevens T. Mason	1835-40
Julia Phelps Mason		
Juliana Trumbull Woodbridge	William Woodbridge	1840-41
Mary Hudun Gordon	James Wright Gordon	1841
Mary Kidder Barry	John S. Barry	1842-46
Lucretia Lawrence Felch	Alpheus Felch	1846-47
	William L. Greenly*	1847
Almira Cadwell Ransom	Epaphroditus Ransom	1848-50
Mary Kidder Barry	John S. Barry	1850-51
Sarah Sabin McClelland	Robert McClelland	1852-53
Marella Stewart Parsons	Andrew Parsons	1853-54
Mary Warden Bingham	Kinsley S. Bingham	1855-58
Angeolina Hascall Wisner	Moses Wisner	1859-60
Sarah Horton Ford Blair	Austin Blair	1861-64
Mary Ann Slocum Crapo	Henry H. Crapo	1865-68
Sibyle Lambard Baldwin	Henry P. Baldwin	1869-72
Frances Newberry Bagley	John J. Bagley	1873-76
Elizabeth Musgrave Croswell	Charles M. Croswell	1877-80
Lucy Peck Jerome	David H. Jerome	1881-82
Harriet Miles Begole	Josiah W. Begole	1883-84
Annette Henry Alger	Russell A. Alger	1885-86
Mary Thompson Luce	Cyrus G. Luce	1887-90
Elizabeth Galloway Winans	Edwin B. Winans	1891-92
Lucretia Winship Rich	John T. Rich	1893-96
Frances Gilbert Pingree	Hazen S. Pingree	1897-00
Allaseba Phelps Bliss	Aaron T. Bliss	1901-04
Martha Davis Warner	Fred M. Warner	1905-10
Lillian Jones Osborn	Chase S. Osborn	1911-12
Helen Gillespie Ferris	Woodbridge N. Ferris	1913-16
Mary Moore Sleeper	Albert E. Sleeper	1917-20
	Alexander J. Groesbeck	1921-26
Helen Kelley Green	Fred W. Green	1927-30
Clara Hantel Brucker	Wilber M. Brucker	1931-32
Josephine White Comstock	William A. Comstock	1933-34
Queena Warner Fitzgerald	Frank D. Fitzgerald	1935-36
Marguerite Murphy Teahan (sister)	Frank Murphy	1937-38
Queena Warner Fitzgerald	Frank D. Fitzgerald	1939
Zora Cooley Dickinson	Luren D. Dickinson	1939-40
Helen Jossman Van Wagoner	Murray D. Van Wagoner	1941-42
Anne O'Brien Kelly	Harry F. Kelly	1943-46
Mae Pierson Sigler	Kim Sigler	1947-48
Nancy Quirk Williams	G. Mennen Williams	1949-60
Alice Nielsen Swainson	John B. Swainson	1961-62
Lenore LaFount Romney	George Romney	1963-69
Helen Wallbank Milliken	William G. Milliken	1969-82
Paula Parker Blanchard	James J. Blanchard	1983-

*Records are not clear on which of Greenly's three wives was first lady.

Michael S. Green/The Detroit News

Governors-in-waiting: The lieutenant governors

*"Tell me," asked a dinner companion of Massachusetts Lt.
Gov. Calvin Coolidge, "what do you do?"*
"I'm the lieutenant governor."
"That's wonderful. Tell me all about it."
"I just did."

The above dialog might reflect a do-nothing role for Calvin Coolidge when he was lieutenant governor of Massachusetts in 1919-20, before he went on to become governor, U.S. vice-president and eventually president. Or it might just reflect the famed reticence of Silent Cal.

Variations of that story are legion across the country, including Michigan. When asked what it was like to be a lame duck lieutenant governor, outgoing Michigan Lt. Gov. James H. Brickley said, "It's like being lieutenant governor." The job of backup governor is not in itself a burdensome one, but the job *can* be a gateway to the governorship — as it was for six lieutenant governors in Michigan's first 150 years of statehood. Only two of them

ever were elected to the governorship — Democrat John B. Swainson and Republican William G. Milliken. Milliken initially inherited the job, upon the resignation of Republican Gov. George Romney, before winning it on his own.

"The old image of the lieutenant governor as a stand-in and ribbon-cutter is no longer valid," said Indiana Lt. Gov. John M. Mutz after he cited the Silent Cal story in a column he wrote for the Washington Post. "Many states are finding important new roles for their lieutenant governors."[1] In Indiana, by law, the lieutenant governor directs the Department of Commerce.

Michigan had no such statutory assignments as of 1987, and, on paper, the lieutenant governor was essentially an

Lt. Gov. Martha Griffiths at a 1986 rally with Gov. James J. Blanchard and First Lady Paula Blanchard, and Sen. Donald Riegle, Jr.

145

GEE, BILL—
IT'S **JUST**
WHAT I'VE
ALWAYS
WANTED

THROW OUT
THE LIFELINE
FEELINGLY

SALVATION
PACKAGE

BRICKLEY

©1982 THE DETROIT NEWS

Draper Hill/The Detroit News

Sometimes a lieutenant governor's tether to a governor can hurt, as it did in 1982 when Gov. William G. Milliken made massive budget cuts that were unpopular with some interest groups.

executive spare tire. The Constitution said only: "The lieutenant governor shall be president of the Senate, but shall have no vote, unless they be equally divided. He (sic) may perform duties requested of him by the governor, but no power vested in the governor shall be delegated."[2]

Starting in 1966, when they began running in tandem,[3] Michigan governors gave their lieutenant governors special assignments and tried to give them high visibility. After all, a vote for one was a vote for both. Romney dispatched Milliken to settle school strikes, and Milliken headed a well-publicized task force that recommended ways to cut government costs. Milliken found work for Brickley (1971-74, 1979-82) and James J. Damman (1975-78), as did Democratic Gov. James J. Blanchard for Martha Griffiths (1983-). They all took on trouble-shooting roles.

Running mates, whether for lieutenant governor or vice-president, don't get gover-

nors or presidents elected. Voters judge the head of the ticket. A candidate for lieutenant governor is essentially an early flash in the campaign pan — one whose biggest moment is when the selection is announced. The selection comes at a time when voters take a close look at the judgment of the newly nominated gubernatorial candidate. A bad choice hurts far more than a good one helps. Often, a candidate for governor wants someone who will bring a degree of geographical or other other special appeal — and won't rock the boat during the campaign or while in office.

Brickley and Griffiths, while not decisive factors in the outcome of their tickets, brought timely assets and are instructive examples in any examination of the office of lieutenant governor. Brickley was a classic example of how a running mate could help a governor — and then be hurt in the end.

As a Catholic and former member of the Detroit City Council, Brickley provided a 1970 balance to outstater and Protestant Milliken, although both the religious and regional factors were less important then than they previously had been. To boot, Brickley was a crime fighter — a former FBI agent, assistant prosecutor and U.S. attorney.

Although more conservative than Milliken on some matters, Brickley was a loyalist. But when the time came for Brickley to run on his own, the tether proved to be troublesome. Economic times were bad. In making the biggest budget cuts in Michigan history, the Milliken-Brickley administration alienated environmental, educational and other interests. Furthermore, much of the wrath of Republican conservatives that fell on liberal-leaning Milliken for his friendship with Democratic Detroit Mayor Coleman A. Young and other "sins" descended on Brickley. Milliken's coalition politics won general elections, but did not transfer to Brickley in the narrow confines of a GOP primary. Times were difficult and the GOP looked increasingly to the right. Brickley lost the nomination to conservative Richard H. Headlee, who, on top of everything else, ran a better campaign.

Blanchard's selection of Griffiths as his running mate in his first campaign in 1982 also was a wise political stroke. For starters, the time was ripe for a woman to be on the ticket to help woo feminists, as well as moderate Republicans and independents who weren't sure where to turn with the

Executive Office

Lt. Gov. James H. Brickley is sworn in in 1979 by Detroit Common Pleas Judge Jessie Slaton as longtime Republican National Committeeman Peter B. Fletcher stands by. (Slaton was among the 269 people killed in 1983 when a Korean airliner was shot down by a Soviet jet fighter after the airliner strayed into Soviet airspace.)

retirement of Milliken and the defeat of Brickley.

Griffiths was an institution in the Michigan Democratic Party, having been, along with her husband, Hicks, among a small band of mavericks in 1948 who helped G. Mennen Williams overthrow ineffective Democratic leadership and launch his unprecedented six terms as governor. As a former judge and congresswoman, she had solid credentials.

Of particular importance to Blanchard was that she had close ties to business, based on her voting record and membership on corporate boards. Then, too, there was the comfortable knowledge that 70-year-old Griffiths would not be politically ambitious and overly interested in Blanchard's pulse rate.

Griffiths later would prove to be somewhat of a loose cannon in that she made Blanchard wince on occasion by speaking out her independent mind. But she was a loyal backup and helpmate, an occasionally aggressive hatchet person for Blanchard, and a stern presiding officer in an often unruly Senate. In the campaign, she was an asset, a fact acknowledged by Headlee, later saying he probably should also have selected a woman to run with him. In 1986, Blanchard's Republican opponent, William Lucas, did select a woman as his running mate, former state Rep. Colleen Engler, who had run unsuccessfully for the gubernatorial nomination earlier that year.

The 1986 campaign marked the first time both major parties had women running for lieutenant governor. Michigan had its first female lieutenant governor in 1940, when Matilda R. Wilson was appointed to the post in the closing days of the administration of Republican Gov. Luren D. Dickinson.

Dickinson was Michigan's longest-serving lieutenant governor, holding the job in 1915-20, 1927-32, and in 1939. He became governor when Gov. Frank D. Fitzgerald died in office. In the 19th century, Lt. Govs. James Wright Gordon, William L. Greenly and Andrew Parsons also functioned as governors when the chief executive resigned. After acting as governor, Whig Gordon became a diplomat in Brazil, where he died in a fall from a balcony; Democrat Greenly became mayor of Adrian and a justice of the peace; and Democrat Parsons served in the state House of Representatives. Dickinson was the first lieutenant governor who succeeded to the governorship and then ran for the office on his own. He lost.

One lieutenant governor to rise to prominence was Philip A. Hart, a former legal adviser to Williams who was lieutenant governor in 1955-58. He later became a U.S. senator and his fame as "conscience of the Senate" was recognized when the Senate named one of its office buildings after him.

Democratic Lt. Gov. T. John Lesinski examines Gov. George Romney's 1964 congressional redistricting plan as Romney briefs legislators on it in his office.

AP

Democrat T. John Lesinski was lieutenant governor in 1961-64 and was the first to occupy the No. 2 spot under Republican Romney, who complained that Lesinski tried to "embarrass" him. Lesinski said, "We kidded around a lot but we never really had any trouble."[4] At the time, a large majority of states had their governors and lieutenant governors run separately. Two of the five lieutenant governors who served under Williams were Republicans. Lesinski was the last lieutenant governor to be chosen in the same election with a governor of another party.

The *Michigan Manual* spells out the selection process and role of the lieutenant governor: "The lieutenant governor is nominated at party convention and elected with the governor. Terms of office, beginning in 1966, changed from two years to four years. S/he must be at least 30 years old and have been a registered voter." It outlines the constitutional provisions on Senate duties and concludes: "The lieutenant governor is a member of the Adminis-

trative Board and would succeed the governor in case of death, impeachment, removal from office or resignation."[5]

The Constitution and manual aside, a lieutenant governor of Michigan, other than presiding part-time in the Senate, does essentially what a governor wants him or her to do. The office has come a long way in Michigan and elsewhere since the days when Silent Cal was No. 2 in Massachusetts, but its occupants still are primarily stand-ins for governors.

As of 1985, seven states did not even have such an office.* In 1986, the Washington Post said it was not apparent "why more and more states have made the candidates for lieutenant governor and governor a kind of package."[6]

It is apparent from Michigan's experience that it works better to have the governor and lieutenant governor offered up as a package — to have them run *and* work together.

* Maine, New Hampshire, New Jersey, Oregon, Tennessee, West Virginia and Wyoming.

MICHIGAN'S LIEUTENANT GOVERNORS

Edward Mundy	Democrat	1835-1840
James W. Gordon[1]	Whig	1841
Thomas J. Drake (acting)	Whig	1841-1842
Origen D. Richardson	Democrat	1842-1846
William L. Greenly[1]	Democrat	1847
Charles P. Bush (acting)	Democrat	1847-1848
William M. Fenton	Democrat	1848-1851
Calvin Britain	Democrat	1852-1853
Andrew Parsons[1]	Democrat	1853
George Griswold (acting)	Democrat	1853-1854
George Coe	Whig	1855-1858
Edmund Fairfield	Republican	1859-1860
James Birney[2]	Republican	1861
Joseph R. Williams (acting)[3]	Republican	1861-1862
Henry T. Backus (acting)	Republican	1862
Charles S. May	Republican	1863-1864
Ebenezer O. Grosvenor	Republican	1865-1866
Dwight May	Republican	1867-1868
Morgan Bates	Republican	1869-1872
Henry H. Holt	Republican	1873-1876
Alonzo Sessions	Republican	1877-1880
Moreau S. Crosby	Republican	1881-1884
Archibald Buttars	Republican	1885-1886
James H. MacDonald[4]	Republican	1887-1889
William Ball (acting)	Republican	1889-1890
John Strong	Democrat	1891-1892
J. Wight Giddings	Republican	1893-1894
Alfred Milnes[5]	Republican	1895
Joseph R. McLaughlin (acting)	Republican	1895-1896
Thomas B. Dunstan	Republican	1897-1898
Orrin W. Robinson	Republican	1899-1902
Alexander Maintland	Republican	1903-1906
Patrick H. Kelley	Republican	1907-1910
John Q. Ross	Republican	1911-1914
Luren D. Dickinson	Republican	1915-1920
Thomas Read	Republican	1921-1924
George W. Welsh	Republican	1925-1926
Luren D. Dickinson	Republican	1927-1932
Allen E. Stebbins	Democrat	1933-1934
Thomas Read	Republican	1935-1936
Leo J. Nowicki	Democrat	1937-1938
Luren D. Dickinson[6]	Republican	1939
Matilda R. Wilson	Republican	1940
Frank Murphy	Democrat	1941-1942
Eugene C. Keyes	Republican	1943-1944
Vernon J. Brown	Republican	1945-1946
Eugene C. Keyes	Republican	1947-1948
John W. Connolly	Democrat	1949-1950
William C. Vandenberg	Republican	1951-1952
Clarence A. Reid	Republican	1953-1954
Philip A. Hart	Democrat	1955-1958
John B. Swainson	Democrat	1959-1960
T. John Lesinski	Democrat	1961-1964
William G. Milliken[7]	Republican	1965-1969
James H. Brickley	Republican	1971-1974
James J. Damman	Republican	1975-1978
James H. Brickley	Republican	1979-1982
Martha W. Griffiths	Democrat	1983-

Notes:
1 Acting Governor
2 Resigned Apr. 3, 1861
3 Died; Henry T. Backus acting Lieutenant Governor
4 Died Jan. 19, 1889
5 Elected to Congress, Apr. 1, 1895; resigned as Lieutenant Governor May 31, 1895
6 Became Governor Mar. 17, 1939; Matilda R. Wilson appointed Nov. 19, 1940, for unexpired term.
7 Became Governor Jan. 22, 1969

Source: Michigan Manual, 1985-86

United Press

Governors and the press

The public press kindled the flame, and its devastation has reached every dwelling within our borders. — **Stevens T. Mason to the Michigan Legislature, Jan. 2, 1838.**

From Michigan's beginnings as a state, its governors have never been able to quite figure out how to deal with the press, especially with negative press. Politicians and the press throughout the nation have used and abused each other on occasion. Michigan in its first 150 years was no exception. "Bad press" troubled most of Michigan's governors at one time or another.

Stevens T. Mason, Michigan's first governor (1835-40), was often the target of criticism, especially on his handling of the state's first internal improvements program. But Mason told the Legislature: "Whilst a public officer should not be too callous to assaults upon his reputation, it is also true, that he should not be too sensitive. His public measures and official acts belong to the public, are always before them, and they will judge them fairly and correctly. And even when his integrity has been assailed,

the vilest and worst of motives attributed to his conduct, he has only to await the development of time, trust to the good sense and justice of the people, and they will right the wrong done him."[1]

Mason did not always wait for the good sense of the people to right the wrongs of the press. He once punched an editor who referred to him as Michigan's "boy governor."

Gov. Moses Wisner (1859-60) complained to the Legislature: "There is a portion of the Northern press which for base, cowardly and selfish purposes, has constantly, for the past six years, instilled into the minds of our Southern brothers the vile libel that the Republican Party is a party of aggression."[2]

In his final message to the Legislature, Gov. Hazen S. Pingree (1897-1900) said: "Every large interest that I have antagonized has been arrayed against me, and the allies

Gov. G. Mennen Williams at a 1952 press conference

151

of those interests, the newspapers of the state, have lost no opportunity to attempt to draw the minds of the people from the real issue by making personal attacks on me and publishing malicious and willful libels, and to belittle my efforts and bring me into disrepute ..."[3]

Much depends, in gubernatorial press relations, on the governor's staff. Gov. G. Mennen Williams (1949-60), reflecting on his unprecedented six terms in office, gave deserved credit to Paul Weber, his cigar-smoking press secretary: "My press secretary was my eyes and ears as well as my voice. He was also no small part of my brain."[4] Williams in his early campaigns had few editorial endorsements and was the target of some hostile state and national media. But Weber was popular with reporters and helped smooth over Williams' sometimes-brittle press relations.

At a gathering of ex-governors, sponsored by the Michigan Historical Commission in 1981, Williams said "probably the kind of coverage you get is dependent upon your ability in doing your job and handling the press. And I only regret that I wasn't as able as the present governor (William G. Milliken), because he certainly is, and I say this with admiration, rather than the pejorative sense, a consummate politician in handling something that is of vital importance to any politician or government administrator, and that is public relations."[5]

The strong suit of Milliken (1969-82) in press relations was in his good personal relations with media representatives, his openness and candor, and deft handling of even the most hostile questions. He seldom complained publicly about press coverage, although he claimed some elements of the press gave distorted coverage to the tainting of food products by the accidental mixing in 1973 of a toxic chemical in cattle feed.

Milliken's successor, Gov. James J. Blanchard (1983-), got off to a rocky start with the Capitol press corps as he grappled with the state's rocky finances. He often was testy in responding to questions and, even after his personal press relations improved,

U.S. Attorney General Frank Murphy, former governor of Michigan, at a 1940 press conference after his appointment to the U.S. Supreme Court.

ACME

Dale Atkins/AP

he continued to be critical of what he considered to be a tendency to accentuate the negative.

Blanchard's image was enhanced by Rick Cole, who served as his press secretary and later chief of staff. Detroit News Lansing Bureau Chief Joanna Firestone wrote in 1985 that Cole "is responsible in no small part for the dramatic turnaround in Blanchard's popularity in Michigan and his emerging national image as a political wunderkind and fiscal magician."[6] This was done by such devices as frequent press "availabilities" for Blanchard outside of Lansing, and periodic guest appearances on network TV shows.

Republican Gov. George Romney (1963-69) was a special case. One word, uttered on a Detroit TV show, rippled across the nation and undermined his bid for the 1968 Republican presidential nomination. Romney said on the *Lou Gordon Show* that he had undergone a "brainwashing" by military and diplomatic officials in Vietnam. In headlines, it came out that Romney admitted to being "brainwashed."

After Romney withdrew from the presidential race, Washington Post columnist David S. Broder wrote: "This Romney was

UPI

Above **Gov. William G. Milliken, Michigan's longest-serving governor, tells a 1981 press conference in his office that he will not seek re-election in 1982.**

Left **Gov. George Romney bids farewell in a 1969 statewide radio-TV address.**

153

certainly not 'brainwashed,' i.e., incapable of distinguishing appearance from reality or of reasoning from evidence to a conclusion. Those who thought that one word epitomized the man missed the mark by a mile."[7]

Romney, speaking to reporters at the Republican National Convention in Miami Beach, was reported to have snapped in a TV interview, "You fellows killed me. I'm a dead duck."[8] So it was understandable when Romney said at the 1981 gathering of ex-governors: "Some press people are like archeologists or anthropologists ... an anthropologist finds a tooth or a jawbone, and he resurrects a whole dinosaur. ... Some press people take a word or a clause, and they manufacture a whole interpretation of a person in public life."[9]

Romney had a point. Unfortunately, perception is everything in politics. Political careers are built on images. In the days of instant and mass media, images can be built overnight — and often on a single episode.

At the meeting of ex-governors, Gov. Murray D. Van Wagoner (1941-42) offered a simple formula for press relations: "If you can't lick them, join them." He quipped that he had good relations with reporters by hiring reporters. For one thing, he said, "any time a handout (press release) came out of our office, it would be written up so they didn't have to rewrite the darn thing. They could take it and print it, because it was written up by a professional."[10] It really doesn't work that way.

David Coates/The Detroit News

To enhance visual presentation in newspapers and on TV, modern governors use charts and other "props" at press conferences. At a 1986 press conference at the Detroit Press Club is Gov. James J. Blanchard and Peter Plastrik, a former Booth newspaper reporter who became president of Blanchard's Michigan Strategic Fund.

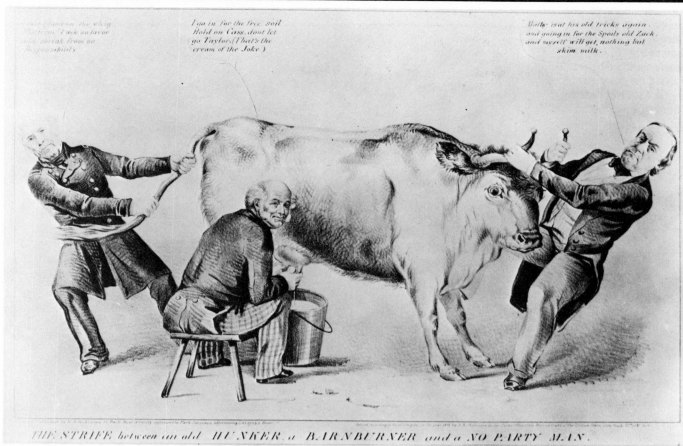

State Archives

The pen and politics:
Governors in cartoon

The pins, needles, stilettos, broadswords and occasional bludgeons are still finding targets in these homogeneous times.

— Detroit News cartoonist Draper Hill, observing a 1986 exhibition of works by 43 political cartoonists.

Benjamin Franklin pioneered political cartooning in America. His classic "Join or Die" drawing of the segments of a snake, published in the Pennsylvania Gazette in 1754, called upon New Englanders to unite against French and Indian forces threatening the western border. It served as a bellows fanning the flames of the young and unruly satirical press.

In the next two centuries or so, much has happened to temper the revolutionary spirit in America, but as Detroit News cartoonist Draper Hill suggested, the institution of political cartooning remains a power to reckon with — as Michigan governors learned throughout the first 150 years of statehood. We continue to depend on graphic commentators to tell us whether the

emperor is wearing clothes. Political cartoonists are perhaps best suited for this sort of wardrobe critique. They have instant impact, far more so than editorial writers. A cartoonist can, in a very direct and simple way, uncover a naked deception.

Jeff MacNelly, political cartoonist for the Chicago Tribune, said that cartoonists "violate every rule of ethical journalism — they misquote, trifle with the truth, make science fiction out of politics and sometimes should be held for personal libel. But when the smoke clears, the political cartoonist has been getting closer to the truth than the guys who write political opinions."[1]

Political cartoonists have a unique relationship with editorial writers. They often have the same boss — the editorial page director — but usually have less

In the 1848 presidential campaign, former Mich. Territorial Gov. Lewis Cass, the Democratic nominee, pulls the horns as Whig nominee Zachary Taylor tugs the tail.

155

Slinging of campaign mud
is a recurrent theme when
the pen looks at politics, as
it was in this 1936 cartoon.
Thomas Nast of *Harper's
Weekly* started the practice
of using the donkey and the
elephant to represent the
Democratic and Republican
parties.

THE SOIL EROSION THIS SUMMER WILL BE TERRIBLE

CAMPAIGN MUD

B.R. Thomas/The Detroit News

editorial control exerted on them. Of course, each editor has a different mangement style, but most cartoonists agreed that they work best when given the creative freedom to cross the bounds of their newspaper's editorial policy.

Frank Williams, cartoonist for the Detroit Free Press from 1943 to 1978, said, "The cartoonist, if he's a good cartoonist, can't be a stenographer. He has to have his own ideas and be interested in his own subject matter."[2] Williams recalled that when he first started drawing for the Free Press, Editor Malcolm Bingay tried to give him cartoon ideas, and pressured him to do a couple of cartoons that Williams thought were not good. They flopped, Williams said, and Bingay never again forced cartoon ideas on him.

The News' Hill agreed. He declared the institution of cartooning "is apt to be at its best when it is irreverent, unpredictable, independent and as unillustrative as possible of the good, gray editorial matter which frames it on the page."[3]

Williams stressed that he thought it best to stay independent of the subjects he drew. "I always steered clear of associations with very many politicians because I was afraid I'd get emotionally involved, either like them or dislike them, and it would show in what I did."[4]

For many cartoonists, there's no danger of becoming overly friendly with their subjects, as they tend not to endear themselves to the people they draw. Tim Menees, the political cartoonist for the Pittsburgh Post-Gazette, said cartoonists are often asked, "Can't you guys ever draw anything *nice* about anybody?" Menees replied, "Yes, but rarely. ... We engage in an imperfect, highly flammable art. It is opinionated, sometimes snide, sometimes cruel. But that's the whole point."[5]

Bill Mauldin, creator of the famous pair of World War II GIs, Willie and Joe, and winner of many cartooning awards, has said that when you make people mad, you make people think. But Williams disagreed. He said, "I've always felt that a light approach would make people think a little more than a hard-hitting cartoon that is more mean than meaningful." Williams thought, too, that a cartoonist must be sensitive to the subject and to the audience: "I don't think the sky is the limit on slugging at somebody."[6]

Quite often, cartoonists are surprised by how forgiving their victims can be. Thomas Nast's cartoons in Harper's Weekly in the 1890s depicted New York political leader Boss William Marcy Tweed as a sack of money. Nast almost single-handedly brought about Tweed's downfall by chronicling his corrupt practices. Tweed had good reason to want to burn every cartoon Nast ever drew, but he reportedly had a complete set of Nast's "Boss Tweed" drawings. Williams attributed this to ego, and likened it to an experience he had with U.S. Sen. Barry Goldwater. After Williams did several "unflattering" cartoons about the Arizona Republican, Goldwater not only sent a letter asking for prints, but sent a check to pay for them.

But not everyone can take the jab of a pen in stride. In 1902, Pennsylvania Gov. Samuel Pennypacker was not amused by a cartoon in the Philadelphia North American that portrayed him as a fat parrot, complete with feathers and beak. The governor had a bill drafted prohibiting "the depicting of men ... as birds or animals." One irreverent Philadelphia cartoonist, Walt McDougall, then started drawing politicians' faces on various vegetables.[7]

Political cartoons are both examples of, and contributors to, the ability that Americans have for seeing humor in their own adversity. In the 10 or 15 seconds that they claim a reader's attention, cartoonists can take the ingredients of a complex, timely issue, boil it down to one or two easily understandable concepts and season it with a memorable dash — a dash that most often is humor.

With that they have taught an important social, economic or political lesson. They have taught us not to take ourselves or our leaders too seriously.

Following are examples of Michigan governors who have been targeted by the pens of Hill, Williams and other Michigan cartoonists.

— Don Weeks

Gov. Hazen S. Pingree said he'd hold his nose and vote for fellow Republican William McKinley for president. This 1900 cartoon suggests he should hold his tongue.

The Detroit News

157

Top **Money is always a factor in campaigns, as it was for Gov. Aaron T. Bliss early in the 20th century.**

Bottom **Gov. Alex J. Groesbeck leads his party on a 1926 road-building crusade.**

B.R. Thomas/The Detroit News

P.N. Cromwell/The Detroit Times

158

P.N. Cromwell/The Detroit Times

P.N. Cromwell/The Detroit Times

Top left **A boost for Fred Green's quest to take the governorship from Alex Groesbeck**

Top right **As governor, Green smokes out lobbyists**

Bottom **William A. Comstock was not the first or last governor to confront a stubborn legislature.**

WANTED, AN EXPERT MULE SKINNER

B.R. Thomas/The Detroit News

B.R. Thomas/The Detroit News

Top **Democrat Jim Farley conveys Franklin D. Roosevelt's plea that former Detroit Mayor Frank Murphy come back to Michigan to run for governor.**

Bottom left **Gov. G. Mennen Williams plunges to payless paydays in 1959.**

Bottom right **The links between John B. Swainson and UAW President Walter Reuther are portrayed in 1960.**

Frank Williams/Detroit Free Press

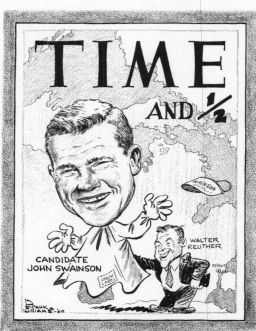

Frank Williams/Detroit Free Press

160

THIS'LL BE SOMETHING TO WATCH! 3B

MICHIGAN

DEM. ADMIN. BOARD

ROMNEY

GOP GOVERNORSHIP

Art Poinier/The Detroit News

BE IT EVER SO HUMBLE

ROMNEY TAX PROGRAM

FISCAL PROBLEM MORTGAGE

MICH.

TAX PAYER

Frank Williams/Detroit Free Press

Top left **Gov. George Romney had to share some powers with the Democrats in the executive branch.**

Top right **To the rescue — the Romney tax program**

Bottom **Labor's influence on Democratic legislators has been a recurring theme of Michigan cartoonists — and an occasional problem for Republican governors, such as William G. Milliken**

COULDN'T YOU JUST USE A RAG LIKE EVERYONE ELSE?

HOUSE DEMOCRATS

UAW

ELECTION YEAR WAX

WORKERS' COMP OINTMENT

©1981 THE DETROIT NEWS

Draper Hill/The Detroit News

161

Top In 1980, thanks in large part to Gov. William G. Milliken, George Bush defeated Ronald Reagan in the Republican presidential primary in Michigan.

Bottom left PBB contamination of milk was a political issue of the 1970's.

Bottom right The budget — be it surplus or deficit — is a favorite theme of cartoonists.

Draper Hill/The Detroit News

Frank Williams/Detroit Free Press

Draper Hill/The Detroit News

Draper Hill/The Detroit News

Top **Governors always like to accentuate the good news, as Gov. James J. Blanchard did in his 1986 re-election year.**

Bottom **A favorite theme of Michigan governors is property tax relief**

Draper Hill/The Detroit News

163

State Archives

The capitals and capitols of Michigan

We stand here as conquerors of forest and swamp.

— Gov. John J. Bagley when construction started on the present Capitol, Oct. 2, 1873.

In 1987, an actor portraying Gov. Stevens T. Mason joined Gov. James J. Blanchard in a celebration at the Capitol in Lansing, marking Michigan's first 150 years as a state. But Mason, Michigan's first elected governor, and the majority of the other 19th century governors, had their offices elsewhere.

Lansing was selected as the capital city only after long debate, but the events leading to construction of the permanent Capitol — dedicated by Gov. Charles M. Croswell Jan. 1, 1879 — were not nearly so smooth as the polished Vermont marble in its corridors. In fact, one governor, Hazen S. Pingree, wanted the state to abandon Lansing as the capital.

Michigan's first Capitol, in Detroit, later became a school.

165

Choosing the capital city

Detroit was the seat of the territorial government and remained the capital temporarily after statehood was achieved in 1837. The state Constitution of 1835 stipulated that a permanent site was to be selected within 10 years. Some legislators wanted the capital to remain where it was because Detroit was the state's most developed city. But others used the same reason to argue that the capital should be moved. Creating a new capital city, they said, would foster outstate settlement, an important consideration during a period when growth was a barometer of success. It also was pointed out that Detroit was vulnerable to attack from Canada if another war with Great Britain were to break out.

As the deadline for choosing the capital drew near, competition was intense. Being named state capital was seen by many communities as a boon for growth and prestige. Arguments were made on behalf of Detroit, Ann Arbor, Battle Creek, Albion, Dexter, Byron, Lyons, Owosso, Jackson and Marshall.

Resolutions were introduced by legislators for practically every city and town in the state. Said one legislator, William W. Upton: "It is almost incredible but there was no exception, the people of each embryo city could see abundant reasons why that city ought to be, and for hoping it would be, selected as the capital of the state."[1]

In the state House, a committee was formed to investigate the issue. It included members from Wayne, Genesee, Washtenaw, Monroe and Ionia counties. Its recommendations were as diverse as its membership. As expected, the committee became deadlocked, and then submitted three separate reports. The first was written by the chairman, George Throop of Wayne County. Not surprisingly, it favored keeping the capital in Detroit. Throop said that moving it "would involve an expenditure of a very large sum of public money." He predicted the cost of such a move would be as high as $200,000.[2] Rep. John D. Pierce of Marshall touted his hometown and warned against the danger of having a border town for the capital. Detroit, he said, "not only lies upon the frontier of the state, but of the United States, being ... in sight of a foreign country."[3] The third report, written by Enos Goodrich of Genesee County, did not single out any location, but urged that the capital be moved closer to the geographical center of the state. Goodrich was one of several anti-Detroit legislators known as the "Northern Rangers" who were sympathetic to James Seymour, a businessman from Flint. Seymour owned land in Lansing Township, Ingham County, that he offered to donate to the state for the new capitol.

With the help of state Rep. Joseph H. Kilbourne of Ingham County, Lansing was added to the many locations vying for the site. Most potential sites included promises of free land, building materials or other inducements, so Seymour's offer was not especially appealing at first. In fact, Lansing seemed a far less likely capital candidate

Top Former Gov. Alpheus Felch (center with white beard) on the steps of the temporary Capitol with fellow members of the planning committee for the permanent Capitol.

Bottom Sketch of the temporary Capitol in Lansing

State Archives

OLD STATE CAPITOL.
Occupied by the Legislature from the Session of 1848 to 1877 inclusive

1881 Michigan Manual

166

State Archives

Left Laying of the corner-stone for the permanent Capitol

Below New Capitol under construction in the 1870's

State Archives

than most.

Few people had ever heard of it. It was largely undeveloped. Other than Seymour's sawmill on the Grand River and a few log buildings, Lansing was little more than trees and swamps. Goodrich said later: "When the Legislature of 1847 was first organized, the man who could have supposed it possible to wrest the capital from Detroit and set it down in the midst of a dense forest on the banks of the Grand River would have been considered a fit subject for an insane asylum."[4]

Seymour's proposal included a map showing Lansing's central location in the state. Red lines on the map reached outward from Lansing and showed its location was equidistant from each of the settled lake ports and towns. This turned out to be a strong argument. But Lansing still was subject to ridicule. Rep. James M. Edmunds, a Whig from Ypsilanti, brought laughter to the chamber when he asked, "Mr. Speaker, will the clerk please read that table of distances again? I did not learn where this place is, although I learned it is a great ways from any other place."[5]

The House voted on 13 sites. At one point, Lyons was chosen the capital by a vote of 30-28, but the House later reversed itself. During the voting one exasperated member suggested Copper Harbor in the Upper Peninsula, but it never came to a vote. As each city was rejected, Lansing gained supporters. Once their personal choices were out of the running, many legislators leaned to Lansing. The "dense forest" of Lansing was the House choice as the capital by a final vote of 48-17.

The bill was sent to the Senate, which also had a difficult time with the issue. As in the House, Lyons at one point received majority Senate support, but the vote was reversed. The same thing happened with Jackson and Marshall. On March 8, 1847, senators voted 51 times without reaching a decision. The next day, however, the Senate finally approved the House bill. A week later, Acting Gov. William L. Greenly signed it.

167

Michigan Avenue looking west in 1878

State Archives

1919

The Detroit News

1987

Don Weeks

The capital debate overlapped two gubernatorial terms. Alpheus Felch was governor when the House voted. But before the Michigan Senate decided on Lansing, he resigned to become a U.S. senator. Lt. Gov. Greenly became acting governor March 3. Even though Felch was gone by the time Lansing was approved, he played an important role. He anticipated that Lansing eventually would be chosen and kept some township land out of the hands of speculators. Some speculators were traveling toward the land office in Marshall on the same train that carried a letter from Felch instructing the land commissioner to withdraw certain sections from the market. The train was involved in an accident, delaying arrival of the speculators until the following morning. However, the letter was delivered before the office opened. The speculators were out of luck.[6]

In the end, Lansing was chosen for some of the same reasons it was criticized. It was centrally located. There also was precedent for this decision. Ohio earlier had chosen Columbus, a relative wilderness area, as its capital. Also, because of the intense rivalries and antagonisms that had developed among the other contenders, legislators were relieved to be able to select a neutral site, one which would offend all equally.

Greenly suggested that, rather than showing "any foresight ... of the immense benefits, which were ultimately to accrue the state," legislators chose Lansing because of "a desire to get rid of the whole subject."[7] A companion bill to the one naming Lansing Township the capital gave the new capital city the name of "Michigan." The new legislative session of 1848 quickly changed the name to "Lansing." The name, like most of the state's residents at the time, came from the East. Lansing Township was named in 1841 by Joseph H. North Jr. after his home town in Tompkins County, N.Y., which was named after John Lansing, a Revolutionary War hero from New York.[8] Turning a swamp into a capital city took some time, and during its early years, Lansing's roads, housing and amenities left much to be desired.

Responding to efforts by some legislators to relocate the capital, the delegates to the 1850 constitutional convention firmly declared, "The seat of government shall be at Lansing, where it is established."[9] That statement may have quelled some of the agitation about moving the capital, but it certainly didn't silence Gov. Pingree. As he

Bill Kuenzel/The Detroit News

Aerial view of the Capitol in 1922

left office in 1901, Pingree, who had a legendary disdain for Lansing, still urged that the capital be relocated. In his farewell message to the Legislature, he said, "I have long been of the opinion that the capital of the state should be removed either to the city of Detroit or the city of Grand Rapids. ... Either city would be more accessible than Lansing, and the living accommodations infinitely better."[10]

The capitols

As soon as Lansing was chosen the capital city in 1847, work commenced on a temporary Capitol at the southwest corner of South Washington and Allegan streets, a few blocks from the present Capitol. Epaphroditus Ransom was the first governor to be inaugurated in the temporary Capitol, in 1848.

The new statehouse was a two-story building with a small dome. The cost, including a 16-foot addition in 1865, was $25,952. Legislators found it such an uncomfortable workplace that they called it "the Barn." Although it was designed to be temporary, it housed state government until completion of the permanent Capitol in 1879. The original building was later used in the manufacture of wood handles until it was destroyed by fire in 1882.[11] According to various accounts, it supposedly required only one wagon to move the state's records from Detroit to Lansing.

One governor after another cited the need for a new and permanent Capitol. On Jan. 5, 1859, Gov. Moses Wisner told legislators, "Your state Capitol was built for a temporary purpose and at a time when it was impractical to build any other. ... What was sufficient for the wants and necessities of the state at that time, no longer answers the purpose. ... I recommend that you make some provision towards the purchasing of

169

materials preparatory to the building of the new Capitol."[12] Two years later, he reiterated the arguments, and recommended that $50,000 be appropriated for each of the next two years to begin work on a new Capitol.

In 1871, at the urging of Gov. Henry P. Baldwin, the Legislature authorized start on a new $1.2-million building. The state advertised for bids, and heard from 80 interested architects around the country. From the 20 sets of designs received, the plans submitted by Elijah E. Meyers of Illinois were chosen on Jan. 24, 1872. Meyers soon moved his family to Detroit, doing business under the name E.E. Meyers and Son.[13]

Meyers was establishing a reputation as a designer of public buildings, having just finished plans for the Freeport, Ill., Courthouse. Michigan's was his first Capitol, but he later designed the Texas Capitol at Austin (built 1885-1888) and the Colorado statehouse (built 1890-1900). In *Temples of Democracy: The State Capitols of the USA,* authors Henry-Russell Hitchcock and William Seale called Meyers "the greatest capitol-builder of the Gilded Age."[14] The Michigan Capitol was described by Meyers as Palladian, a classical style with its origin in the architecture of Greece and Rome. Its dome and spire reached to 276 feet. Including porticos and steps, the building measured 420-by-273 feet. Its materials included English glass, tin from Wales and limestone from Illinois.

The cornerstone was laid Oct. 2, 1873, in a ceremony that marked the beginning of construction. Gov. John J. Bagley, addressing the estimated 30,000 people who had come from all over Michigan, proclaimed, "We stand here as conquerors of forest and swamp, and can proudly say, 'If thou seekest a pleasant peninsula, seek it here.'"[15]

The Capitol was completed in 1878 at a cost of $1,510,131. Charles M. Croswell was the first governor to be inaugurated there.

The Capitol was remodeled and modernized periodically during its first century. Gaslights were replaced by electric lamps when the building was wired in 1905. In 1953, Gov. G. Mennen Williams pushed a button to bathe the dome with light from 37 floodlights.

But as changes were made, the original design underwent change as well. The floodlights were more energy-efficient than the 735 24-watt bulbs that had previously lighted the dome. But they necessitated removal of small domes on the north and south wing roofs that, in the blaze of floodlights, cast shadows on the main dome.

Original designs were painted, plastered or paneled over, including those in the governor's office, where one occupant after another remodeled and partitioned with scant concern for the past. Stained glass ceilings in the House and Senate chambers were replaced by wooden panels. To provide more office space, many floors were cut in half, making two stories fit into one.

The exterior lines of the Capitol were distorted by air-conditioners protruding from windows and walls, and by temporary mobile home-type offices added to the west end of the building in 1967. The temporary offices were replaced by more modern modular office units in 1983.

Step by step, layer after layer, inside and out, the integrity of Elijah Meyers' design was compromised. But the Capitol had many friends whose concern over the architectural abominations led to a restoration movement that gained momentum in Michigan's sesquicentennial year.

Calling the Capitol a "symbol of Michigan's history and greatness," Sen. William Sederburg of East Lansing in February 1987 announced proposals for restoration of the Capitol. "It's appropriate," he said, "that we begin preserving this 108-year gem during this, our sesquicentennial year."

— *Don Weeks*

A 1928 night scene at the Capitol. Bulbs were replaced by floodlights in 1953.

The Detroit News

Mackinac Island Park Commission

Residences of the governor: Lansing and Mackinac Island

(A governor) needs a home here, and ought to have a mansion, which is at least as respectable as the mansions most private citizens occupy ...
— **Ex-Gov. Austin Blair, speaking at the 1879 Dedication of the Capitol.**

Civil War Gov. Austin Blair was not the only governor to fuss about the state's failure to provide a residence for its governor. Aaron T. Bliss complained in 1903 that a governor should not have to invest in Lansing real estate for "temporary purposes." He said, "It is in the interest of the state that the governor should have his home in the capital during his term, and the state should build and maintain an official residence for him."[1]

Gov. Chase S. Osborn lamented in 1911 that the length of a governor's term "does not warrant a personal establishment" in Lansing. "The chief executive," he said, "should be required to reside in Lansing, and it would be fair and proper to provide a home for him, as is done in many other states."[2]

The Legislature periodically considered, but rejected, the idea. In 1969, Howard Sober, who became wealthy by trucking cars from factories to auto dealers, gave his rambling Lansing house at 2520 Oxford in the fashionable Moores River Drive neighborhood in southwest Lansing to the state for use as the official governor's mansion.

The 10-room, one-story, house was built in 1959 on 3.2 acres overlooking the Grand River. In 1965, the last time it was assessed before Sober gave it to the state, the property had an assessed value of $90,000.[3] The market value in 1969 was estimated at $400,000. Sober stipulated that he be paid $250,000 for the furnishings, including Chinese art objects.[4] A state study indicated the cost of building a suitable residence would be as high as $350,000.

Ultimately, a complicated funding arrangement led to acquisition of the "free" house. Wealthy individuals, part of a committee headed by ex-governors, pledged to raise the money for the furnishings. When private fund-raising efforts fizzled, the Legislature in 1973 appropriated the necessary funds to reimburse those who had signed pledges, but Atty. Gen. Frank J. Kelley ruled the appropriation was drafted improperly. Later that year, Gov. William G. Milliken, first governor to live in the official residence, signed a bill that included $210,000 for the furnishings.

There was no such hassle over the state's earlier acquisition of the best fringe benefit

This 24-room Mackinac Island house, pictured about 1910 shortly after it was built, was purchased in 1945 as a summer residence for governors. In the background is the Grand Hotel.

UPI

Mackinac Island Park Commission

Top Official Governors' Residence in Lansing, pictured when acquired in 1969

Bottom Governors' Summer Residence, Mackinac Island, as refurbished in 1970's

provided any U.S. governor — the 24-room, three-story Victorian house perched on a Mackinac Island bluff overlooking the Straits of Mackinac. It was purchased by the state in 1945 at the original early 1900's construction cost of $15,000 as the governor's summer residence. At the time, the residence was in such poor condition that extensive repairs and restoration were undertaken, with help from prison inmates.

Gov. Harry F. Kelly was the first governor to stay at the summer residence, which he used to help host a national governors' conference. Massachusetts Sen. John F. Kennedy met there with Gov. G. Mennen Williams in 1960, winning Williams' pledge of support for his successful campaign for president.

In 1975, President Gerald R. Ford stayed overnight at the Mackinac Island residence as Milliken's guest, but only after Secret Service agents ordered a few changes be made to ensure presidential safety. Strips of tape were put in the bathtub off the master bedroom to guard against a presidential slip. Loose bricks were firmed up along steps leading to the second story.

It has been tradition each summer for Boy Scouts to raise and lower the flag daily at the summer residence. Gov. James J. Blanchard once was in a Scout detail that handled the duties while Williams was in residence there. The tradition was amended somewhat during the Milliken administration. At the urging of First Lady Helen Milliken, occasional use of Girl Scouts was started.

The long white porch overlooking the Straits of Mackinac is known as "Michigan's front porch" and has a view shared by thousands of visitors. Many a deal has been cut by governors who wooed legislators invited to the residence. Many a program has been drafted by gubernatorial staffs sitting in front of its massive fireplaces.

It took the state of Michigan a long time to do it, but it handsomely corrected the hardships experienced by Blair, Bliss, Osborn, and other early Michigan governors. Gov. Hazen S. Pingree complained at the turn of the century about lack of accommodations in Lansing, and grumbled to the Legislature it was hard to get a decent hot bath there.

Much later, Michigan governors had a sprawling official residence in Lansing with a sunken circular pink ceramic bathtub and a shower equipped with multiple shower heads at several levels to reach the gubernatorial body from many angles — and a slip-proof Mackinac Island bathtub with a presidential seal of approval.

Gubernatorial perks have come a long way since Pingree's day.

White House

Grand Hotel

Left "Michigan's Front Porch" at the Governors' Summer Residence overlooks the Mackinac Island harbor and a busy shipping lane. On the porch in 1967 are, left to right, Govs. William Scranton of Penn., Nelson Rockefeller of NY, George Romney of Mich., and John Chafee of RI.

Above In 1975, on the east end of the porch are Gov. William G. Milliken and President Gerald R. Ford.

A Michigan tradition:
Governors on Opening Day

Fred Green, 1928

The Detroit News

Frank Murphy, 1932

The Detroit News

Luren Dickinson, 1939

Bill Kuenzel/The Detroit News

Bill Kuenzel/The Detroit News

Frank D. Fitzgerald and Detroit Tiger Manager Mickey Cochrane, 1935

G. Mennen Williams, 1958

Carl Wienke/The Detroit News

George Romney, 1966

Drayton Holcomb/The Detroit News

The Detroit News

John B. Swainson with son Stephen, and Tiger second baseman Jake Wood, 1961

G. Mennen Williams, 1953

Scott MacGregor/The Detroit News

William T. Anderson/The Detroit News

James J. Blanchard, 1987

Epilogue

I remember what it was like to be elected governor and immediately face an enormous revenue shortfall. It has happened before.

— President Ronald Reagan, former governor of California, to the nation's governors, Feb. 27, 1983.

I t happened from California to New York, all across the nation, as it occurred so often in Michigan's first 150 years of statehood: Governors encountered revenue shortfalls and lingering deficits.

Many governors rode into office on a wave of popularity, only to ride for an eventual financial fall. Stevens T. Mason brought Michigan to statehood in 1837, and then left office amid controversy after encountering setbacks in financing ambitious development plans. Part of his problem was the banking Panic of 1837. Other governors faced the impact on Michigan of such financial crises as the depression of the 1870s, the worldwide financial panic and Great Depression of the 1930s, and back-to-back recessions in the 1970s and 1980s.

Gov. John S. Barry reported in 1842 that "embarrassments of no ordinary magnitude oppress the finances of the state." Gov. John J. Bagley in 1875: "A financial crisis of more than ordinary severity has been encountered by every section of the country, and the best thought of the nation has been taxed for measures of relief — to a large extent unsuccessfully." Gov. John T. Rich in 1893: "Michigan confronted an empty treasury." Gov. Fred W. Green, upon taking office in 1927: "The state is not paying its bills." Gov. Frank D. Fitzgerald in 1939: "We cannot feed the hungry with an empty treasury. ... It is imperative that we start at once to put our financial house in order."

Periodically, the house was put in order by Michigan governors and legislators, only to tumble again. Gov. G. Mennen Williams was elected to an unprecedented six terms and was able to proclaim that in many areas he brought Michigan "into the 20th century." But in his last term, Michigan had a 1959 cash crisis and payless paydays for state workers. As a reporter covering the Capitol for United Press International, I did not realize at the time that an earlier Michigan governor had encountered payless paydays. In 1908, Gov. Fred M. Warner reported to the Legislature that pay for state employees had to be "withheld a few weeks."

Warner's payless paydays were among the discoveries from scanning State of the State and other messages of Michigan's first 43 governors. The archives reverberate with echoes of governors blaming inherited economic woes on the national economy, or on their predecessors — depending on the political affiliations of the incoming and outgoing governors and presidents. Another recurring theme of the Michigan governorship: Economic diversification. If Michigan diversified as much as each succeeding governor said it should, it would lead the nation in production of about everything except oranges.

Many other issues persisted throughout the Michigan governorship. Some, such as road-building, confronted all governors. Others cropped up occasionally. In 1987, a Michigan issue, particularly in Detroit, was the presence of guns in schools. It also was a concern 100 years earlier, prompting Gov. Cyrus G. Luce to tell the Legislature in 1887: "... boys of all ages are ready upon the least provocation to use the deadly weapon. Schoolteachers and schoolboys go to their duties and lessons armed."

Of more interest than reading the pronouncements of governors was learning something about their lives, especially how they became politicians. Many were profoundly influenced in that pursuit by their parents, and their youth. Mason, born into Virginia aristocracy, was still a young man when he became governor. From his office, he maintained a correspondence with his parents that sometimes read like a boy writing home from summer camp.

Alexander J. Groesbeck's mother was the dominate influence on his early years. William G. Milliken followed his grandfather and father to the state Senate, but his mother was a strong influence in instilling a rare quality among politicians — civility. Milliken and

Williams both decided as young men that they wanted to become governor. James J. Blanchard's mother gently encouraged his boyhood interest in politics after his father abandoned the family.

There were many notable physical exploits among Michigan's governors, starting with territorial Gov. Lewis Cass' trip from Detroit to Minnesota by canoe...Mason, branded "Young Hotspur" by President Andrew Jackson, abandoning a sleigh in a snowstorm and mounting a horse to continue a trek from Michigan to the nation's capital..."Rough-and-Ready" Edwin B. Winans prospecting for California gold, once putting supplies on his back and continuing on when pack horses collapsed under him, and once accidentally shooting himself in the chest and shoulder when a stagecoach rolled over...Hazen S. Pingree and Aaron T. Bliss each spending six months in Confederate prisons ... Harry F. Kelly wounded and held prisoner by Germans, escaping, getting wounded again, and then losing a leg ... John B. Swainson losing both legs in World War II, and breaking his jaw and a rib — and then writing home to say, "There are guys here worse off than me ...." An undersized George Romney going out for a football team that had no uniform small enough for him, and a coach who praised the "grit" that carried Romney far in later life.

Civil War Gov. Austin Blair, who mustered Michigan to help preserve human rights and the Union, richly deserved his honor as the only Michigan governor to have a statue erected on the Capitol grounds. But, as was true with so many of Michigan's other governors, he feuded with his party upon leaving office. Interestingly, some of the biggest battles of the Michigan governorship were between progressive Republican governors and conservative Republican senators.

Michigan's first Republican governor, Kinsley S. Bingham, was plagued in 1857 by intra-party frictions between Detroiters and outstaters. As a Michigan Historical Commission account recalled, "There was disaffection in the Republican party throughout the state." Democrats had similar problems on occasion, but one of the recurring stories of Michigan politics has been disaffection between notable Republican governors and the Republican Party:

Blair fought to preserve the union but could not preserve the unity of his own party; after leaving office, Chase S. Osborn helped elect Democrat Frank Murphy as governor; also, after leaving office, Groesbeck helped Democrat Williams defeat Republican Sigler.

Pingree was one Republican governor who proved popular with the people but not his party. After spats with the Legislature — especially those he called the "Immortal 19" in the Senate — and the courts, he went off to Africa to hunt elephants, and died in London before returning home. He was honored with a statue in Detroit, with an inscription that memorialized him as "Idol of the People."

Few Michigan governors were so honored. Their portraits were placed in the Capitol. But as the years went by, the newer portraits were placed in choice space in the rotunda and the older ones were moved farther and farther from the center of attention. By the time Michigan celebrated its sesquicentennial in 1987, some gubernatorial portraits had been rotated out of the Capitol and into storage.

It is hoped that through words and pictures, this book has helped bring *all* of Michigan's Stewards of the State out of storage and into current thought, however briefly.

Bibliography

(The State Archives) is both the memory and the consciousness of state government ... In a very real sense, the archives is the protector of the people's liberty.

— **Martha M. Bigelow, director, Michigan History Bureau***

A treasury of the stewardship of Michigan can be found in the State Archives in Lansing, the Michigan Historical Collections at the University of Michigan's Bentley Historical Library in Ann Arbor, the Burton Historical Collection in the Detroit Public Library, the Michigan State Library, and local libraries, historical societies and museums. These repositories were important sources for this effort to chronicle the words and careers of Michigan's governors.

The author also drew from publications and other sources that are cited in the footnotes. Several references deserve mention as sources for biographical and other collective information on Michigan governors for various periods. (It is recommended that more than one source be consulted because some contain conflicting dates, spellings and other information.)

Of particular value were the four volumes, published in the 1925-27 period, of *Messages of the Governors of Michigan,* edited by George N. Fuller and published by the Michigan Historical Commission. They contain selected legislative messages beginning with territorial Gov. Lewis Cass in 1825 and concluding with Gov. Fred W. Green in 1927. These volumes also contain lengthy biographical sketches, found as well in another commission publication, *Governors of the Territory and State of Michigan.* Brief sketches on early governors can be found in the two volumes of *Michigan Biographies* published by the commission in 1924.

Also of value on early governors is *General History of the State of Michigan: With Biographical Sketches* compiled by Charles Richard Tuttle, published by R.D.S. Tyler & Co, and printed in 1873 by the Detroit Free Press Company. Another source of lengthy sketches on many 19th century governors is *Representative Men of Michigan,* the Michigan volume of the *American Biographical History of Eminent and Self-Made Men,* published in 1878 by Western Biographical Publishing Co. The title reflects the glowing approach to the sketching of careers of politicians of the day.

The *Biographical Directory of the Governors of the United States,* edited by Robert Sobel and John Raimo and published by Meckler Books, is a good starting point for basic information on governors into the 1980s.

Highlights of actions taken by many governors, and the eras in which they served, are contained in the 1980 printing of *Michigan, A History of the Wolverine State* by Willis F. Dunbar and George S. May, published by William B. Eerdmans Publishing Co., and F. Clever Bald's *Michigan in Four Centuries,* published in 1954 by Harper & Brothers.

Michigan History magazine, showcase publication of the Michigan History Bureau of the Michigan Department of State, is a valuable source on governors. In addition to its occasional articles on individual governors, it published sketches on the first 42 governors in its January/February issue in 1980. The *Michigan Manual,* published by the Michigan Department of Management and Budget (and its predecessor agencies) every two years, includes a brief biography of the sitting governor and lieutenant governor, the names and terms of all governors beginning with the territorial period, gubernatorial election results beginning with 1835, and county-by-county election results from the most recent primary and general elections.

Another useful biennial publication is *The Book of the States,* published by the Council of State Governments. It contains updated information on the powers, duties and other aspects of governors of all of the states.

*In preface to *A Guide to the State Archives of Michigan: State Records,* Michigan Department of State, 1977.

Footnotes

Michigan and the American Governorship

1. Williams, statement at the Michigan Historical Commission Day "Gathering of Governors" at Michigan State University Nov. 17, 1981, attended by ex-Govs. Murray D. Van Wagoner, John B. Swainson and George Romney, and then-Gov. William G. Milliken.
2. Milliken, State of the State Message, Jan. 14, 1982.
3. Debates in the federal convention of 1787 as reported by James Madison in *Documents Illustrative of the Formation of the Union of the United States,* Charles C. Tansill, ed.
4. Roy Glashan, *American Governors and Gubernatorial Elections, 1775-1975,* Stillwater, Minn., 1975, p.150.
5. Lipson, University of Chicago Press, 1939, p.6.
6. Solomon, remarks before National Municipal League, Denver, Nov. 15, 1977.
7. Most comparisons of gubernatorial powers in this book are drawn from the *1986-87 Book of the States,* published by the Council of State Governments, Lexington, Ky., 1986.
8. Glashan, Ibid.
9. Solomon, "Governors: 1960-70," *National Civic Review,* March 1971.
10. Solomon, Ibid.
11. Larry Sabato, *Good-by to Good-Time Charlie: The American Governor Transformed, 1950-75,* Lexington Books, 1978.
12. Blair, excerpt of 1879 speech at the dedication of the Capitol in Lansing, reprinted in The Detroit News, May 23, 1948.
13. Blanchard, *Budget Message of the Governor,* Jan. 28, 1987.
14. Kallenbach, *The American Chief Executive: The Presidency and the Governorship,* Harper & Row, New York, 1966.
15. Weeks, a study by the author, "Outstanding Governors of the 20th Century," originally presented as a paper at the 1981 meeting of the Southern Political Science Association and published in 1982 by the National Governors' Association, Washington, D.C. (The governors were Robert M. LaFollette, R-Wis., 1901-06; Woodrow Wilson, D-N.J., 1911-13; Alfred E. Smith, D-N.Y., 1919-21, 1923-28; Huey Long, D-La., 1928-32; Earl Warren, R-Calif., 1943-53; Thomas E. Dewey, R-N.Y., 1943-54; Nelson A. Rockefeller, R-N.Y., 1959-73; Terry Sanford, D-N.C., 1961-65; Daniel J. Evans, R-Wash., 1965-77; and Reubin Askew, D-Fla., 1971-79).
16. Sabato, Ibid.
17. Peirce, *The Megastates of America,* W.W. Norton & Co., New York, 1972.
18. Weeks, from Institute of Politics study.

The Territorial Governors

1. Alan S. Brown, "Governor Simcoe, Michigan and Canadian Defense," Michigan History magazine, March/April, 1983.
2. Willis F. Dunbar/George S. May, *Michigan, A History of the Wolverine State,* William B. Eerdmans Co., Grand Rapids, 1980. p.135, 139.
3. Catton, *Michigan, A History,* W.W. Norton & Co., New York, 1982, p.62.
4. Catton, Ibid.
5. Dunbar/May, Ibid., p.187.
6. Charles Richard Tuttle, *General History of the State of Michigan,* R.D.S. Tyler & Co., Detroit, 1873, p.20.
7. Benjamin F. Comfort (principal of Cass Technical High School), *Lewis Cass and the Indian Treaties,* the Charles F. May Co., Detroit, 1923, p.23.
8. Comfort, Ibid., p.27, citing an 1856 account from W.L.G. Smith's *Life and Times of Lewis Cass.*

Michigan's Elected Governors.

Stevens T. Mason

1. Patricia J. Baker, "Stevens Thomson Mason," *Famous Michiganians,* Series 1, No. 5, Michigan History Division, Michigan Department of State, Lansing, 1983, p.2.
2. George N. Fuller, ed., *Governors of the Territory and State of Michigan,* Bulletin No. 16, Michigan Historical Commission, Lansing, 1928, p.46.
3. Lawton T. Hemans, *Life and Times of Stevens Thomson Mason, The Boy Governor of Michigan,* Michigan Historical Commission, Lansing, 1920, p.218.
4. Hemans, Ibid.
5. Willis F. Dunbar/George S. May, *Michigan, A History of the Wolverine State,* William B. Eerdmans Co., Grand Rapids, 1980, p.251.
6. Baker, Ibid., p.1.
7. Jackson, Presidential message to Congress, dated December 1836.
8. Dunbar/May, Ibid., p.195.
9. Hemans, Ibid., p.218-219.
10. Hemans, Ibid., p.94-97.
11. Jean Frazier, Michigan History magazine, January/February issue, 1980, p.31.
12. Bruce Catton, *Michigan, A History,* W.W. Norton & Co., New York, 1984, p.109.
13. Hemans, Ibid., p.153.
14. Hemans, Ibid., p.509. (Also noted: *Stevens Thomson Mason, Misunderstood Patriot,* by Kent Sagendorph, E.P. Dutton, New York, 1947.)

William Woodbridge

1. Emily George, R.S.M., *William Woodbridge, Michigan's Connecticut Yankee,* Michigan History Division, Michigan Department of State, Lansing, 1979, p.43.
2. Patricia J. Baker, "Stevens Thomson Mason," *Famous Michiganians* Series 1, No. 5, Michigan History Division, Michigan Department of State, Lansing, 1983, p.4
3. Charles Lanman, *The Life of William Woodbridge,* Blanchard & Mohun, Washington, 1867.
4. George, Ibid., quoting from a Woodbridge address to the New England Society of Michigan, p.76.
5. George, Ibid., p.69.
6. Charles Richard Tuttle, *General History of the State of Michigan,* R.D.S. Tyler & Co., Detroit, 1873, p.630.
7. Mrs. Neil McMillan of Grosse Pointe, the former Juliana Woodbridge Moring, who was named after Woodbridge's wife, Juliana. In a statement to author Feb. 3, 1987.

James Wright Gordon

1. *Michigan Biographies,* Michigan Historical Commission, Lansing, 1924, Vol. I, p.338.
2. Lawton T. Hemans, *Life and Times of Stevens T.*

Mason, The Boy Governor of Michigan, Michigan Historical Commission, Lansing, 1920, p.496.
3. Emily George, *William Woodbridge, Michigan's Connecticut Yankee,* Michigan History Division, Department of State, Lansing, 1979, p.55.
4. Charles Richard Tuttle, *General History of the State of Michigan,* R.D.S. Tyler & Co., Detroit, 1873, p.701.
5. *Governors of the Territory and State of Michigan,* Michigan Historical Commission, Bulletin No. 16, George N. Fuller, ed., Lansing, 1928.
6. *Executive Journal for the Annual Session of 1841,* Michigan Senate, 1841.
7. Documents in Michigan State Archives.
8. George N. Fuller, *Messages of the Governors of Michigan,* Michigan Historical Commission, Lansing, 1925, Vol. I, p.421.
9. Charlie Cain, "What Happened to the Old Guv's Body?" The Detroit News, Sept. 12, 1984. p.3-A.
10. Cain, Ibid.

John F. Barry

1. George N. Fuller, *Messages of the Governors of Michigan,* Vol. I., Michigan Historical Commission, Lansing, 1925, p.431.
2. Willis F. Dunbar/George S. May, *Michigan, A History of the Wolverine State,* William B. Eerdmans Co., Grand Rapids, 1980, p.281.

Alpheus Felch

1. George N. Fuller, *Messages of the Governors of Michigan,* Vol. II, Michigan Historical Commission, Lansing, 1926, p.25-26.
2. Claudius B. Grant, *Governors of the Territory and State of Michigan,* Bulletin No. 16, Michigan Historical Commission, Lansing, 1928, p.59.

William L. Greenly

1. Lawton T. Hemans, *Life and Times of Stevens T. Mason, The Boy Governor of Michigan,* Michigan Historical Commission, Lansing, 1920, p.511.
2. Dudley A. Siddall, *Governors of Michigan,* April 2, 1916, an article in Greenly folder at the Burton Historical Collection, Detroit.
3. *Michigan Biographies,* Michigan Historical Commission, Lansing, 1924, Vol. I, p.351.

Epaphroditus Ransom

1. *Michigan Biographies,* Michigan Historical Commission, Vol. II, Lansing, 1924, p.219.
2. George N. Fuller, ed., *Messages of the Governors of Michigan,* Michigan Historical Commission, Lansing, 1926, Vol. 2, p.96-97.
3. Fuller, Ibid., p.121.
4. Willis F. Dunbar/George S. May, *Michigan, A History of the Wolverine State,* William B. Eerdmans Co., Grand Rapids, 1980, p.319.
5. Fuller, Ibid., p.109.
6. Fuller, Ibid., p.109-110.
7. Dunbar/May, Ibid., p.351.

Robert McClelland

1. George N. Fuller, *Messages of the Governors of Michigan,* Michigan Historical Commission, Lansing, 1926, Vol. II, p.222.
2. Charles Richard Tuttle, *General History of the State of Michigan,* R.D.S. Tyler & Co., Detroit, 1873, p.431.
3. I.P. Christiancy, author of McClelland sketch in George N. Fuller's *Governors of the Territory and State of Michigan,* Michigan Historical Commission, Lansing, 1928, p.78.

Andrew Parsons

1. George N. Fuller, *Messages of the Governors of Michigan,* Michigan Historical Commission, 1926, Vol. II, p.255-56.
2. Fuller, Ibid., p.271-72
3. Charles Richard Tuttle, *General History of the State of Michigan,* R.D.S. Tyler & Co., Detroit, 1873, p.48.

Kinsley S. Bingham

1. George N. Fuller, *Messages of the Governors of Michigan,* Michigan Historical Commission, Lansing, 1926, Vol. II, p.315.
2. George N. Fuller, *Governors of the Territory and State of Michigan,* Michigan Historical Commission, Lansing, 1928, p.81.
3. Willis F. Dunbar/George S. May, Michigan, *A History of the Wolverine State,* William B. Eerdmans Co., Grand Rapids, 1980, p.363.

Moses Wisner

1. George N. Fuller, *Messages of the Governors of Michigan,* Michigan Historical Commission, Lansing, 1926, Vol. II, p.412-13.
2. Eric Freedman, "Wisner had a proud past," The Detroit News, Jan. 19, 1987, p.3-B.
3. Fuller, Ibid., p.389.
4. Fuller, Ibid., p.382.
5. Fuller, Ibid., p.360.
6. Michigan Biographies, Michigan Historical Commission, Lansing, Vol. II, p.462.
7. Fuller, Ibid., p.410.
8. Fuller, Ibid., p.411.

Austin Blair

1. George N. Fuller, *Messages of the Governors of Michigan,* Michigan Historical Commission, Lansing, 1926, Vol. II, p.442.
2. Fuller, Ibid., p.441.
3. Fuller, Ibid., p.430.
4. Fuller, Ibid., p.446.
5. Fuller, Ibid., p.452.
6. Will Muller, "Unsung GOP Liberal," The Detroit News, Aug. 12, 1959.
7. Muller, Ibid.
8. Stout was nominated "against his earnest protest," according to Michigan Biographies, Michigan Historical Commission, Lansing, 1824, Vol. II, p.334.
9. Arnold J. Levin, The Detroit News, May 23, 1948.
10. Muller, Ibid.
11. Frederick D. Williams, Michigan History magazine, January/February 1980, p.34.
12. Fuller, Ibid., p.473.
13. Fuller, Ibid., p.459.

Henry H. Crapo

1. Martin Lewis, *Lumberman from Flint: The Michigan Career of Henry H. Crapo,* Wayne State University Press, Detroit, 1956. p.145.
2. Lewis, Ibid., p.165, 167.
3. Henry Howland Crapo (grandson of Crapo), *The Story of Henry Howland Crapo 1804-1869,* Thomas Todd Co., Boston, 1933.
4. George N. Fuller, *Messages of the Governors of Michigan,* Michigan Historical Commission, Lansing, 1926. Vol. II, p.526-27.
5. Robert Sobel and John Raimo, *Biographical Directory of the Governors of the United States 1789-1978,* Meckler Books, Westport, Conn., Vol. II, p.749.
6. Crapo, Ibid., p.251
7. The Detroit News, May 20, 1955.

Henry P. Baldwin

1. George N. Fuller, *Messages of the Governors of Michigan,* Michigan Historical Commission, Lansing, 1927, Vol. III, p.112.
2. Willis F. Dunbar/George S. May, *Michigan, A History of the Wolverine State,* William B. Eerdmans Co., Grand Rapids, 1980, p.408.
3. Fuller, Ibid., p.108.

John J. Bagley

1. George N. Fuller, *Messages of the Governors of Michigan,* Michigan Historical Commission, Lansing, 1927, Vol. III, p.192
2. Fuller, Ibid., p.235.
3. George S. May, *A Most Unique Machine: The Michigan Origins of the American Automobile Industry,* Grand Rapids, 1975, p.81.
4. Fuller, Ibid., p.267

Charles M. Croswell

1. George N. Fuller, *Messages of the Governors of Michigan,* Michigan Historical Commission, Lansing, 1927, Vol. III, p.336.
2. Fuller, Ibid., p.330.
3. Fuller, Ibid., p.335.

David H. Jerome

1. George N. Fuller, *Messages of the Governors of Michigan,* Michigan Historical Commission, Lansing, Vol. III, p.433.
2. Fuller, Ibid., p.420.
3. Willis F. Dunbar/George S. May, *Michigan: A History of the Wolverine State,* William B. Eerdmans Co., Grand Rapids, 1980, p.408.

Josiah W. Begole

1. Eric Freedman, The Detroit News, Oct. 6, 1986, p.B1.
2. The full text of the letter, along with a detailed account of the role it played in the campaign and how it later was discovered, was reported by John Fitzgibbon of The Detroit News, May 28, 1924.
3. George N. Fuller, *Messages of the Governors of Michigan,* Michigan Historical Commission, Lansing, 1927, Vol. III, p.481.
4. Fuller, Ibid.

Russell A. Alger

1. Rodney Bell, Michigan History magazine, January/February, 1980, p.36.
2. George N. Fuller, *Messages of the Governors of Michigan,* Michigan Historical Commission, Lansing, 1927, Vol. III, p.534.
3. Fuller, Ibid., 559.
4. Fuller, Ibid., p.560.

Cyrus. G. Luce

1. *Michigan Biographies,* Michigan Historical Commission, Lansing, 1924, Vol. II, p.40.
2. Robert Sobel/John Raimo, *Biographical Directory of the Governors of the United States 1789-1978,* Meckler Books, Westport, Conn., Vol. II, p.754.
3. George N. Fuller, *Messages of the Governors of Michigan,* Michigan Historical Commission, Lansing, 1927, Vol. III, p.577.
4. Fuller, Ibid., p.642.

Edwin B. Winans

1. George N. Fuller, *Messages of the Governors of Michigan,* Michigan Historical Commission, Lansing, 1927, Vol. III, p.656-57.
2. *Governors of the Territory and State of Michigan,* Michigan Historical Commission, edited by George N. Fuller, Lansing, 1928, p.142.
3. An interview with Howard Hovey in Brighton reported by Lawrence McCracken, Detroit Free Press, Aug. 14, 1938.
4. Fuller, Ibid., p.657.

John T. Rich

1. George N. Fuller, *Messages of the Governors of Michigan,* Michigan Historical Commission, Lansing, 1927, Vol. III, p.699.
2. Fuller, Ibid., p.714.
3. John Fitzgibbon, a biographical sketch in the files of The Detroit News.
4. Fitzgibbon, Ibid.

Hazen S. Pingree

1. George N. Fuller, *Messages of the Governors of Michigan,* Michigan Historical Commission, Lansing, 1927, Vol. IV, p.235, 203.
2. Fuller, Ibid., p.290-91.
3. Fuller, Ibid., p.310-11.
4. Cyril and Marjorie Player, *The Life Story of Hazen S. Pingree,* The Detroit News, Jan. 3, 1932.
5. Fuller, Ibid., p.289.
6. Melvin G. Holli, Michigan History magazine, January/February 1980, p.39. (Holli is author of *Reform in Detroit: Hazen S. Pingree and Urban Politics,* Oxford University Press, 1969). Although Pingree was quoted as using these words, it was not documented that it was a direct quote. Rep. Lawton T. Hemans, author of several historical works, was quoted in the April 6, 1901, Lansing State Republican as saying: "What can you do with a man who, when he is cited to answer a charge of contempt says: 'To hell with your court and your contempt' and sails off to Africa?"
7. Cyril and Marjorie Player, *Hazen Pingree: The Biography of an American Commonplace,* bound, 357-page typed manuscript in the Catlin Library of The Detroit News, 1931, p.353.
8. Player, Ibid., p.357.
9. The Detroit News, June 19, 1901.

Aaron T. Bliss

1. George N. Fuller, *Messages of the Governors of Michigan,* Michigan Historical Commission, Lansing, 1927, Vol. IV, p.377.
2. Bliss, speech before the Gridley Club, Ionia, Jan. 31, 1902.
3. Willis F. Dunbar/George S. May, *Michigan: A History of the Wolverine State,* William B. Eerdmans Co., Grand Rapids, 1980, p.516.
4. William Stocking, *Under the Oaks,* a commemorative book published by the Detroit Tribune, Detroit, 1904, p.147.

Fred M. Warner

1. George N. Fuller, *Messages of the Governors of Michigan,* Michigan Historical Commission, Lansing, 1927, Vol. IV, p.411.
2. Fuller, Ibid., p.495.
3. Fuller, Ibid., p.492.

Chase S. Osborn

1. Robert M. Warner, *Chase Salmon Osborn: 1860-1949,* University of Michigan, Ann Arbor, 1960, p.26.
2. Warner, Ibid., p.3.
3. Osborn, *The Iron Hunter,* Macmillan Co., New York, 1919, p.103.
4. Saralee R. Howard-Filler, Michigan History magazine, May/June 1983, p.13.
5. Willis F. Dunbar/George S. May, *Michigan: A History of the Wolverine State,* William B. Eerdmans Co., Grand Rapids, 1980, p.552.

6. George N. Fuller, *Messages of the Governors of Michigan,* Michigan Historical Commission, Lansing, Vol. IV, 1927, p.597.
7. Fuller, Ibid., p.634.

Woodbridge N. Ferris

1. The Associated Press, an obituary, March 23, 1928.
2. *From His History as Told by Himself,* a biographical sketch written by Woodbridge N. Ferris and distributed during his 1914 re-election campaign.
3. Ferris, Ibid.
4. George N. Fuller, *Messages of the Governors of Michigan,* Michigan Historical Commission, Lansing, Vol. IV, 1927, p.692.
5. Fuller, Ibid., p.693.
6. Fuller, Ibid., p.671.
7. Will Muller, The Detroit News, Dec. 18, 1968.
8. Ferris made the remark to Jay G. Hayden of The Detroit News, who reported them March 23, 1928.

Albert E. Sleeper

1. George N. Fuller, *Messages of the Governors of Michigan,* Michigan Historical Commission, Lansing, Vol. IV, 1927, p.728-29.
2. Fuller, Ibid., 730.
3. John Fitzgibbon, The Detroit News, June 29, 1919.

Alexander J. Groesbeck

1. George N. Fuller, *Messages of the Governors of Michigan,* Michigan Historical Commission, Lansing, Vol. IV, p.776.
2. Fuller, Ibid., p.800-01.
3. Fuller, Ibid., p.848.
4. Carl Muller, The Detroit News, March 11, 1953.
5. Thomas E. Brown, Michigan History magazine, January/February, 1980, p.40.
6. The Detroit News, April 21, 1926.
7. Frank Woodford, *Alex J. Groesbeck: Portrait of a Public Man,* Wayne State University Press, Detroit, 1962, p. 242.
8. In a 1986 interview with the author.

Fred W. Green

1. George N. Fuller, *Messages of the Governors of Michigan,* Michigan Historical Commission, Lansing, 1927, Vol. IV, p.848.
2. Fuller, Ibid., p.925-26.
3. The Detroit News, April 7, 1927.
4. Fuller, Ibid., p.861.
5. Michigan History magazine, January/February 1980, p.41.

Wilber M. Brucker

1. F. Clever Bald, *Michigan in Four Centuries,* Harper & Brothers, New York, 1954, p.404.
2. Will Muller, The Detroit News, Oct. 29, 1968, p.4B.
3. Printed version of governor's message to the Legislature, March 29, 1932, p.3.
4. The Detroit News, Oct. 19, 1968, p.4B.
5. The Detroit News, Oct. 30, 1968.

William A. Comstock

1. From printed version of the governor's Feb. 19, 1934, message to the Legislature, p.2.
2. Jan. 3, 1935. Final message to the Legislature, p.8.
3. Willah Weddon, *First Ladies of Michigan,* The Printers, Grand Rapids, 1977, p.322.
4. W.A. Markland, The Detroit News, Sept. 16, 1934.

Frank D. Fitzgerald

1. Message to the Legislature, Jan. 5, 1939, p.7-8 of printed version.
2. The Detroit News, March 17, 1939.

3. Frank M. Fitzgerald (Fitzgerald's grandson), *A Rememberance of Governor Fitzgerald of Grand Ledge,* Grand Ledge Area Historical Society, 1985, p.23.
4. Message to the Legislature, Ibid., p.4.
5. Frank M. Fitzgerald, Ibid., p.5.

Frank Murphy

1. From an address delivered over radio station WABC, New York City, and the Columbia Broadcasting System, Sept. 24, 1937.
2. New York Times, March 13, 1937.
3. Sidney Fine, Michigan History magazine, January/February, 1980, p.43.
4. Frank McNaughton, *Mennen Williams of Michigan,* Oceana Publications Inc., New York, 1960, p.73.
5. Sidney Fine, *Frank Murphy: The Washington Years,* University of Michigan Press, Ann Arbor, 1984, p.236.

Luren D. Dickinson

1. William Kulsea, *The governors: 50 years covering the statehouse,* an article in Michigan Business magazine, December 1985, p.25.
2. Kulsea, Ibid., p.26.
3. The Associated Press, March 17, 1940, as published in the Detroit Free Press.
4. W.A. Markland, The Detroit News, April 23, 1939.
5. Willah Weddon, *First Ladies of Michigan,* The Printers, Grand Rapids, 1977, p.27.
6. Kulsea, Ibid., p.26.

Murray D. Van Wagoner

1. Comment in a 1985 interview with the author.
2. Message to the Legislature in Extraordinary Session, Jan. 19, 1942.
3. Frank McNaughton, *Mennen Williams of Michigan,* Oceana Publications Inc., New York, 1960, p.96.
4. Roddy Ray, the Detroit Free Press, June 9, 1983, p.3A.

Harry F. Kelly

1. Feb. 4, 1946, Message to the Legislature in Extraordinary Session, p.4.
2. Feb. 5, 1945, Message to the Michigan Legislature, p.10.
3. Hub M. George, the Detroit Free Press, Oct. 25, 1942.

Kim Sigler

1. Message to the Legislature in Extraordinary Session, March 16, 1948, p.7.
2. Will Muller, The Detroit News, Dec. 11, 1953.
3. Muller, Ibid.
4. William Kulsea, Michigan Business magazine, January 1987, p.21.

G. Mennen Williams

1. Interview with the author in 1985. Most quotes in this sketch are from interviews with the author unless otherwise noted.
2. Message to the Legislature, Jan. 4, 1951, p.1, 6.
3. Message to the Legislature, Jan. 15, 1953, p.2-3.
4. The Detroit News, Feb. 23, 1986, p.6B, a feature on Williams at age 75 by the author.
5. Frank McNaughton, *Mennen Williams of Michigan,* Oceana Publications Inc., New York City, 1960, p.105.

John B. Swainson

1. Statement to the Michigan Historical Commission's "Gathering of Governors" at Michigan State University Nov. 17, 1981.

2. Message to the Michigan Legislature, Feb. 1, 1961, p.3.
3. Ibid., p.1.
4. From a letter Swainson wrote Dec. 2, 1944, while hospitalized in England.
5. Feb. 2, 1987, during the second of two interviews with the author.
6. Remer Tyson, "Hero, Governor, Felon — Fate Baffles John Swainson," Detroit Free Press, Dec. 18, 1977.

George Romney

1. D. Duane Angel, *Romney, A Political Biography,* Exposition Press, New York, 1967, p.181.
2. Tom Mahoney, *The Story of George Romney,* Harper & Brothers, New York, 1960, p.71. (Further information on the relationship of George and Lenore Romney can be found in *Giving Time a Chance: The Secret of a Lasting Marriage,* by Ronna Romney and Beppie Harrison, Bantam Books, New York, 1985.)
3. Mahoney, Ibid., p.69.
4. Speech to National Parking Association, Detroit, June 5, 1957.
5. Message to the Legislature, Jan. 10, 1963, p.2-3.
6. Message to the Legislature, Jan. 17, 1964, p.1.
7. Message to the Legislature, Jan. 14, 1965, p.1.
8. Message to the Legislature, Jan. 13, 1966, p.1.
9. In a 1987 discussion with the author. Most of Romney's comments in this sketch, unless otherwise noted, came during such discussions.
10. Statement at a "Gathering of Governors" sponsored by the Michigan Historical Commission at Michigan State University, Nov. 17, 1981.
11. The Detroit News, Oct. 27, 1968. (Also noted: *Romney's Way,* by George T. Harris, Prentice-Hall, Englewood Cliffs, 1968; *George Romney: Mormon in Politics,* by Clark R. Mollenhoff, Meredity Press, New York, 1968; and *The Romney Riddle,* Berwyn Publishers, Detroit, 1967. The latter was described by the Columbus Dispatch as "an arsenal of ammunition for anti-Romney forces.")

William G. Milliken

1. Dan Angel, *William G. Milliken, A Touch of Steel,* Public Affairs Press, Warren, 1970, p.76.
2. Message to the Legislature, Jan. 9, 1969.
3. Hillel Levin, "Milliken: The Man You Never Knew," Monthly Detroit magazine, February 1982, p.49.
4. John Broder, "The Milliken Years," a special issue of Michigan, The Magazine of The Detroit News, Dec. 5, 1982, p.28.
5. Special message on economy and budget, March 10, 1982.
6. The Detroit News, Dec. 23, 1981.
7. Willis F. Dunbar and George S. May, *Michigan: A History of the Wolverine State,* William B. Eerdmans Co., Grand Rapids, 1980, p.667.
8. William Kulsea, "The Governors: From Sigler to Blanchard," part two of a series published by Michigan Business magazine, January 1987, p.26-27.

James J. Blanchard

1. Joanna Firestone, "Bringing Up Jamie, the Blanchard Only a Mother Could Know," Michigan, the magazine of The Detroit News, Nov. 10, 1985, p.11.
2. In an interview with the author. Such interviews are the sources of most Blanchard quotes unless otherwise indicated.
3. Firestone, Ibid., p.10.
4. Firestone, Ibid., p.10.
5. Tim Jones, the Detroit Free Press, Dec. 28, 1986.

Michigan's first ladies

1. Lawton T. Hemans, *Life and Times of Stevens Thomson Mason: The Boy Governor of Michigan.* Michigan Historical Commission, 1920. p.154.
2. Ibid.
3. Willah Weddon, *First Ladies of Michigan,* The Printers, Grand Rapids, 1977, p.70.
4. "St. Joseph in Homespun," University of Michigan Bentley Historical Library. Quoted in *First Ladies of Michigan,* Willah Weddon, The Printers, Grand Rapids, 1977, p.75.
5. Weddon, Ibid., p.67.
6. Ibid., p.61.
7. Ibid., p.57.
8. Ibid., p.39.
9. Ibid., p.34.
10. Ibid., p.24-25.
11. Ibid., p.19.
12. Robert L. Pisor, The Detroit News, Jan. 20, 1970.
13. Weddon, Ibid., p.14.

Governors-in-waiting:
The lieutenant governors

1. John H. Mutz, "We Do Too Need Lt. Governors," The Washington Post, April 28, 1986.
2. Constitution of the state of Michigan, Article V, Section 25.
3. The Constitution, Article V, Section 21, said, "In the general election one vote shall be cast jointly for the candidates for governor and lieutenant governor nominated by the same party."
4. In a column by the author, The Detroit News, Jan. 20, 1987.
5. 1985-86 Michigan Manual, Department of Management and Budget, Lansing, p.171.
6. The Washington Post, April 14, 1986.

Governors and the press

1. George N. Fuller, *Messages of the Governors of Michigan,* Michigan Historical Commission, Lansing, 1925, Vol. I, p.217.
2. Fuller, Ibid., 1926, Vol. II, p.409.
3. Fuller, Ibid., Vol. IV, 1927, p.310.
4. G. Mennen Williams, "A Governor's Notes," Institute of Public Administration, University of Michigan, Ann Arbor, p.16.
5. Williams, at Michigan State University, Nov. 17, 1981.
6. Joanna Firestone, "The 'deputy governor' sells his boss," The Detroit News, April 1, 1985.
7. David S. Broder, as published in the Grand Rapids Press, March 5, 1968.
8. Willard Baird, the Lansing State Journal, Aug. 7, 1968.
9. George Romney, at Michigan State University, Nov. 17, 1981.
10. Murray D. Van Wagoner, at Michigan State University, Nov. 17, 1981.

The Pen and Politics:
Governors in Cartoon

1. Jerry Adler. Newsweek Oct. 13, 1980, p.74
2. Feb. 28, 1987, interview with the author.
3. *The Art of Opinion.* Booklet accompanying the International Cartoon Exhibit, sponsored by the Pittsburgh Post-Gazette and the Toledo Blade. 1986. p.4.
4. Feb. 28, 1987, interview with the author.
5. *The Art of Opinion.* p.3
6. Feb. 28, 1987, interview with the author.
7. Adler, Ibid., p.78.

The capitals and the capitols

1. William H. Upton, Michigan History magazine, summer 1939, Vol. 23, p.276.
2. Justin L. Kestenbaum, "Advance in the Wilderness," Michigan History magazine, November/December 1986, Vol. 70, p.48.
3. Kestenbaum, Ibid., p.48.
4. Kestenbaum, Ibid., p.45.
5. Upton, Ibid., p.283.
6. George N. Fuller, *Messages of the Governors of Michigan* Michigan Historical Commission, Lansing, 1926, Vol. II, p.15-16.
7. Kestenbaum, Ibid., p.51.
8. Walter Romig, *Michigan Place Names.* Grosse Pointe, Walter Romig Publisher, 1973, p.318.
9. Roger Rosentrater, *Michigan's 83 Counties: Ingham County.* Michigan History magazine, Vol. 67, p.9.
10. Fuller, Ibid., Vol IV, p.276-278.
11. Birt Darling, *City in the Forest: The Story of Lansing,* Stratford House, New York, 1950, p.119.
12. Fuller, Ibid., Vol. II, p.367-368.
13. Henry-Russell Hitchcock and William Seale, *Temples of Democracy: The State Capitols of the USA,* Harcourt Brace Jovanovich, New York, 1976, p.175-176.
14. Hitchcock/Seale, Ibid., p.174.
15. Rosentrater, Ibid., p.11.

Residences of the governors

1. George N. Fuller, *Messages of the Governors of Michigan,* Michigan Historical Commission, Lansing, Vol. IV., p.358.
2. Fuller, Ibid., p.592.
3. Lansing State Journal, Sept. 3, 1986, reporting Sober's death at age 90.
4. Al Sandner, The Detroit News, Feb. 7 and March 12, 1969.

Index of Names

E

Edmunds, James M., 34, 167
Edwards, George, 87
Eisenhower, Dwight D., 91
Engler, Colleen, 147
Engler, John, 136

F

Farnsworth, Elon, 25
Farrell, Larry, 77, 114
Felch, Alpheus, 30, 32, 34, 37, 40, 168
Felch, Lucretia W. (Lawrence), 30, 143
Fenton, William M., 48
Ferency, Zolton, 122, 134
Ferris, Helen Frances (Gillespie), 80,
    139, 143
Ferris, Woodbridge N., 74, 78, 80-81,
    85, 89
Fine, Sidney, 99, 101
Firestone, Joanna, 153
Fisher, Spencer O., 67
Fitzgerald, Frank D., 32, 94, 96-97, 99-
    100, 102-103, 137, 147, 179
Fitzgerald, Frank M., 94, 97, 102, 138,
    147
Fitzgerald, John Warner, 94, 96
Fitzgerald, Queena Maud (Warner),
    94, 143
Fitzgerald, Thomas, 26
Fitzgerald, William, 128, 134
Ford, Gerald R., 125, 172
Ford, Henry, 73, 79
Frazier, Jean, 19
Frensdorf, Edward, 85
Fry, Edward, 107
Fuller, Philo C., 28

G

George, Emily, 26
Gilpin, Henry D., 14
Glazier, Frank P., 74
Goldwater, Barry, 122, 157
Goodrich, Enos, 166-67
Gordon, James Wright, 26-27, 32, 116,
    147
Gordon, Mary (Hudun), 26, 143
Grant, Claudius B., 30
Grant, Ulysses, 51
Green, Allison, 127
Green, Fred W., 3, 87-91, 96, 134, 179
Green, Helen A. (Kelly), 88, 143
Greenly, Elizabeth W. (Hubbard), 32
Greenly, Maria (Hunt), 32

Greenly, Sarah A. (Dascomb), 32
Greenly, William L., 26, 32, 147,
    167-68
Gridley, Townsend E., 36
Griffin, Robert P., 115, 128
Griffiths, Hicks, 112, 147
Griffiths, Martha, 103, 112, 146-47
Groesbeck, Alexander J., 3, 60, 77, 81,
    84- 89, 91, 96, 112, 180

H

Haggerty, John, 77, 87
Hamilton, Alexander, 1
Hare, James M., 117
Harrison, Gen. William Henry, 7, 25
Hart, Phillip A., 125, 147
Hatfield, Mark, 2
Hayes, Rutherford B., 4, 46
Headlee, Richard H., 134, 146-47
Hemans, Lawton T., 15, 18, 75, 77
Henry, Patrick, 14
Hill, Draper, 155-57
Hoffa, James R., 113-14
Holloway, Frederick M., 56
Hooper, Warren G., 107
Hoover, Herbert, 84, 91
Horner, John S., 14-15
Houghton, Douglass, 18
Huber, Robert J., 133
Hull, Gen. William, 9

J

Jackson, 9, 11, 14, 17-18, 21, 44, 180
Jefferson, Thomas, 4
Jeffries, Edward J., 106
Jerome, David H., 56, 58, 60, 62
Jerome, Lucy (Peck), 56, 143
Johnson, Andrew, 4
Johnson, Lyndon B., 115, 122, 124

K

Kallenbach, Joseph E., 4
Kelley, Frank J., 133-34, 171
Kelly, Anne V. (O'Brien), 106, 139, 143
Kelly, Harry, 1, 105-07, 113, 124, 172,
    180
Kennedy, John F., 114-15, 172
Kimmerle, Charles H., 75
Knox, Frank, 77
Kulsea, William, 102-03, 109, 131

These pictures of Kuenzel in 1906 and 1951 were published July 22, 1951, in a Detroit News pictorial section in connection with Detroit's 250th birthday celebration. City Historian George W. Stark wrote that Kuenzel's "nose for news is still keen and the experience of the years ready in any emergency."

Tribute

One of the keenest eyes on Michigan politics was the camera of William A. Kuenzel, a Detroit News photographer for much of the first half of the 20th century. Frank Angelo, who for 16 years was managing editor of the Detroit Free Press, called Kuenzel "one of the pioneers of photo journalism." Photo journalism contributed significantly to this book, which contains many of Kuenzel's pioneering pictures, including his 1922 aerial photograph of the state Capitol on Page 169.

This page is offered as a tribute to Bill Kuenzel and the many other photographers who did so much to capture memorable moments of the Michigan governorship.